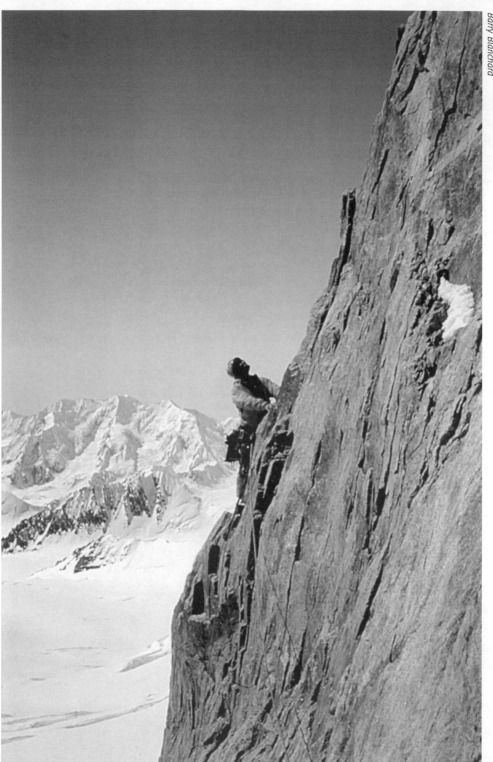

Traditional Lead Climbing

A Rock Climber's Guide to Taking the Sharp End of the Rope

Heidi Pesterfield

WILDERNESS PRESS · BERKELEY, CA

Traditional Lead Climbing: A Rock Climber's Guide to Taking the Sharp End of the Rope

1st EDITION September 2002
2nd EDITION August 2007
  2nd printing November 2008

Copyright © 2002 and 2007 by Heidi Pesterfield

Front cover photo copyright © 2007 by Simon Carter
Back cover photo copyright © 2007 by Topher Donahue
Frontispiece photo copyright © 2007 by Barry Blanchard
Illustrations: Tami Knight
Instructional photos: Lisa Dearing and Carl Davis
Other interior photos, except where noted, by author
Book design: Jaan Hitt
Cover design: Larry B. Van Dyke
Book production: Hayden Foell and Larry B. Van Dyke
Book editor: Laura Shauger
Technical editor of Chapter 8: Jeff Achey

ISBN 978-0-89997-442-2

Manufactured in China

Published by: **Wilderness Press**
               1345 8th Street
               Berkeley, CA 94710
               (800) 443-7227; FAX (510) 558-1696
               info@wildernesspress.com
               www.wildernesspress.com

Visit our website for a complete listing of our books and for ordering information.

Cover photos: Sean Isaac on the Grand Wall's Split Pillar, the Stawamus Chief, British
                 Columbia *(front);* Meg Noffsinger in Boulder Canyon, Colorado *(back)*
Frontispiece: Mark Wilford in the St. Elias Range, Alaska

Library of Congress Cataloging-in-Publication Data
   Pesterfield, Heidi, 1962–
   Traditional lead climbing : a rock climber's guide to taking the sharp end of the rope /
   Heidi Pesterfield.—2nd ed.
      p. cm.
   Includes bibliographical references and index.
   ISBN 978-0-89997-442-2 (pbk.)
      1. Rock climbing—Handbooks, manuals, etc. I. Title.
   GV200.2.P47 2007
   796.522'3—dc22
                                                                    2007004958

In memory of Carol Jean Pesterfield

CONTENTS

ACKNOWLEDGMENTS

Without the gracious assistance and never-ending support of the following individuals, this book would have never been possible: Carl Davis, Catherine Davis, Lisa Dearing, Doug Robinson, and the staff of Wilderness Press, especially Paul Backhurst, Jaan Hitt, Jannie Dresser, Roslyn Bullas, and Laura Shauger.

Additional thanks to: Jeff Achey; Julie Anderson; The Backcountry in Truckee, California; Brian Bax; Phebe Bell; Noah Bigwood; Maureen Bokeland; Tom Carter; Pete Chasse; Beth Christman; Ann Clemmer; Scott Cosgrove; Mike Davis; Steph Davis; Mimi DeGravelle; Joe Dolister; Topher Donahue; Heidi Ettlinger; Chris Falkenstein; Sharon Forsythe; Sue Fox; Patience Gribble; Regan Grillig; Steve Grossman; Sunshine Sunday Hansen; Jan Holan; Myrna Johnson; Ron Kauk; Bridget Kerr; Tim "Shaggy" Kipp; Tami Knight; Allison Kreutzen; Susie Lancaster; Elaine Lee; Bill McChesney; Billy McCollough; Dave Nettle; The Outdoor Industry Association (previously the Outdoor Recreation Coalition of America); Sarah Patterson; Mike Pennings; Holly Samson; Alia Selke; Hans Standtiemer; Squamish Fish; Peter Thompson; Greg "Thor" Tirdel; and Abby Watkins.

FOREWORD

As I hung from the sloping hold, my sweating fingers began to slowly grease off. My oversized hiking boots skated across the rock futilely searching for purchase as my right leg began a steadily increasing sewing machine Elvis twitch. Looking to the right, I could see the big hold I had to get to, but it seemed impossibly far away and with that first specter of doubt my arms immediately turned to Jell-O. As I awkwardly shifted my clunky rack of Hexes off to the side, I accidentally flicked the rope and watched in dismay as all the nice shiny stoppers and hexes I had placed lifted out of the crack and slid down the rope taking the last of my hopes with them. Below me, tucked in the midst of a jumble of boulders, my best friend clutched the rope in a hip belay with all my protection hung out like laundry on the long loop of slack. If I harbored any illusion of confidence at that point, it vanished as the look on my friend's face summed up my grim situation. I looked down into that maw of granite blocks 80 feet below and made the most broken promise a climber makes: "If I get out of this alive, I swear I'll never do it again."

For a brief moment, I actually started to calculate where I would hit and what my chances of survival would be when something deep and powerful within me arose of its own accord and took over. I felt both a surge and a calm that magically welded my mind, body, and desire into a single point and, in a move that took only a second but formed a memory that has lasted a lifetime, I reached across and climbed to easier ground. As I pulled myself onto the summit—physically and emotionally spent, I was already breaking the promise that seemed so reasonable just seconds earlier. It was 1974 in Joshua Tree National Monument; I had just survived my first epic lead and I wanted more.

"Play for more than you can afford to lose, and you will learn the game"— Winston Churchill could have just as easily been talking about traditional lead climbing as World War II. In the 30-plus years since that transforming lead at age 16, a blend of fear, elation, confidence, and uncertainty has drawn me to the mountains and rock walls of the world. Again and again, I risk a life I cannot afford to lose but equally cannot afford to live without a journey that excites my soul.

While learning the game of traditional lead climbing, I have formed my finest friendships, discovered my strengths, and found myself perched between rock and sky in some of the most amazing places on earth—not to mention being treated to many grand, memorable, and suffering epics. My traditional climbing and life have been shaped by great climbers of the past in their writing and images, bold climbers of today with their inspiring accomplishments, my partners who have shared both challenge and adventure, and, of course, by mother nature who can be wonderfully gentle or surprisingly harsh.

"The best way to avoid epics is to gain experience and the best way to gain experience is to have a few epics…": this saying is a blessing in disguise to a traditional lead climber for it promises that the learning curve will last a lifetime and that the excitement and discovery you unlock as a beginner will always be there. With its wealth of technical information, safe procedures, and excellent firsthand advice from experienced climbers, *Traditional Lead Climbing* is the perfect book to help you lead out on many fine climbs and give you a base of knowledge that will help you turn those epics that may await you into learning adventures.

Good climbing!

—Dave Nettle
Tahoe City, CA
February 5, 2007

Since his first traditional lead climb in 1973 in the southern Sierra backcountry, Dave Nettle has climbed in Patagonia, Canada, and the Dolomites, as well as in the Sierra Nevada backcountry and Yosemite Valley. Dave began mountaineering in the late 1970s and has climbed in Alaska, Nepal, and South America. He has thru-hiked the PCT, the Continental Divide Trail, and the Great Divide Trail. An internationally certified rope access technician, he is the lead instructor, teaching people to work at height on ropes, for Ropeworks, Inc. His writing has been published in *Climbing*, *Rock & Ice*, and the *American Alpine Journal*.

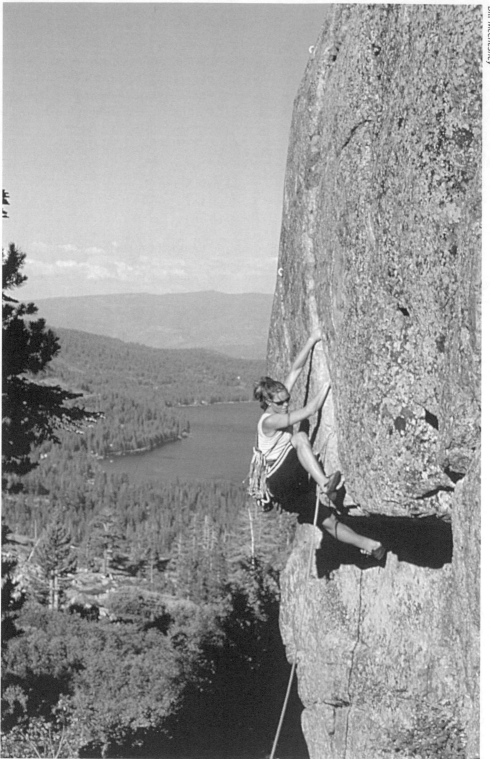

Bill McChesney

Allison Kreutzen at Donner Summit, California

Introduction

Most seasoned rock climbers agree that lead climbing often evokes a state of consciousness so focused that many compare it to the act of meditation. Life is distilled to pure simplicity when you lead a climb. In this concentrated state, free from both internal and external distractions, you rediscover your innate ability to experience the present moment. Zen practice never seemed so easy. Offering yourself to the rock wall above, you navigate up mysterious rock pathways, shifting your focus between motor skills and intellect. Emotions emerge and dissolve, spilling in and out of your consciousness. Angst, fear, confidence, relief—each feeling fades into the past as swiftly as it emerges.

Moving skyward, the objective of taking "the sharp end" becomes more obvious. Leading is a game of exploration and discovery. Linking together a chain of holds not visible from the ground, you deftly navigate over bulges and plug your feet and fingers into cracks, all the while looking for ideal protection and rest opportunities. Decisions are made intuitively, as your body embraces a ritual memory entirely its own: placing or forgoing safeguards, resting or not resting, moving right, left, or easing back down to a stance. Your personal orchestration of each individual route as the leader is a creative and unique process. No two lead adventures are alike.

Leading gives you opportunities for independence and freedom. Without leading skills, your climbing experience is limited to top-roping or following others. A partnership in which one team member takes every lead cannot be as fulfilling as sharing lead responsibilities.

And top-roping opportunities are limited by logistics: arriving with only top-roping gear to explore the celebrated granite cracks of Yosemite Valley, the soaring sandstone towers of southern Utah, or even Bouox's famed limestone pockets in France is like arriving at Northern California's Pebble Beach Golf Course with a croquet mallet.

A climber who successfully completes a challenging lead possesses an almost ethereal clarity. The climber who was disagreeable at the base sheds all emotional baggage by the summit. The formerly reticent individual is animated and talkative. Your postlead "buzz" defines the phrase "on cloud nine" in a way that Merriam or Webster never could. Meet the leader.

Spanning almost two decades, my rock climbing experience features venues that support various styles and methods. Some highlights include bouldering at Hueco Tanks in Texas and Fontainbleu, bolt clipping in southern France, free climbing on desert towers, big-wall climbing in Yosemite Valley, and climbing backcountry routes in the Dolomites, the Rockies, the Alps, and the Sierra Nevada. While each is a treasured memory, most cherished are the free-climbing experiences that required what is known today as traditional (trad) lead climbing skills.

Trad lead climbing is fundamentally about placing your own protection and anchors. While you may clip an occasional bolt or piton already in place as you lead, you mostly place your own gear; you set Stoppers, camming devices, Hexes, and other devices into cracks as temporary anchors to protect yourself from long falls. As the leader, you must balance technical gear skills with physical capabilities while remaining relaxed and focused.

Despite its many joys, traditional lead climbing happens to be one of the more dangerous climbing activities. While it offers you adventures aplenty, you enter an arena where risks are extremely high and mistakes unforgiving. Therefore, without expert guidance, learning to lead with gear will be frustrating and could be life-threatening.

I first became motivated to write this book when several newcomers asked me to recommend a book that would teach them specifically how to lead with gear. I was certain such a book existed and erroneously recommended *The Art of Leading*, which turned out to be a short video. After some research I learned that, while the information is available in chapters of several instructional texts, a book had not been written. Now it has.

Another reason I wrote this book stems from my own challenges learning to lead in Yosemite National Park in 1984—a few years prior to the advent of sport climbing (before gear-leading was referred to as "traditional"). It was a dangerous and frightening undertaking, but I didn't know it at the time. I was young and, like many of my friends, far too consumed in the glory of it all to realize the risks I took. I haphazardly borrowed equipment from (understandably) hesitant friends, and thrashed my way up anything relatively "easy," which, in Yosemite Valley, amounts to a humble smattering of routes you can count on two hands. The instructional information available at this time was sparse, and what was available wasn't as accessible as resources are today. Although the copies I owned were obscenely outdated, *Basic Rockcraft* and *Advanced Rockcraft* were my bibles, and probably helped save me numerous times.

Today, learning to lead with gear doesn't have to be the dangerous undertaking it was for me. Besides progressive developments in climbing technology, climbers learning to lead in this century have a tremendous amount of instructional information available in frequently updated books, videos, and CD-ROMs, as well as on the Web. Comprehensive classes offered through guiding services and accredited outdoor programs can provide the new leader with excellent information and hands-on experience in relatively safe environments. Learn about all the resources available to you and take advantage of them.

It took me 10 years to develop competence as a leader; the skills required are many. Traditional leading is a major undertaking—one significantly more complex than sport climbing, bouldering, or top-roping. This complexity differential is perhaps best illustrated by the analogy of open-ocean (blue-water) sailing to sailing in a bay, where land is always in sight, swells are gentle, and challenges predictable. Like open-ocean sailing, traditional lead climbing involves discovery, adventure, and risk. Without a commitment to learning, your chances of staying alive, let alone truly enjoying yourself, are slim. To embark upon learning this is to commit to a lifetime of education.

It is virtually impossible to gain the skills of an expert trad leader in one season, or even in a year. After five years, you'll realize there's even more to learn. And in 10 years, you'll still be making mistakes you thought only beginners made. Accidents can happen even to very experienced and seasoned climbers. Statistics compiled in Canada and the U.S. in 1997 indicate that climbing accidents occur equally among beginner, intermediate, and advanced climbers, a fact that should deter you from complacency at any climbing skill level.

HOW TO USE THIS BOOK

This book is intended for the intermediate, nonleading rock climber who has a desire to lead with gear. It's also ideal for the climber whose leading experience has been limited to clipping bolts in a sport-climbing setting. It is not designed to provide instruction for beginner climbers with little or no prior experience. You should own and have working knowledge of basic climbing equipment, including a harness, rope, belay device, and carabiners. General comprehension of simple systems like belaying, top-roping, and leading is essential, and a desire to absorb an enormous amount of new technical information won't hurt. If you struggle to grasp technical concepts, don't worry. You'll get it. It might just take longer and require more repetition. If you've got outdoor climbing experience, you have a significant advantage over those who do not. You'll be even more ahead of the game if you've followed and cleaned trad routes or set up removable top-rope anchors. If you're transitioning from the artificial to the organic realm, you've got a lot of work to do. Indoor gym climbing only vaguely resembles climbing on real rock, and the mountain environment where the majority of trad areas exist is a unique setting unlike any other. In addition to their climbing practices, transitional climbers will benefit from cultivating other outdoor interests like backpacking to help develop their high country instincts.

If you're in a hurry to take the sharp end on a traditional route, the guidance in this book may not work for you. But if you embrace the status of beginner and are patient enough to learn this unique and multifaceted craft at a moderate pace, you've got the right book. Just keep in mind the information here cannot replace the mentoring of a trained professional. Use the book to supplement other resources.

In the same vein, none of the information in this book is valuable without repeated application on the rock. You could memorize every last word ever published on trad leading, but without regular, hands-on practice, every trip to the crags will be like your first. By all means—read all the climbing literature you can get your hands on. Tie knots in your living room, and practice anchoring and self-rescue off your sun deck. Just don't believe that those sessions will ever replace real-time experience on the rock.

For learning purposes, this book refers to traditional lead climbing synonymously with gear-leading. Also, the techniques described refer specifically to roped free climbing on rock, using a single lead line, unless otherwise stated. More details about the origin of trad free climbing and how it differs from other methods and styles are discussed in Chapter 1. In the context of modern climbing, it is necessary to describe sport climbing in order to define traditional climbing. A style or methodology doesn't receive the label "traditional" unless it is the earlier standard, and a new and different trend (in this case, sport climbing) arises to define it as such. Comparisons help you differentiate the two styles.

This book relies on a linear approach to learning that emphasizes slow and steady progress with the guidance of a mentor or experienced trad climber. Chapters 1 and 2 explain where traditional leading fits into the realm of roped rock climbing as a whole, and details the psychosocial joys and challenges involved. After reading these chapters, you might ask yourself, do I have what it takes? Chapter 3 describes the hardware and tools you'll need. Chapter 4 explains the process of transitioning from the gym to the outdoors, and Chapter 5 emphasizes technical skill building in low-risk environments. By the end of

Chapter 6, you'll be prepared for your first single-pitch lead without relying on a back-up top-rope.

Chapters 7 and 8 are devoted to more advanced trad lead skills, including multipitch techniques, and an introduction to the fundamentals of self-rescue. Chapter 9 provides information on knot and rope craft, while discussions of ratings, climbing etiquette, and impact and access issues are found in Chapter 10. Following the main text is an afterword that encourages you on your journey as a traditional lead climber and appendices, as well as a glossary of common climbing vernacular. Throughout the book, each time I introduce a technical term or jargon, it appears in *bold italics*, indicating that it's defined in the glossary.

Some of the most valuable information in this book stems from the gleanings of several of America's most talented traditional leaders, presented throughout the book in the form of advice and tales of their own learning. These contributors shed light on numerous facets of traditional leading, from partnerships to more technical information on placing gear, falling, and retreating.

The information presented in this book is not intended to be used as a set of protocols you can fall back on at every turn. Trad climbers are most successful when they alternate between protocol and judgment-based decisions. In your beginning years, it's certainly wise to lean heavily toward protocol. But with more experience, your judgment and intuition will mature, giving you the ability to make wise and thoughtful assessments of each situation without relying as heavily on protocol. Book-smart novices expect to be safe on the rocks if, at every turn, they simply do what the protocol suggests. Although probably intelligent and talented, these folks are often some of the most dangerous climbers out there: they never allow their judgment and intuition to blossom. Eventually they run into a problem they don't ever recall reading about. Though ready to initiate a canned solution, they are stumped when the solution requires logic and a combination of skills they possess.

Keep in mind that most of us are out there pursuing these techniques because we want to have fun. Don't take yourself too seriously, laugh a lot, be safe, and enjoy the journey.

Chapter 1

Rock Climbing 101

What is traditional ("trad") climbing, and what is its relationship to sport climbing? To free climbing? To aid climbing? Where do leading and top-roping fit into the picture? Aspiring rock climbers currently entering the sport frequently ask these questions. To learn the answers, you can begin by examining roles within the typical climbing partnership, as well as by studying fundamental ascent systems and methods. But the paradigm doesn't really come into focus without some sort of historical context. By exploring the recent evolution of the roped rock-climbing experience, you gain a general understanding of the most common techniques and styles used today.

Dave Nettle Collection

ROLES & SYSTEMS

Leading is a roped ascent system with two people fulfilling roles as *leader* and *belayer* and, sometimes, *follower*. In another system known as *top-roping*, the partnership involves a climber and belayer.

Top-Roping

If you are the belayed climber in this system, a rope redirected through an anchor above protects you from a

7

serious fall. While your anchored belayer might be situated above you if you are following a route, the belayer is more commonly below you via a *yo-yo* or "slingshot" arrangement. *(See illustrations below.)*

An anchor is established atop a climb—no longer than half the distance of the length of the rope—for the yo-yo top-rope. A climber either leads the route (see "Leading" on facing page) or hikes up to access the summit. If the climber attains the top via hiking, he or she threads the rope halfway through the anchor and tosses the rope strands to the ground.

The belayer of a yo-yo arrangement is situated at the base of the route and threads a *bight* (or fold) of the rope through his or her *belay device*. The rope runs up through the anchor and back down to the climber who ties into the other end. The top-rope belayer takes in slack rope as the climber ascends. If the climber falls, the

THE "YO-YO" TOP-ROPE CLIMB

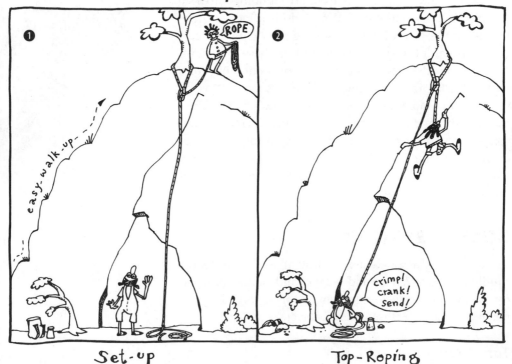

Set-up   Top-Roping

belayer engages the device's braking mechanism and, if properly belayed, the climber falls only the distance that the rope stretches.

Leading

Leading provides the answer to the age-old non-climber question "How do they get their ropes up there?" It is the only method for rigging a top-rope on a climb if its summit cannot be attained by walking or scrambling. Here's how it works: The belayer pays out rope through a belay device at the bottom of the climb as the leader, tied to one end of the rope, moves up the rock. The leader clips the rope into preestablished *bolts*, or places pieces of *protection* in *cracks* and crevices en route to the *belay stance*, where anchors are either preexisting or created on the spot with the leader's remaining gear. *(See illustrations below.)*

The Lead Climb

Leading   Cleaning (following)

If the leader falls "on lead," the belayer engages the braking mechanism, so that the rope is halted at the last piece of protection placed. If the piece is secure, the length of the fall will equal the distance above the last piece of protection placed, multiplied by two, plus rope stretch. For instance, if a fall occurs 7 feet above the leader's last piece, the approximate length of the fall is 14 feet, plus several inches of rope stretch. (*See illustrations below.*)

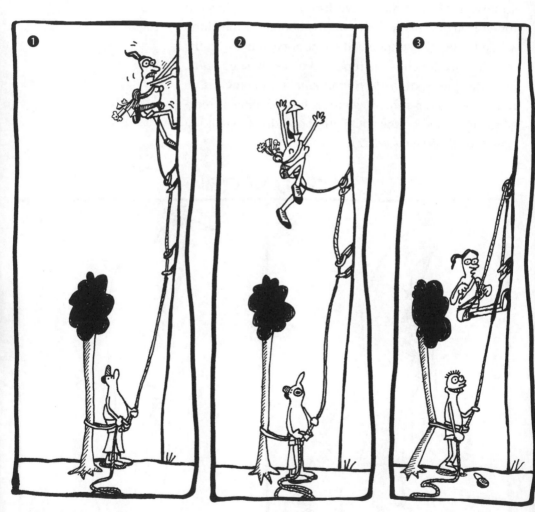

A typical lead fall

Once the leader is anchored at the top of the climb, the partners' roles change. Shifting into belayer mode, the leader provides a top-rope for his or her partner, who then takes on the role of *second*, or follower *(illustration, p. 9)*. The second is responsible for *cleaning* (removing) lead gear. Another option if route criteria allows is for the leader to lower from the anchor, cleaning the route as he or she descends, thereby establishing a yo-yo top-rope.

The second (follower) in action

BASIC ASCENT METHODS

Roped climbers attain summits via one of two ascent methods: free climbing or direct-aid climbing (or sometimes a combination of both). In general, the extent to which climbers rely on equipment best defines each method. When free climbing, equipment is used passively, while aid climbing requires active reliance on gear. Free climbing is the most common ascent method used by the majority of climbers today. Both methods might be used on a single route, most commonly on *big walls*.

Free Climbing

Free climbing is often confused with *free soloing*, the act of climbing without a rope and protection. However, free climbing involves roped climbers who wear harnesses and use belay systems and climbing hardware for safety.

Free climbing can occur either on lead or top-rope. Traditionally, free climbing means that you attempt to ascend a route by relying on your own strength, using hand- and footholds for purchase. The rope, protection points, and anchors are used passively as backups, arresting your fall should a mistake occur. But there are modern ascent tactics in which free climbers use equipment for periodic rests between a series of moves (see "Sport Climbing," p. 17 and Appendix 2).

Most free climbing today involves *clean lead ascents*, meaning to ascend without the use of *pitons* (pins) as protection. From the turn of the 20th century through the mid-1960s, pitons were carried up free routes and hammered into cracks for lead protection. But during the early '70s, preservation issues related to the increasing rock damage resulting from hammering fueled what is known as the "clean climbing revolution" (see Appendix 1). The elimination of pitons on free climbs was eventually supported by the mass production of alternate, lightweight hardware that climbers could place into cracks and remove with relative ease, all without a hammer. I discuss these devices along with other equipment in Chapter 3.

Pitons are still used occasionally on free routes, particularly on first ascents where leaders lack opportunities to place low-impact hardware. In such cases, a leader will often choose a piton over the more time-consuming and expensive option of placing a bolt.

Direct-Aid Climbing

Direct-aid, a.k.a. *artificial climbing (see illustration, left),* is another method of ascent. Aid techniques provide options when the wall is too steep or blank to allow passage via free climbing. In this method, you place a piece of lead protection, clip yourself directly into it, and then literally lean back and rest (hang) on it. To get higher to place your next piece, you ascend a pair of webbing "ladders" called *étriers* (aiders). Upward progress is slow in aid climbing as pieces cannot be placed more than a body-length apart. On harder routes, you'll frequently place lead protection that can hold only the weight of your body to get high enough to place a better piece that will hold a potential fall. Used in big wall climbing, aid climbing is sometimes alternated with free climbing on such routes.

The ascent of the second in aid climbing is supported by the use of mechanical ascenders, known generically as *Jumars*. These devices slide up the rope but not down it. Piton craft is still common on some big walls. Clean-aid (sans pitons) ascents are also popular, providing significant challenges for climbers up for the task. Severely scarred piton cracks are notoriously difficult to protect with clean-climbing gear.

Direct-aid climbing

ALPINE CLIMBING

Alpine climbing (a.k.a. *mountaineering*) involves climbing on varied terrain in a mountain setting. Snow, ice, and rock are all part of the alpine game. Many alpine routes involve a combination of free climbing and aid climbing, while others are strictly free. The combination of these factors place alpine climbing in a category all its own. The free climbing style employed in alpine climbing is "traditional" in origin (see "Traditional Free Climbing," p. 14). An alpine route exclusively involving ice is referred to as *ice climbing*, which utilizes its own distinct tools and methods of ascent.

Two distinct mountaineering styles based on speed and resource reliance help define how a party or team reaches its intended summit. Expedition-style refers to an ascent involving a large team, massive resources (gear, food, radios, etc.), and long periods of time. Alpine-style refers to a small team (usually no more than three climbers) using little gear and few resources, which allows them to move quickly up and down a mountain.

FREE CLIMBING STYLES

The development of new and diverse styles has marked 20th-century climbing. In *Basic Rockcraft*, Royal Robbins defines a "style" as the sum of methods and equipment used, plus the degree of adventure involved in the ascent. The emergence of a new climbing style often follows technological advances that allow climbers to accomplish more difficult routes, usually with increased safety.

The development of tools as complex as the nylon rope and the *spring-loaded camming device (SLCD)*, and as simple as the *hip belay* and sticky rubber have all ushered in tremendous changes. But no development has resulted in changes more momentous than that of the drill and expansion bolt. Several decades after their introduction, the drill and expansion bolt gave rise to the two distinctive free climbing styles dominant at crags today—*traditional free climbing* and *sport climbing*.

Existing under the free climbing umbrella, traditional free and sport climbing employ similar principles of ascent and roles but vastly different techniques, tools, skills, and first-ascent methods. *(See illustrations 1 and 2, p. 16)*. Prior to the widespread development of sport climbing in the 1980s, "traditional" rock climbing remained virtually undefined. As sport climbing's popularity increased worldwide, descriptive labels became necessary to distinguish the styles. Labels like "adventure climbing," "classic climbing," and "gear-leading" were frequently used to describe trad ascents, while "modern free climbing" was used occasionally to describe sport climbing. Today the terms "traditional" and "sport" are well anchored in climbing vernacular.

Traditional Free Climbing

In his June 1999 article in *Climbing* No. 186, writer Jeff Achey describes the concept of traditional climbing with disarming frankness: "Bolts and hardware don't grow naturally on cliffs. One of the defining characteristics of trad climbing is that you climb raw rock, and protect your own ass."[1] Traditional free climbing involves ascending a route from the *ground-up*, spontaneously placing pieces of removable protection from the rack wherever you deem necessary or as the rock yields. A traditional rack varies depending on the route and the climbing area. It is generally composed of an assortment of standard clean-climbing hardware of varying sizes and brands in combination with *runners* (a.k.a. slings), *quickdraws*, and *carabiners*. The trad climbing rack is discussed at length in Chapter 3.

Though numerous elements are involved in a masterful trad lead, placing secure and solid protection while maintaining mental and physical composure tops the list. Ernest Hemingway's description of courage as "grace under pressure" best portrays the successful trad leader, who balances the physical demands of climbing with the mental tasks of deciding where and how to place gear. The complexity of placing solid protection involves several factors: knowing when to stop and place a piece; knowing how to rest efficiently; deciding

how to use what's available on the rock and from your
rack creatively; understanding the mechanics of each
piece of protection; and evaluating gear size, fit, and
rock quality. All these factors play a role in the integrity
of each lead.

Traditional routes commonly, but not always, follow
crack systems. Climbers on traditional routes frequently
encounter *faces* protected by runnered trees, tied-off
natural rock protrusions like horns and knobs (chickenheads) and/or clipped bolts placed on lead (hence the
term "ground up"). Most trad climbs involve some of
each, depending on the morphology of the rock.

Trad climbs vary in length and are measured in terms
of pitches. A *pitch* is the distance between belay stances
(anchors) and generally does not exceed the length of the
rope. Trad routes can be a single pitch, or a combination
of several. Except when a yo-yo system is established on
certain single-pitch routes, a partner is required to follow
a trad lead to clean protection. If the route continues for
more than one pitch, partners will generally swap gear
and roles at the top of each. The second now becomes the
leader, and the leader becomes the follower. This is the
multipitch concept, discussed at length in Chapter 6.

Trad climbs are determined by the natural existing
features of the rock; therefore, some routes may involve
climbing sections that are either difficult or impossible to
protect. Such sections are called *runouts* and may present themselves at any time between belay anchors. For
instance, the security of a hand-sized crack may peter
out into an insidious difficult-to-protect groove. Or the
pimply features on a knobby face can diminish gradually, taking on the peaches-and-cream complexion of a
smooth wall that will not accept protection. Although
many traditional routes offer ample opportunity for protection, most trad leaders accept the fact that runouts are
often part of the game. They must always be prepared
to climb carefully through sections where protection is
sparse and potential falls are long and possibly of great
consequence.

Though belay anchors on traditional routes are sometimes pre-established with *fixed gear* such as bolts and
pitons, most routes require the establishment of removable protection. The traditional leader is constantly in

❶ Traditional free climbing

❷ Sport climbing

Traditional free and sport climbing employ similar principles of ascent and roles but vastly different techniques, tools, and skills.

gear-conservation mode to leave enough equipment to adequately protect the rest of the climb and create a safe belay anchor. The *anchor* (a.k.a. the *belay*) is located at the end of each pitch.

Communication can be difficult on traditional routes. As the leader, you often climb out of your belayer's sight and range of hearing. Your belayer's visual clue to your progress is sometimes limited to the inch-by-inch movement of the rope slithering up and across the rock face, disappearing around a corner or over a bulge.

Sport Climbing

Sport climbs occur on generously bolted routes that are usually established by *rap-bolting*, the permanent placement of bolts on walls accessed from above via rappeling. Yet some sport routes are established "on lead," usually with the assistance of direct-aid. Sport climbs are almost always protected exclusively by bolts although some might require the placement of a piece of gear or two. Most involve steep-face climbing on vertical-to-overhanging surfaces.

The abundance of closely placed bolts on sport routes eliminates much of the danger that climbers face in traditional routes, where placing protection is critical, complex, and time-consuming. Because gear responsibilities are fewer when leading a sport route, climbers can focus on continuity and difficulty; they can push their physical and mental limits and risk relatively safe, short falls, usually with minimal consequences.

A standard sport rack typically consists of several quickdraws assembled with specialized lightweight carabiners for clipping bolts and anchors. The equipment theme in sport climbing is "go light."

Most sport routes require less than half the length of a standard rope, providing leaders the option of a relatively easy retreat, by having the belayer lower them from any bolt. Since they use less than half the rope length, they can, after they reach the top, descend via lowering, establishing a yo-yo top-rope to protect subsequent climbers. Typically, the sport belayer is situated directly below the leader and is close enough for relaxed casual communication.

Sport climbs are often rehearsed at length. The leader "works" a route that he or she was previously unable to climb without falling or hanging on the rope. Working a route entails requesting frequent tension from your belayer so you can rest (hang) between difficult sections. Your eventual goal is to climb the route in one push from bottom to top with no falls or hangs. Known as the *red-point*, this mastery can take hours, days, or even months to achieve. Other styles of working routes, some of which are employed on traditional, as well as on sport, routes are discussed in Appendix 2.

Although the dangerous elements of traditional free climbing dwarf those of sport climbing, leading sport routes can still be hazardous. Improperly *back-clipping* bolts can result in the disconnection of the rope from carabiners on quickdraws, and erroneous rope positioning can flip the leader upside down if a fall occurs, making head injuries likely without a helmet. Bolts can be *manky* (old and deteriorating), compromising their strength and security. In addition, some first-ascent parties fail to space bolts close enough to protect the leader safely at all points on the route, resulting in the rare but occasional runout sport route.

GROWING PAINS

Recent Changes

Like other changes in climbing history, the emergence in the 1980s of sport climbing did not occur overnight. Trends that laid the groundwork for this new method were in the works years before, mostly in Europe but also on a more covert level in the U.S. (see Appendix 3).

Once sport climbing caught on, conspicuous changes occurred rapidly within the sport, as well as in the climbing industry. First, the continuous-move difficulty ceiling was broken as talented, visionary sport pioneers used new tactics to establish routes previously considered unclimbable. New bolted climbing areas developed seemingly overnight, and ratings everywhere shot skyward. Then, a plethora of specialized gear and apparel erupted on the outdoor retail market to arm and outfit sport climbers. Of course, the indoor-climbing concept spread like wildfire, inspiring mainstream interest and an eventual dissolution of climbing's former daredevil reputation. Eventually, these changes helped to launch the sport of climbing into the largest popularity explosion in its history.

Resistance & Ethical Debates

Changes within the sport were initially met with heated debates by two predominant factions whose voices have accompanied almost every new development in the sport since the early 1900s. The first group was made up of climbers who wholeheartedly embraced new technologies and methods as a way to push the sport's standards and complete more difficult routes. The second included those who consider themselves purists, seeking aesthetics in a "less is more" adventure. Some of the latter believe that the less they rely on technology, the more valuable their experience will be. Some free climbers of this faction suggest that if climbers can't succeed on a route without bringing the difficulty level down to their ability, perhaps they should climb something easier. Doug Robinson describes this principle elegantly in *A Night on the Ground: A Day in the Open*:

> *Technology is imposed on the land, but technique means conforming to the landscape. They work in opposite directions, one forcing a passage while the other discovers it. The goal of developing technique is to conform to the most improbable landscape by means of the greatest degree of skill and boldness supported by the least equipment.*[2]

A fierce volley of ethical accusations and criticism ensued for several years over establishing routes on rappel, specifically, and sport-climbing tactics in general. Traditionalists were paranoid that the rap-bolters' enthusiasm might transform their favorite walls into a grid of bolts, attracting swarms of people to otherwise quiet and serene crags. Sport aficionados complained that traditionalist dinosaurs, clinging to outdated methods, prevented the sport from moving forward. Trad climbers accused sport climbers of diminishing the value of achievement within the sport; sport pioneers and their young, talented protégés defended new tactics by thumbing their noses at old-schoolers with every new 5.13 they established. These heated debates were fueled by extreme emotions, probably comparable to the notorious debates in Yosemite Valley regarding the reliance on bolts and the use of fixed ropes on big walls in the 1960s (see Appendix 4).

Around 1988 I recall feeling pressure to choose one style or the other. But with time, tempers softened and the tenor of the debates changed. Both factions slowly came to embrace the "to each his own" aphorism, probably realizing that the choices climbers were making had less to do with ethics than with style. As a result, rap-bolted routes and sport-climbing tactics slowly became more and more accepted. Today most climbers tolerate and perhaps even enjoy both styles of free climbing.

Rock Climbing Today

Since the advent of sport climbing, the popularity of all facets of rock climbing has skyrocketed. According to a study conducted by the Outdoor Industry Association (OIA, formerly the Outdoor Recreation Coalition of America) with Leisure Trends and the Gallup organization, in 1998, 1.1 million people in the U.S. were climbing enthusiasts (those owning a harness and rope who went climbing more than six times that year). In 1999, 5.7 million people participated in the sport at least once during the year. In 2001, Gallup and Leisure Trends began tracking climbers who specifically climbed with a rope and harness on natural rock surface outdoors. Participation in this category of climbing (which excludes bouldering and indoor climbing) remained consistent between 2001 and 2005 at around 5 million participants. While virtually no scientific studies were conducted prior to these dates for comparison purposes, longtime climbers know that these figures reflect a tremendous increase.

Now that you have a clear picture of what modern roped rock climbing looks like today, you're ready to take a closer look at traditional lead climbing—its unique joys and challenges. In delving into the psyche of the traditional leader, Chapter 2 examines trad leading's relationship to adventure, psychology, and personal ambition.

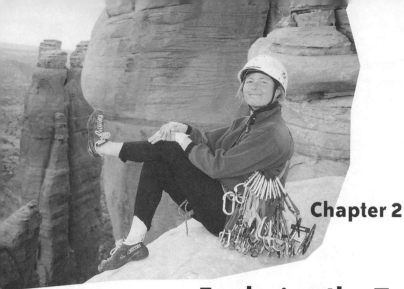

Chapter 2

Exploring the Traditional Lead Experience

A CLOSER LOOK

Traditional climbing is a complex and demanding endeavor spurring adventure, camaraderie, creativity, intuition, spontaneity, and commitment. It challenges you to be honest about your limitations and entices you by providing access to extraordinary places. It can be an extremely rewarding and joyous experience, or it can be a hair-raising joyride. It is always dangerous. Jeff Achey neatly summarizes the experience:

Key to the feeling [of traditional climbing] is invoking the spirit of mountain and crag, the inherent hazards and joys. As a trad climber you can't be squeamish. You'll be up on cliffs when it rains. You'll use loose handholds. On a great day maybe you'll get lost, cold, scared, and hungry. And when you make it back, a can of beans never tasted so good, and the campfire feels like the warm embrace of Mother Earth herself.[3]

Adventure

It's obvious that the risks of trad leading far out-weigh those of the sport lead. Why take the added risks? *Adventure*. But how do you define adventure in relation to climbing? When you set off on a traditional lead climb, you open the door to the unknown. This is the true embodiment of adventure at the crags. From the ground you may not be able to see the entire pitch. You may not know if an established anchor awaits you at the top or whether you need to conserve gear to build your own. How well you read the rock from the ground will determine whether you bring the right gear. You'll rely on your topo map, as well as your own navigational skills and intuition to find your way upward. As you ascend, the route unfolds unexpectedly, one move at a time—each corner turned or bulge surmounted chal-lenges you. If you run into trouble, you have little choice but to accept responsibility, get into action, and execute a solution. This is adventure.

Conversely, on sport turf you connect the dots up a line of pre-placed bolts with few surprises. In what is essentially a gymnastic exercise, you can see every bolt—even the anchors at the top. You know exactly how many quickdraws to bring. You know that your partner will lower you to the ground when you're ready—whether it be at the anchors or when you're simply too spent to make the next move. This may be fun, but it's not adventure.

Commitment

The risk-taking inherent in trad leading keeps com-mitment levels high. On a sport lead, if you're climb-ing poorly or the weather takes a turn for the worse, you can almost always retreat with ease. This is rarely the case when you lead a trad route. While you may be able to retreat by lowering back down to the belay, you can't depend upon it. Often there aren't solid gear options left when you run out of steam. Sometimes the route traverses so much that lowering wouldn't put you anywhere near your belayer. Most commonly you've used more than half the rope and a quick descent to the belay isn't an option. A trad lead commitment to both the summit and your partner must be bona fide. You must always climb at your best because, if you don't, your life may be at risk.

Creativity

The craft of the traditional lead is enticing because it provides vast opportunities for individual expression and creativity. Every gear-lead is itself a unique creation—a masterpiece, if you will. Free to place the pieces that you want, where you want, and when, you can stand or rest here or there. You can place a piece here if you're short, or up there if you're taller. You can muscle your way up the flake because you're better at cracks, or tiptoe around it because you're a slab master. You can jam the crack straight on, or lay it back. You can place two pieces because the move ahead looks difficult or the landing dangerous, or forgo protection for several feet when the terrain is less challenging and speed essential.

A little creativity accomplishes a lot if unexpected and complex challenges arise on lead. With hard-won experience, a solid leader's repertoire of solutions expands as his or her toolbox shrinks. Instead of relying on technology, experienced climbers solve problems with innovation. For example, when protection is difficult or sparse, trad leaders are challenged to create solutions with just a handful of resources. I've watched such leaders weave intricate chains of lead gear on routes rumored by novices to be void of protection, or runout. Similar to the way a master potter envisions infinite possibilities in a lump of clay, an experienced leader, fueled by a similar creative force, identifies safe pathways up seemingly blank stone canvases.

Simplicity

A true master trad leader doesn't need a slew of gadgets or the latest, greatest technical toy to get to the top of any climb. Self-rescue (see Chapter 8) epitomizes the concept of simplicity. A few cords, carabiners, and knots combined with knowledge of a few basic concepts is all you need to rescue yourself from any bad situation almost anywhere—quite amazing when you consider the amount of gear rescue professionals use in the front-country.

I've learned the value of simplicity in climbing through varied experiences, some unpleasant. I think the one that really shifted my climbing approach to embrace a "less is more" attitude occurred several years ago in Yosemite Valley. One fall day a friend and I decided to climb the northwest face of Higher Cathedral Rock, a "moderate" Grade IV in the valley that spits overzealous climbers from its walls regularly like a slot machine. After a pre-dawn march to the base, we were disappointed to greet two Levi–clad gentlemen sporting a slim rack of Hexes and a few old forged Friends at the base of the route. I don't even think they had belay devices. Arrogantly, we asked the team if they'd mind much if we went ahead of them. We were certain we would be the faster party, we told them. After all, my partner and I thought, we had the big cams we knew were essential for the notorious off-width near the top. Heck, these guys didn't even have a pack. Politely one of them responded, "We won't hold you up, if you don't hold us up." We were bummed but were forced into making peace with images of impatiently climbing on their heels, sharing cramped belay ledges, and a possible walk-off in the dark. In the end, only the latter came to pass. After the first pitch, we never saw the team again, and after a long, difficult day, we spent nearly the entire night finding our way down the tricky descent.

Multidimensionality

The traditional gear-lead has numerous facets. With a number of priorities constantly jockeying for your attention as leader, your focus shifts rapidly between climbing movement, placing protection, and route finding. Each requires a degree of technical and physical prowess that is impossible without remaining calm and focused. Add to this list weather considerations, rack organization, partner communication, energy and gear conservation, rope positioning, runnering, evaluation of rock quality, and anchoring, and you can understand why many leaders are overwhelmed on their first few trad forays. The challenge lies in working toward careful prioritizing, attempting to remain flexible, and mastering the delicate skill of shifting from one concept to the other and back without sacrificing mindfulness.

Camaraderie

Friendships built within the complex emotional framework of a shared adventure are gifts of traditional climbing. Swapping leads on multipitch routes has fast-forwarded more friendships than I can count. Even an afternoon of climbing single trad pitches can provide the basis of a lifetime friendship, opening the door to a sort of intimacy less common outside the realm of adventure. Here's an analogy: Spending an afternoon sport cragging is like spending an afternoon on a guided tour with an acquaintance on a paved bike path in a city park. A day spent swinging leads on a multipitch trad climb is like sharing a maniacal rickshaw ride down the unpaved backstreets of Katmandu with another traveler, unsure if the driver is sober or knows your destination. As trad-climbing partners, you're vulnerable and exposed to each other. Fear, joy, and trust meld to create an unforgettable experience. This quality of traditional leading makes time shared on the crags extremely precious and sacred, and traditional climbs memorable.

Access

Beyond its adventure, the one aspect that draws my heart to traditional climbing is access. Trad leading skills are key in ascending routes in some of the most spectacular environments on the planet. While there are some lovely sport climbing locales, many spires, towers, and ridges in wilderness settings can only be ascended by means of traditional gear routes. Long routes on such crags are generally incompatible with sport climbing simply because of logistics. The vast majority of established rock climbing routes in the world involve gear placement.

PSYCHOLOGICAL FACTORS

The psychological fitness required of the trad leader involves a unique ability to concentrate on the task at hand, shift from one task to another, cope with fear and danger, and honor personal limitations.

Concentration

Concentration is a skill required of all leaders. Traditional leads in particular demand a climber's utmost attention because even slight distractions can lead to dire consequences. Obstacles that make focusing difficult generally stem from internal distractions, holding us captive in either the past or the future. Your mind generates distractions that take a variety of forms. On some days, you wonder whether or not you have the skills to succeed on the chosen route. Other days you mentally rehash the argument you had with a loved one earlier in the day, thinking of all the things you should have said but didn't. And sometimes your mind will avoid the present moment by creating lists—what to buy at the store for dinner, climbing areas you'd like to visit, routes you'd like to climb, jobs for which you'd like apply—and the lists go on.

To lead climb effectively you need ways to screen out distractions. You could explore the finer points of stabilizing the mind through relaxation and breathing techniques. Meditating regularly can also improve concentration skills by enhancing awareness. As you develop the ability to relax on lead, you notice that in the present moment your busy mind stabilizes, your focus increases, and your performance becomes enhanced.

Decision-Making & Multitasking

On gear-leads be prepared to make split-second decisions while juggling a multitude of equally important tasks. Your success will stem from confidence and intuition gained from experience and time on the rock. Most decisions you make as the leader will affect the safety of both you and your partner. In the beginning, the multitasking nature of trad leading will overwhelm you. You'll wonder how to ever focus on the physical aspect of climbing itself. For awhile the trad lead will be all about gear and you'll barely remember making moves between pieces. As your skills develop over time, though, your movements take on a natural flow—you're able to focus on the climbing at hand while calmly addressing other tasks as they arise. When decision-making becomes second nature, situations that once were colossal are easily resolved.

Climber: Steph Davis

Years Trad Free Climbing: 15

Favorite Trad Climbing Areas: Indian Creek & the Diamond on Long's Peak

Most Respected Trad Free Climber: Layton Kor

Kennan Harvey

Talking Yourself Through Fear & Suffering

To stay mentally focused during hard trad leads, I've had to cope effectively with two common stumbling blocks: fear and suffering. The techniques I use to negotiate both issues involve talking to myself. When I'm most successful negotiating with pain and suffering, I actually hear my voice inside my head—it's that calculated.

Fear—If I'm really afraid, I try to moderate my breathing and concentrate on the nuts and bolts of safety. I run down a mental checklist in my head to make sure the basics are covered. Is my protection the best that it can possibly be? Is the rope positioned properly? Am I using all the best footholds and handholds? Sometimes when you're really scared, you just can't see—it's as if you've become blinded by fear. So if you calm your mind long enough to bring these three basic things into focus, you will reinforce your feeling of being safe, which in turn makes you less afraid.

Suffering—Some climbs—long desert crack climbs spring to mind—are hard because the climbing actually hurts. The pitch may be quite safe but, as it drags on and the physical pain increases, deep down inside you begin to think of giving up—you lose interest in getting to the top. When I'm grinding through something like this, I remember that when it's over I'll be glad I persevered. As a waitress in Moab, my mantra for pushing through on Indian Creek pitches was would you like some more iced tea? When my muscles are screaming, my body is hurting, and I'm having a hard time finding motivation to keep going, I remind myself that I'd given up on law school, a Ph.D., and many other opportunities so that I could be doing this, so I damn well better give it my all!

—Steph Davis

Coping with Fear & Danger

For the traditional leader, ineffectively coping with fear threatens safety, let alone success. Yet fear can be healthy. By fostering your respect for (and attention to) the mountains and nature, it keeps you alive. But at its worst, it's a liability morphing into terror, then panic and, soon, paralysis. To lead trad routes you must manage and channel fear into a useful energy that doesn't undermine your goals.

Climber Marc Twight describes how to use self-discipline to harness fear and transform it into a source of strength:

> *To climb through fear, to point fear up instead of down, you need to maintain the desire and strength, the will and discipline, to go until the end of the pitch. If you are scared, reinforce your confidence by biting off what you know you can chew. Successfully swallowing it will encourage you to take another bite, another pitch. . . . Trust in your skill, and give yourself up to the action.*[4]

Although Twight addresses extreme alpine climbing, his description of manipulating fear can apply in nearly any climbing scenario. If you are the type of person likely to respond to urgent situations with thoughtful action rather than immobilization, you're probably capable of transforming fear into fuel to keep you safe and moving upward, a little at a time.

AMBITION

By providing the momentum needed to attain goals and gain confidence, ambition plays a positive role in your life, whether you express it by attending a job interview, giving a presentation at work, or running a marathon. In climbing, ambition lets you progress in skill level as you're willing to tackle increasingly difficult routes. To advance safely in the trad leading sphere though, you must balance your ambition with a healthy dose of reason.

Honoring Personal Limitations

Problems develop when the excitement of achieving a climbing goal interferes with a clear appraisal of your capabilities. According to American Alpine Club (AAC) data for the past five years, climbers misjudging their abilities is one of the most common contributing causes of reported accidents in both the U.S. and Canada.

Sometimes the desire to say you've done one route or another, coupled with the satisfaction of checking it off your list, is more attractive than the immense effort and preparation necessary to actually *do* the route. During my first season in Yosemite, I found myself so enthralled by talk of big walls that I committed myself to a route high above the valley floor where I, unskilled and frightened, faced tasks I was completely unprepared for. A route that most climbers at that time completed in a day and a half took my partner and me three days. My overzealous will to "have done" a big wall, together with my misappraised abilities, endangered us. I became so flustered while attempting to follow a traversing aid pitch that I panicked and froze, requiring my partner to rappel down to help me. After our ropes became a tangled macramé, we spent our last daylight hour disentangling the mess. We discovered at one point to our horror that we had both untied from the rope and clipped off the same, single, fixed piton, circa 1950, no doubt.

A few days later, after miraculously summiting unharmed, we were safely back down on the valley floor. When an experienced local climber commented that I "had no business going up there," I recall being miffed. Years later I realized this person had been right. Being accepted by my peers for having done a big wall at the time completely overshadowed my awareness that I didn't have adequate experience or skills. A year later I returned to the valley with many more skills and experience on the rock, and safely completed two additional walls in decent time and with no major *epics*.

Questioning Motives

Thinking your climbing goals through requires rigorous awareness of your motives, as well as your skill level. Had I taken the time to think through my first big wall adventure, I would have recognized I had more

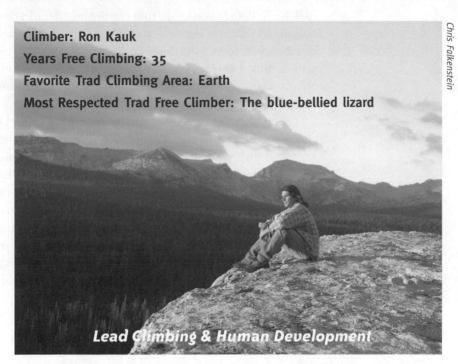

Climber: Ron Kauk

Years Free Climbing: 35

Favorite Trad Climbing Area: Earth

Most Respected Trad Free Climber: The blue-bellied lizard

Chris Falkenstein

Lead Climbing & Human Development

Leading allows you the opportunity to work in a balanced way with all of the elements of your humanness: emotion, judgment, ability, ego. It's an unbelievable teacher and educator. That's the beauty of bothering yourself to put on a rack and climb up a rock really—all this potential human development. The way you are on lead is a direct reflection of your approach to everyday life. Are you organized? Are you respectful toward the natural world? Are you hurried? Flexible? Humble? Are you trying to prove something to someone else? Egos are very tricky. They can sneak up on you and play games with your mind. Just when you're convinced you are operating without ego is often the time when it's bigger than ever, simply because you believe this. It's nuts! If you become egotistical about your achievements and believe you are superior because you have something more than everyone else, you're in trouble. You miss the point, and any positive aspect of your experience will backfire. You could actually become arrogant enough that your ego will walk you right off the side of a cliff. As a new leader, follow your own experience and avoid comparing yourself to anyone else. Your true strength will shine in your ability to humble yourself and connect with the natural world with balance and respect. We're all equal whether you believe it or not.

—Ron Kauk

work to do before taking on that challenge. I would have recognized that my ego was convincing me that I could do whatever made me look cool. Some very dangerous intentions can be veiled by ambition. Tilted heavily toward desire, they are often light on reason and humility.

When you find yourself at the base of a challenging route desiring to climb it because so and so is at the crags and you want to show off, because everyone else you know has led it, or simply because you'd like to tick it off your list, take a minute to adequately assess your abilities. Remember there's a lot more at stake on trad climbs. Are you puffed up with unbalanced ambition? Are you succumbing to peer pressure? A climber who lives to climb another day can walk away from a trad climb thinking *Not today* or *I'm not ready*. A climber who walks away can always return another time when he or she feels ready.

Chapter 3

Tools of the Trad

Mike Davis Collection

Traditional leading requires specific gear. Your previous climbing experience has most likely resulted in the acquisition of a harness, shoes, belay device, *chalk bag*, rope, and perhaps a modest rack for top-roping. If you're coming into the trad realm by means of sport climbing, you may have a few more items. Although some crossover use is possible, climbing gear has become so highly specialized that you're probably going to need an entirely new set of tools, specifically chosen with traditional lead climbing in mind.

GENERAL GEAR CONSIDERATIONS

The accumulation of trad lead climbing gear doesn't usually happen in a day. This shopping spree is bound to last several years. Discovering exactly what to buy and why takes some effort. Cost is also a consideration. You may want to be absolutely sure you thoroughly dig trad climbing before you invest. If you're gung ho, there's really little you can do to ease the financial crunch unless you hook up with a friend who's on a similar quest. Finally, once you get your gear, you need to do what you can to keep it by marking it in such a way that it is easily identified as yours.

33

Cost

Some relish the task of acquiring the necessary accoutrements for trad leading (especially self-styled gearheads or equipment nerds), but nearly everyone balks at the costly investment. If you gear-lead with a trustworthy friend, you can cut your initial costs in half. I'm not recommending sharing gear but rather each climber owning half of the gear to complete a rack. After the initial investment, you can both leisurely fill out your individual racks over time. This way you find out what products you prefer without emptying your pocketbook. But you both still need your own personal harness, shoes, chalk bag, *rappel device*, and *nut tool*.

Research

Thorough research prior to any large purchase is always a good idea. You may become overwhelmed and confused though by the abundance of gear on the market, the technicality of the products, and the massive amounts of information available, particularly on the Internet. You may or may not find valuable information by visiting climbing chat rooms, newsgroups, forums, and the like. It's difficult to trust what you read in these online salons since it's almost impossible to confirm the contributors' experience level. Local rock guides are usually good sources, as are small, independent retail mountaineering shops where employees tend to be fairly knowledgeable. Product reviews in climbing magazines usually feature informed opinions, but of course you must remember that panning an item could potentially hurt the publication's relationship with their valued advertisers. You should also be wary of online publications that rely on advertisers.

For detailed technical information on strength ratings and testing, refer to the manufacturers' catalogs and Websites. Some companies provide more details than others. Unless you're a mechanical engineer, metallurgist, or physicist, don't expect to be able to understand typical research and development findings easily. Beware, also, of making choices based solely on strength comparisons or any other single quality. Strength ratings are relative and situational.

Before purchasing trad gear, consider the following criteria:

1. **Versatility.** Can the item serve more than one purpose? (For example, some belay devices can double as rappel devices, and you can use some carabiners in applications from racking gear and leading to self-rescue).

2. **Market longevity.** How long has the item been around? When it comes to manufacturing climbing gear, wisdom comes with age. Purchase brands and products with longevity on the market. These items have spent a lot of time in research and development labs and in the hands of product testers. If a product has been around awhile, it has usually gone through several stages of refinement.

3. **Home-Crag Friendliness.** Ultimately, the gear you choose must suit the type of rock on which you'll most frequently be leading. What works best in the narrow, nonuniform cracks in Eldorado Canyon is a disaster in Indian Creek's splitter, parallel cracks. Talk to a trusted local.

4. **Crossover Use.** Will your partners recognize and feel comfortable using the gear you purchase for your rack? This factor is another good reason to consider market longevity—products that have been around longer are likely widely used and therefore generally familiar to many leaders.

Before using your gear, read the directions carefully and thoroughly. Learn how to properly care for and store your items and when to recognize that retirement is in order. Sometimes gear may be damaged internally but have few external signs of wear and tear. World-class climber Todd Skinner might still be alive if his well-worn harness had been put out to pasture before it broke mid-rappel in a tragic accident in Yosemite Valley in 2006. The American Mountain Guides Association (AMGA) recommends replacing nylon items every five years and hardware every 10, regardless of use. When in doubt, retire it.

Identification

To identify your gear, mark hardware and runners with colored electrical tape. Some climbers prefer to etch their initials into hardware—this lasts forever but takes a significant time commitment. Sort gear after every climb to ensure it stays in your possession. I am now a fanatic about sorting, after years of slow but steady gear loss. No one intentionally "adopts" your gear, it just happens when so much is community property.

BASIC EQUIPMENT

Purchasing all this gear won't be as traumatic if you approach it piecemeal. Begin by fulfilling the basic trad needs: You'll want a comfortable, hearty harness; a good pair of all-around trad shoes that work well on slabs and in cracks; a lightweight belay device that doubles as a rappel device; and a big locking carabiner to attach the device to your harness. You'll also need to purchase a rope. Finally, a nut tool, wide-mouthed chalkbag, and gear sling complete your basic trad ensemble.

Shoes

Find a knowledgeable salesperson with traditional climbing experience to help you choose a pair of shoes for trad routes. Most salespeople offering to help with climbing boots are unqualified to do so, especially in larger chain stores. When making such a pricey investment, you want to walk out with the right pair. If you can't find an informed sales clerk, bring along someone with trad savvy, or at least first obtain a few style and brand recommendations from someone you trust. Another option might be to borrow or rent a pair of shoes to see how they feel on real rock. This is an optimal solution, though it limits size and brand options.

Since traditional cragging involves varied terrain, an all-round model is often a good starter shoe. Look for a moderately stiff pair you think you'll be able to tolerate wearing all day. Most of these are going to have a substantial midsole to support the foot as your muscles develop. You'll probably want to avoid choosing a pair that has an extremely cambered design (which resembles the arched spine of an angry cat), mainly because it lacks the support and comfort of good beginner trad climbing shoes. Modeled after a foot with down-curled toes, extremely cambered boots are used for high performance sport climbing.

A high-top boot that protects your ankles in cracks is a wise choice, especially if you'll be climbing a lot of cracks that are hand-size and larger. Unfortunately, only a few manufacturers still make high tops. Slippers are ideal for bouldering and on short, thin crack routes, but I don't recommend them as your primary trad-climbing shoe. They're not as versatile, will really hurt your feet in wider cracks and on long routes, and will wear much faster since they are usually made with significantly less rubber than lace-ups.

Consider purchasing a second, more specialized pair for terrain on which you'll be climbing most. Eventually, you'll want to have at least two pairs of trad shoes on hand anyway—one to take the place of a pair that's blown out and needs repair. Most veteran climbers own several pairs for a variety of venues. Your second pair for trad cragging may be a bit softer—perhaps a pair with a more flexible midsole for increased sensitivity and fancy footwork. Or, if you find yourself frequently on wide cracks and long routes, a more specialized, super stiff boot might serve you well.

Beware of salespeople convincing you to buy a size so tight that your feet scream out in pain. While climbing boots are not designed to be as comfortable as street shoes, the trad fit should be snug, not painful. If your toes curl in the toe box, try a larger shoe. Spend some time in the boots you're considering; take a stroll around the shop a few times. Do some bouldering if the shop has an artificial wall for that purpose.

Although you're looking for comfort, make sure the fit isn't sloppy. If your feet slide around or rotate inside the boots when you lace them, they're probably too big. Most climbing shoes stretch a little but not a lot. Stretch occurs mostly in width, and more with shoes sans lining. Socks are a personal choice. I don't wear them but my boots collect perspiration odor, and I suffer when temperatures drop. If you prefer socks, try a thin, polyester-blend liner sock. The bulkier the sock, the more sensitivity is lost.

Harness

Choose a harness for trad climbing with five important features: a padded waist belt, a minimum of two gear loops, one rear *haul loop*, and easily released, padded leg loops. Leg loops that easily unhitch are essential for when nature calls and are an absolute must for women. They also allow their wearer to put on another layer of clothing without unbuckling his or her harness. Surprisingly, some available harnesses do not offer this feature. Many harnesses on the market also lack a haul loop. In terms of padding, you will definitely appreciate the comfort of wide, significantly padded waist belts and leg loops on long routes, at hanging belays, and on descents that require multiple rappels. While adjustable leg loops are not absolutely necessary, they do allow adjustment for the varied thickness of your clothing. And if you gain or lose a few pounds, you probably won't have to purchase a new harness.

A properly fitting harness should be snug but not tight. If possible, try on the harness you're thinking of purchasing and, literally, hang in it. If the waist belt rides high up on your ribs, or if the leg loops tend to dangle loosely below your crotch instead of becoming taut, try something smaller. The waist belt should have at least a 3-inch (7.5-millimeter) tail after doubling back.

Female climbers should closely examine what manufacturer's market as "women's harnesses" before purchasing one. Often the "special" features of these gender-specific items amount to nothing more than a harness shaved down to the bare minimum with very little padding. Such harnesses can prove to be extremely uncomfortable, particularly in the trad climbing environment.

Belay/Rappel Device

Tubes, plates, figure eights, mechanized auto-locking, and a few others make up the vast assortment of belay devices on the market today. When selecting one, first consider:

1. **Ease of use.** Is the device known for easy rope feeding? Your partner counts on this. The leader needs rope fed out quickly and smoothly at all times, particularly when he or she is runout, teetering on a small stance, and trying to coax the rope into the safe cradle of a carabiner.

2. **Design.** You're going to be carrying it around for hundreds of feet at a time. Is it light? Is it bulky?

3. **Versatility.** Can it double as a rappel device? It should, as rappelling is a common practice on the trad front.

The ideal device is lightweight, lacks bulk, and can be used for rappelling. You must also be able to feed out rope smoothly and quickly without sacrificing too much braking quality.

Various tube model belay devices

The aforementioned criteria eliminate most mechanized camming devices (such as the GriGri). The average figure eight is bulky and tends to twist the rope. Now consider the diameter of your rope. What remains is still a considerable lot. I am partial to tube and plate models *(see photo, top right)*. While you want a device that has both excellent braking capability and allows for easy rope-feeding, you can't have both. Unfortunately when you buy a device featuring one of these attributes, you sacrifice the other. If a device allows effortless rope feeding, a more alert, proactive belayer is required for optimal braking. There is certainly nothing wrong with this. In fact the majority of trad climbers I know, including guides, prefer such a device (like Black Diamond's ATC), known by some as a "slick" device. Other devices (like Wild Country's VC Pro) offer increased braking quality; if a belayer isn't paying attention and does little to arrest a partner's fall, the device cinches down significantly anyway. The tradeoff is that it's trickier to feed rope through these devices, particularly after braking. These units are sometimes described as "grabbing" devices. Between the two are "intermediate" devices like HB's Sprung Sticht Plate, lacking somewhat in easy feed-out, but a good piece of gear, nevertheless, in the hands of a skilled belayer.

With such a huge variety of specialized gear, when you gain a desirable feature, you often give up another. My favorites are "slick" tube devices (like the ATC-XP and XP Guide) featuring unilateral grooves that offer increased friction when you need it (on steep terrain with thinner ropes) and less when you don't (low-angle terrain, yo-yo top-roping, and thicker ropes). If you decide on a tube device, choose one with thick walls for optimal heat dissipation. Narrow-walled devices heat up to flesh-searing temperatures and are subject to grooving that can create undetectable sharp edges that can harm your rope. The good thing about belay devices is that they are relatively inexpensive. If you're unhappy with your choice, you won't have to sell the farm to get a different one.

Locking Carabiners

Assortment of large locking carabiners

You must use a locking carabiner (*locker*)—the bigger, the better—as your primary carabiner, linking you to your partner while belaying and to the rope while rappelling. Choose one with a large diameter opening to easily accommodate more knots and slings if needed. A variety of lock styles are available, the most common of which is the screw gate. These are fine, as long as you are diligent about locking them, and choose a "gate lock" instead of a "nose lock." The latter can become stuck in the gate-locked position. Spring-loaded auto-locking 'biners are also available. I like both styles. If you choose an auto-locker but also have screw gates on your rack, be sure you don't get so used to the mindless auto-lock feature that you neglect to close the other gates manually.

Another locking carabiner is necessary for clipping yourself into anchors. Although it doesn't need to be as big as your primary locker, the larger it is the more versatile it will be. Eventually, you'll need a few more medium-sized lockers for self-rescue, as well as one small one for key lead pieces.

Ropes

Lead-climbing ropes must be dynamic (rather than static)—they stretch to absorb shock and dissipate energy generated by a fall. Made from nylon, they have a kern-mantle construction: a tough inner core (kern) that is the main load-bearing portion of the rope and an outer sheath (mantle) that protects it from abrasion.

Most trad leaders use either a single-rope or double-rope system for leading, with a twin-rope system being less common. Each system has its pros and cons. Throughout this book, I refer predominantly to the single-rope system, which requires ropes identified by a circled number "1" on a label located at one end of the rope.

The standard length of lead ropes for general rock climbing is gradually shifting from 165 feet (50 meters) to 200 feet (60 meters). Although most pitches (especially in the U.S.) are still 165 feet or less, I wouldn't recommend a length less than 200 feet, especially if you plan on traveling, as newer routes (both sport and trad) in many other countries frequently surpass 50 meters.

In general, the larger the diameter of a rope, the stronger and more durable it is. Rarely seen anymore except in recreational settings are the 11-millimeter workhorses used frequently on big walls, where ropes suffer significant abuse from hauling and ascending. A 10-millimeter rope is a good choice for all-round trad purposes, although some climbers use smaller-diameter single ropes for backcountry ascents or for red-point attempts when weight might be a factor. By going light, you sacrifice durability and may have to retire your rope sooner than with a larger diameter cord.

Though a "dry" rope costs more, I prefer it over a "nondry" cord for trad climbing, particularly if you climb multipitch mountainous routes or in areas prone to thunderstorms. Dry ropes receive a treatment that helps prevent rainwater absorption. When a rope has absorbed a lot of water, it becomes heavier and less able to cushion a fall. And in very cold conditions, absorbed water can freeze, making the rope weaker and less manageable. While some treatments wear off with use, products can be purchased and applied to rejuvenate it.

Lead ropes are available in solid colors, bicolors, or bipatterns. The latter assist climbers in quickly locating the midpoint of their ropes. This excellent timesaving feature, which costs a bit more, may also increase safety. If you don't have the extra cash, purchase Blue Water's special rope pen (made without damaging chemicals), mark your rope's center, and reapply as necessary.

Each type of lead rope is tested to failure (until it breaks) and assigned a strength rating based on the number of falls it tolerates. The average ranges from seven to nine and, as you might guess, larger diameter ropes tend to tolerate more falls. So, it is crucial for climbers to be diligent about recording each significant leader fall and retire lead ropes accordingly. (See Chapter 6 for more information on ropes and lead falls.)

Besides fall ratings, ropes are also rated for "maximum impact force" and "static elongation." Static elongation refers to the amount a rope stretches during strength testing when weighted by a load of 176 pounds (80 kilograms). A low rating means the rope won't stretch as much under load, a favorable characteristic for ropes used specifically for rappelling, hauling, and ascending. A higher elongation rating, which means the rope stretches more under load and is more comfortable for a climber, is desirable for leading.

Maximum-impact force is the force transmitted to a climber during a fall. The lower the impact force, the more the rope absorbs energy generated in a fall, transmitting less to the system and the climber. Since gear isn't always optimal in the trad lead setting, a rope rated for lower maximum impact is preferable in some situations but not necessarily required. Because a lower maximum-impact force translates into more rope stretch, the downside may be a longer fall. (More information on rope strength and loads is discussed in Chapter 6.)

Many climbers who lead on a single rope own a second, smaller-diameter rope specifically for use as a *trail line*. This rope is used for descents requiring double-rope rappels, for hauling a pack, or simply as a backup for unplanned retreats. Your trail line can also be utilized as an emergency lead line should your primary rope become damaged. For this reason you'll want a dynamic trail rope on which you'd feel fairly comfortable leading in an emergency. Personally, I'd lead on a single 9 millimeter in an emergency, but I cringe at the thought of taking the *sharp end* on anything smaller. Others feel differently based on the unlikelihood of such an occurrence and are willing to go lighter.

Handle all climbing ropes with care: avoid stepping on them, and keep them clean and out of the dirt. Rope bags are nice for casual cragging, but don't fit easily into a pack. I carry a square yard of inexpensive nylon tarp material to keep my rope out of the dirt. Immediately retire ropes with damaged sheaths or exposed cores. Exposure to excessive heat (above 120°F or 50°C), sunlight (ultraviolet light), solvents, or chemicals including uric acid (found in urine) should also dictate retirement. Other signs of excessive wear that indicate the need for replacement include inconsistency in texture, unusual stiffness or softness, and glossy marks on the sheath. Wash your rope in a bathtub with warm water and no soap. Allow it to dry uncoiled in a warm, dry location out of the sun. Never put your rope in a dryer.

The Sterling Rope Company recommends these general guidelines for rope retirement based on use periods:

- Three months to six months when used extensively or daily

- About two to three years when used regularly on weekends

- About three to five years when used occasionally

According to Sterling, the actual working life of a rope should never exceed five years.

Helmet

As Russ Walling of FISH Products says, "Helmets are cool." "Brain buckets" have been available for years but the majority of climbers early on couldn't be bothered—they were uncomfortable, heavy, claustrophobic, and hindered your sight. To top it off, they also looked geeky. Years ago a partner of mine demanded to know in frustration as her helmet slumped over her eyes, "When are the bike helmet people going to get together with the climbing helmet makers?"

Sometime in the mid-1990s climbers began to care more about their noggins than fashion and comfort, and helmets began to sell like gangbusters. In response, manufacturers began funneling more energy into helmet design, resulting in several lightweight fiberglass-blend models—which are honestly quite comfortable—featuring high-tech ventilation and adjustment systems. Since then, manufacturers have made helmets even lighter and more comfortable by developing options using molded polyurethane "foam" core similar to today's bicycle helmets. It seems the jury's still out on these items, but some critics report that while they offer better protection against side impacts (most likely the result of falling), they offer significantly less penetration resistance and impact protection (to protect you from falling rock or gear). A foam-core helmet is rated for one-time impact; after any such incident, it must be retired. More often than not the damage is visible. While their hard-shell cousins seem to be able to withstand more abuse, they too, should be retired after a single major impact, even though there may be no visible signs of demise. I still prefer fiberglass-blend models. When choosing a helmet, find an adjustable model that fits your head best and is approved by either the *CEN* or the *UIAA* or perhaps even both. Don't order a helmet from a catalog unless you've tried it on and are certain you like the design. Don't end up with a helmet you hate—it's too easy to leave an unsatisfactory helmet at the base of a climb if you even bring it to the site.

Make sure your helmet adjusts properly for a snug fit. One gear supplier told me his company performed its own tests on helmets and discovered that some, although UIAA-approved, fit poorly after all the manufacturer's directions were followed. If, after adjustments, your helmet shifts even slightly to the back or side of your head, it's not going to provide the proper protection.

A helmet protects you from more than just rockfall. The most common climbing head injuries occur as the result of lead climbing falls. Perhaps the new lightweight helmets will gain favor in some settings in the future because of this fact. Still you must consider that a falling carabiner or a shard of ice rocketing down the face of a climb on a warm spring day can crack a skull as well. But, since a helmet cannot protect you from extreme impact forces, do what you can to stay out of harm's way (see "Rockfall," p. 183).

Chalk Bag

Choose a chalk bag on the larger side. Smaller bags are usually designed with sport climbers in mind, who rarely need to chalk up more than their finger tips. Widemouthed bags are generally preferred by traditional lead climbers because the design allows climbers to coat their entire hands easily. Attach the bag to your waist with tubular nylon webbing instead of purchasing a belt with a plastic buckle. Thread it through both the bag and your belay/rappel loop and secure with a ring bend (see "Knots

& Hitches", p. 221). Now it functions as a harness back-up and provides an extra sling if you run low on lead!

Nut Tool

Gear-leading requires that the follower carry a nut tool to extract snug nut placements (and sometimes cams) while cleaning each pitch. I always carry my own rather than sharing it with a partner. Many suitable designs are available. Buy one with a hooked tip for removing stuck cams and larger nuts with eyeholes (see Chapter 5, p. 113). Keep your nut tool on its own carabiner and attached with about 1 foot (30 centimeters) of small-diameter accessory cord. The tool can then be clipped short for carrying or extended for use *(see photos 1 and 2)*.

Gear Sling

Your *gear sling* should be padded and adjustable. Some companies offer fleece-lined comfort while others make closed-cell-foam slings. Since trad parties need only one rack at a time, you frequently share your rack with a partner, who may not be your size. Before adjustable gear slings I schlepped my way up routes with gear dangling halfway to my knees, like a kid playing dress-up in adult clothes. I finished each climb with the blackest and bluest thighs seen outside of a shelter. Other women and smaller-framed men can attest to the misery they experienced prior to adjustable gear slings.

One particular type of gear sling on the market today features sectioned loops. Though I've never used a sectioned gear sling, many climbers like them. Still, a petite friend told me that this style didn't work well on her small frame.

Nut tool clipped short (top) and extended (bottom)

THE RACK

In climbing terms, the rack is not a torture device, a pair of antlers, nor a place to hang your fleece. The climber's rack loosely refers to the collection of hardware you bring up on lead with you on your gear sling. Your rack is comprised of gear with which you'll build anchors and pieces you'll place intermittently on lead between belays.

It also includes metal snap-links (specifically, carabiners) used to connect hardware to software like the rope, runners, and cords (described in the next section).

Spring-Loaded Camming Devices (SLCDs)

The invention of the SLCD in the mid-1970s revolutionized gear-leading like no other hardware breakthrough. Cams offer protection where nothing else fits, are easy and fast to place once you learn how, and, if placed correctly, are simple to remove.

With a plethora of SLCDs to choose from, most are versatile enough for general use while some excel for specific applications. Specialty offset devices work wonders in thin, corrugated cracks and flares but teeter helplessly in parallel-sided splitters. A fat, 4-cam device offering 35 percent more surface contact than like-sized cams perfectly addresses desert sandstone climbers' needs, but try to get this piece to work in a granite pin scar.

With so many choices available, you may be tempted to own a few of each. For a starter rack, though, stick with just a few brands. Cam manufacturers, curiously, don't share the same sizing scale; owning various brands, therefore, means constantly translating from one size range to another. A fairly uniform cam rack in the beginning of your trad career gets you comfortable with a few designs' sizing ranges, color codes, and technical capabilities. Also, if you mix and match brands, your cams won't hang uniformly, making it more difficult while leading to view the cams at a glance. You can find comprehensive comparison charts of SLCDs online.

Assorted SLCDs

Most SLCD manufacturers offer two stem designs: the U-stem and the central cable. Stem designs probably won't mean much to you as a new trad leader. After some tinkering on lead, however, you may develop a preference. Some stems are more flexible, while others are longer. Triggers vary, too, a detail that is mostly a personal preference depending primarily on hand size. Since operating triggers on some SLCDs may be awkward if you have large hands, spend some time in stores pulling those of various brands before you buy. Or, better yet, borrow an assortment from friends and try them out at your local crags.

SLCDs are available with 2, 3, or 4 cams. Generally, the fewer the cams, the more narrow the head profile. Two-cam units fill a unique specialty need and are discussed at the end of this chapter. Three-cam units have narrow heads that fit well. They are ideal in rounded pin scars and shallow pods. Four-cam units are usually more stable (less likely to pivot), and some possess holding power superior to that of 3-cam units, but they are not as versatile. I prefer a combination because 3-cam SLCDs work wonders at most of the crags I frequent. Talk to local climbers to determine your need for 3-cam units. For larger sizes (1 inch and up), I recommend 4-cam units unless the features at your home crag dictate otherwise.

The dual-axle design, currently sold only by Black Diamond, offers the greatest expansion range of all SLCDs. The drawback of these beauties is that they are slightly heavier than similar-size cams, as well as more expensive. Yet the flexibility gained from having wider expansion is worth the extra weight and money for new leaders.

A standard SLCD rack adequate for most trad climbing areas has two cams of each size up to approximately 3 inches and one for sizes 3–4.5 inches. Because this optimal rack makes for an enormous initial investment, you might consider purchasing your 1.5- to 3-inch sizes first and filling in the remaining gaps with less expensive Stoppers (nuts), Hexes, and Tri-Cams.

A final word on cam purchase: SLCD manufacturers who have been making cams for a long time (like Wild Country, Black Diamond, Colorado Custom Hardware, and Metolius) have an edge over those newer to the game. While other brands can be as good, you have to carefully weigh these purchases when you're hemorrhaging money for gear you hope will last a long time.

Stoppers

Stoppers (a.k.a. *nuts*, *tapers*, or *chocks*) are considered "passive" gear because they have no moving parts. For your trad rack, start with a combination of curved and straight Stoppers.

Various Stoppers (nuts)

Though curved nuts aren't any stronger than straight ones are, they tend to set better, wrapping around tiny inconsistencies inside the crack. For general terrain, carry doubles of small and medium sizes (¼-¾ inch or 6–21 millimeters) and singles of micro and larger sizes.

Before purchasing nuts under ¼ inch (6 millimeters), consider the type of rock on which you'll most often be climbing. If you lead on granite, the superior metal choice for micro nuts is steel or a steel blend. Steel won't deform under stress, while softer metals can shear out of a granite crack. If you're leading on softer rock such as limestone, use brass, bronze, or copper-infused Stoppers because force generated onto a steel nut placement in soft rock can shatter the rock around it.

Offset nuts made by companies like DMM and Hugh Banner (HB) are great specialty pieces that you may choose to add to your standard wired selection eventually. These asymmetrical gems are designed to lock into the rock's subtle irregularities, and work great if you're dealing with sections of corrugated, bottlenecked cracks that aren't parallel.

❶
Lowe Tri-Cams

Hexcentrics & Tri-Cams

Tri-Cams (see photo 1) and ***Hexcentrics*** (Hexes) *(see photo 2)* are known as "passive" camming devices and are lighter and far less expensive than SLCDs. Smaller Tri-Cams work particularly well in shallow flares and pin scars. The latest Black Diamond Hex design fits into four different crack configurations and works best in tapered slots. Metolius makes a curved design. The drawbacks of these devices are that they are much less versatile than SLCDs and take time, patience, and thought to place correctly.

❷
Hexcentrics

Carabiners

Consider strength and versatility when choosing carabiners for your trad rack. A combination of standard and asymetrically shaped Ds *(see photo 3)* is a good choice for most of your 'biner collection. A few ovals *(see photo 4, top of facing page)* come in handy for racking Stoppers, performing ***carabiner brake*** rappels (see Chapter 9), and

❸
Standard (above) and
asymetrical (below)
D carabiners

accommodating multiple knots or webbing. Yet ovals are not as strong as standard Ds. Asymmetrical Ds generally have larger gate openings than standard Ds so clipping is easier. Smaller at one end than the other, they also tend to be somewhat lighter. However, they aren't as versatile as your standard D.

A carabiner is strongest along its vertical axis. A D-shaped 'biner is stronger than an oval because its shape shifts the load close to the spine and away from its weakest point, the gate. Carabiners have closed- and open-gate strength ratings because gates sometimes open unexpectedly (see Chapter 5). The average strength rating of a 'biner with its gate closed is almost three times that of the same one open.

Oval carabiners

Bent-gate and wire-gate carabiners *(see photo 5)* are not as versatile as others but frequently make their way onto trad climbers' racks. The wire-gate 'biner has a very high strength-to-weight ratio and boasts an unsurpassed gate opening for its size. Bent gates are easy to clip with one hand from a precarious position when leading, and unclip just as easily. They are used widely in sport climbing. Bent gates are designed specifically for clipping into the rope while climbing, so their use is limited to being the component of a quick-draw or an SLCD sling. Because they lack versatility, I don't carry many on my trad rack. Also, the smaller diameter of some

Bent-gate (left) and wire-gate (right) carabiners

extremely light bent-gate models significantly reduces the strength of the rope: running the rope over a carabiner with a diameter of 10 millimeters or less will reduce its strength by 30 percent or greater.

How many total carabiners will you need? Aside from a 'biner for each SLCD and a couple on which to rack your Stoppers, consider purchasing 20–25 "single" (or free) carabiners for your starter rack. If the pitches are longer in your home cragging area, or if you're going to pursue multipitch routes in which simultaneous belays eat up more of your single carabiners, purchase a few more.

RUNNERS & CORDAGE

Runners (slings) are used with carabiners to create links between your rope and your anchors and between your rope and lead protection. A section of tubular webbing is either sewn or tied into a loop to create a typical runner. A *cordelette* is typically an 18- to 25-foot (6- to 8-meter) loop of cord used to create a *SERENE* anchor. (SERENE stands for Safe/Secure, Equalized, Redundant, Easy, and No Extension.) The *Web-o-lette* is a 10-foot (250-centimeter) length of Spectra webbing with loops sewn at either end that is also used in building such anchors. Chapter 6 explains how to use both the Web-o-lette and the cordelette to build SERENE anchors.

Modern Materials

For years, climbers relied on runners made from nylon webbing to link ropes to hardware. Enter the tough-as-steel Spectra, one of the strongest materials in the world (bulletproof vests are made from Spectra). Developed in the 1980s, this fiber is a more durable and less bulky runner option with low water-absorption and significant abrasion resistance. Because of its low melting point and vulnerability to ultraviolet (UV) light, climbing gear manufacturers began using Spectra-

nylon blends. (Nylon is more resistant to UV light.) These eventually came to include trademarked brands such as Vectran, Titan, Dyneema, Ultratape, and Supertape. Today, manufacturers are working with additional specialty fibers with many of the same qualities as Spectra, plus a higher resistance to UV light and increased *tensile strength*. These materials like Kevlar, Vectran, and Technora are typically combined with other more supple materials like nylon and sold under brand names such as Dynex, Tech Cord, and Gemini2. One downfall of these materials is that tests have shown they experience a significant decrease in strength with use, meaning you must monitor, retire, and replace them frequently. Some tend to be quite stiff, too, making for difficult handling.

Quickdraws (left) and tied and sewn runners (right)

Recommended Runner Specs

In most cases, trad leaders will benefit from carrying three different lengths of runners on their racks. I refer to these as 4-inch (10-centimeter) quickdraws, 24-inch (60-centimeter) full- or shoulder-length runners, and 48-inch (120-centimeter) double runners. (Sewn lengths may vary slightly depending on the manufacturer). Typical runner material widths range from $^{11}\!/_{16}$ to 1 inch. All things considered, I recommend a combination of tied 1-inch tubular nylon runners, some sewn $^9\!/_{16}$-inch nylon runners, and a few sewn $^9\!/_{16}$-inch Spectra runners and quickdraws.

Sewn runners are made by industrial machines joining webbing together with sewn rows of zigzags called *"bar tacks."* Tied runners allow you to beef up a questionable fixed anchor (you'd need to untie it to thread it through the anchor and then retie it) or for some other improvised solutions to unforeseen problems. In a pinch, several knotted runners can be untied and retied to create one giant runner. I suggest using beefy 1-inch webbing for tied full-length runners because knots reduce their overall strength (bar tacks don't). When using stronger 1-inch webbing, this reduction is insignificant. To tie a runner, use either a ring bend (a.k.a. water knot) or a double fisherman's knot. (Consult Chapter 9 for instructions.) A double fisherman takes more material to tie but, once tightened, will rarely loosen on its own. The ring bend requires less webbing to tie but wiggles loose (or "creeps") more readily, especially when freshly tied. The ring bend is also a bit bulkier than the slender double fisherman. Always leave a 4-inch tail at each end of the knot. Constantly monitor your sling's knots, especially new ring bends, to ensure they remain secure. Spectra should not be cut and tied together; its coefficient of friction is too low to efficiently hold a knot (Translation: It's too slippery).

It's a good idea to have a decent number of sewn $^9\!/_{16}$-inch full-length runners on hand simply because of their versatility. With a much less slippery surface area than Spectra, nylon runners are better suited for self-locking friction hitches in self-rescue scenarios (see Chapter 8) and for slinging natural rock features like protruding horns and knobs (chickenheads) for use as anchors and

Creating a quickdraw from a tripled standard shoulder-length runner

lead protection. They're more likely to stay put than their slick Spectra cousins. In addition, the narrower ⁹⁄₁₆-inch width makes runnering natural rock features easier.

It's also nice to have Spectra on your rack simply because it's strong, durable, and resists abrasion. Spectra fiber is a good material for quickdraws since you'll never sling a feature or need to make a friction hitch with a quickdraw (it's too short). For the majority of your quickdraws though, I recommend tripling full-length slings to create quickdraw-length runners. After all, you can make a long runner shorter, but you can't make a short runner longer. You'll soon discover that running out of long runners on lead is a common but avoidable occurrence for new leaders. To make a quickdraw *(see photos 1–3, p. 51)* out of a tripled shoulder-length runner, begin with a runner with a carabiner at each end. Grasp the lower 'biner and bring it up through the top carabiner. Carefully thread a third of the sling through this upper carabiner and then back down to join the other two loops. Now gather the two loops together and secure them with the bottom carabiner. When you need a quickdraw twice that length, unclip one of the loops and extend. Unclip two loops and extend them when you need a full-length sling.

The number of double runners you need depends upon the terrain. In areas where there are many roofs, traverses, and/or blocky, wandering 4th class sections, you'll want several. They are essential on most backcountry routes. For leading at areas where the routes tend to be fairly direct, you may just need one. Long slings are difficult to carry over your shoulder. To make them more compact for carrying *(see photos 1–5, facing page)*, while holding the sling taut by grasping each end with an index finger, twist both ends simultaneously in opposite directions. After three or four twists, join both ends together with a single 'biner, allowing the strands to spiral around.

Cordelette & Web-o-lette

Both the *cordelette* and the *Web-o-lette* are viable options for creating trad anchors. The average nylon cordelette tends to be bulky and awkward to disassemble and carry but is a versatile piece of gear to have on hand,

You can make your extra-long runners compact for carrying on a single carabiner by doubling and twisting them.

particularly in rescue situations. The Mountain Tool's Web-o-lette is much less bulky hence easier to carry and is significantly easier to disassemble (the knot comes out easier and there's less material to deal with). It's not all that versatile, however, and is a tad short for use when anchor components are far from one another. It's also been criticized because of its weaker single strands (compared to the stronger double strands of the cordelette). I own both but tend to use my cordelette far more often. A cordelette can be made from any number of materials. All things considered, I recommend basic 7-millimeter nylon cord. It's inexpensive, performs well in strength testing, and lasts longer than many other materials. Buy it pre-cut or in bulk and secure it with a well-dressed water knot with 4-inch tails. (See Chapter 9 for knot instructions.) The Web-o-lette is made from a Spectra-Dacron blend.

SPECIALTY ITEMS

Numerous niche items fulfill the specialized needs of lead climbers wishing to protect odd or more advanced features. *Off-widths* (cracks larger than a cupped-hand jam), piton-scars, pods, and *huecos* (holes) are examples of features difficult to protect with gear from a standard rack. Two-cam SLCDs are an ideal solution for protecting pods, piton-scars, and small *huecos*. They have been

Specialty off-width protection

the topic of tech buzz for many years and are now available in three small sizes. *Big Bros* and oversized cams (larger than 4½ inches) are options for use in off-widths *(see photo, left)*. A Big Bro is an expandable tube that is screwed into place but also has camming properties. Big Bros and large specialty cams have made it possible for climbers to safely lead some wide and cavernous *testpieces*, previously led by the bold free climbers of the 1970s with little protection. Offset SLCDs (on each unit, one set of the four cams is a different size than the other set) are also coveted pieces for pin-scar protection. These items, however, are highly specialized and are not generally found or needed on a beginning leader's rack.

Chapter 4

Into the Wild:
From the Gym to the
Great Outdoors

Venturing outdoors is the obvious progression
for gym climbers left unsatisfied after a day of
pulling on plastic holds. Nonetheless, leaving the gym
for the trad climbing environment is a big undertaking,
especially if your ultimate goal is leading. Indoor skills
and perceptions must be revamped to suit the demands
of the trad arena. Initially, the transition from the gym
to trad rock requires as much unlearning as it does
learning. Skills such as belaying, communication, and
movement must be altered to suit this new terrain and
its unique qualities. Nevertheless, most of the basic skills
are in place, awaiting refinement with the assistance of
a skilled mentor or guide. Finally, you must examine
your willingness to accept the higher risk level of the
outdoor environment and accept responsibility for all
of your decisions and actions. When things go wrong
outdoors, there's no manager to complain to. Many of
the things you come to expect at the gym—safe top-rope
set-ups, a climate-controlled environment, holds that
won't break, climbs that are well-protected, partners
that have "passed" a belay test—cannot be guaranteed.
Outside, you are responsible for these things and much,
much more.

RISK & RESPONSIBILITY

Visits to climbing gyms instill an almost unequivocal sense of security in nearly every customer. The majority of visitors are confident that they will leave the gym with wounds no more debilitating than a bruised ego and a pair of flamed forearms. This confidence is earned by the fact that climbing occurs in a controlled and supervised setting under the umbrella of a well-insured operation prepared to accept responsibility for most mishaps. Risk levels increase outdoors, especially in trad settings, where objective dangers lurk in unsupervised settings. This reality should result in a healthy decrease in perceived security. Unfortunately, that often doesn't occur until something goes terribly wrong and there's no one to blame. In the beginning, each outdoor novice's safe return from an outdoor adventure tends to reinforce a false sense of security. Nearly every experienced outdoor climber, though, can recall his or her first mishap when this belief was shattered. Such incidents are often the result of poor decisions involving route or partner choice or lack of respect for objective dangers such as weather or rockfall.

While climbers can't directly control objective dangers, they can consider the potential dangers in every choice they confront and make decisions accordingly. For example, climbing a route in the mountains in early spring may place climbers at risk of rockfall due to snowmelt. Weather patterns and forecasts might indicate a potential afternoon lightning storm that puts climbers on multipitch routes at risk because a quick retreat is impossible. Climbing below another party puts climbers at risk of being the target of falling hardware and dislodged debris. A short autumn day might not be the best time of year to commit to a long route because of shorter daylight hours.

In short, you can't control the weather, but you can choose to climb a short route or not climb at all. You can't control the amount of daylight hours available in each day, but you can choose a route you're sure to summit long before dark. You can't control natural rockfall, but you can be aware of the circumstances that cause it. It doesn't seem like it's your fault if a climber drops a cam and hits you on the head, but you made the choice to climb below another party, a formidable risk.

Based on the choices they make at every turn, climbers themselves are ultimately responsible for their destiny, no matter what the circumstance. Excuses uttered on trad turf, in particular, are lost to the wind. This frightens a lot of people. Climbing outside can be disconcerting for many in our litigious society unaccustomed to accepting responsibility for their actions. Even when a mishap is the result of your partner's poor judgment, the fact that you chose to climb with this person remains your responsibility. The good news is that the natural by-products of this level of accountability include maturity and integrity. It's my experience that taking responsibility creates a sense of capability, inner strength, and worthiness. Deciding to take your skills outdoors is noble, as long as you're willing to take full responsibility for your choices at every turn.

MOVEMENT

The majority of climbing on trad stone requires almost an entirely new set of movement skills. First you must learn to view the rock differently than you did the gym wall. Gym walls are mostly vertical to overhanging, with conspicuous holds (often marked with brightly colored tape) and few cracks. Outdoor terrain is often far more varied, but the features and holds are not always as easy to identify if all you've ever known is the gym environment. Most gym climbers I take on their first outdoor climbs struggle with the terrain differences. The most frequent challenge is a perceived lack of holds. Outdoor holds aren't boldly colored with swirling, modular shapes. They aren't marked with color-coded arrows, nor attached with bolts. Nevertheless, they exist in abundance and in numerous forms—some subtle, others obvious. Outside you'll see knobs, nubbins, dishes, scoops, edges, flakes, shelves, pockets, ripples, holes, ribs, and grooves—all awaiting your discovery. Ironically, what initially appeared to the outdoor newcomer as a scarcity of holds eventually becomes a wealth of options unimaginable in the gym. Obviously it's not the climbing surface that changes, but rather the viewpoint of the new outdoor climber. The keener your ability to identify these features, the easier it is to use them.

Slab and crack climbing can be more of a challenge for the accomplished gym climber. If you flash 5.10 regularly on artificial walls, you may be frustrated when you fail on a 5.8 trad climb outdoors. But take heart: Going from vertical climbs on plastic to crack climbs on rock is like asking a prima ballerina to demonstrate her strength by taking on a professional wrestler in the ring. Refined crack technique, even at a moderate difficulty level, takes a lot of practice and has little to do with actual strength. The same goes for slab climbing, which demands tenuous balance, intricate footwork, and little reliance on your upper body.

The only real magic in mastering these trad techniques is to practice them on real rock, however uncomfortable or inconvenient. When I first meet guided clients without much of an agenda, one of my first questions is: "On what type of terrain are you most comfortable climbing?" If it's steep face, I usually suggest working on cracks. If it's steep cracks or overhanging face, I'll guide them gently toward slab terrain. Do this favor for yourself, and you'll start to become a well-rounded trad climber.

Slab Climbing

Slab climbing is a form of face climbing on low-angle terrain *(see photo, facing page, top)*. Some climbers categorize any wall less than vertical as a slab. Generally, slab techniques work best on walls less than 80 degrees. These walls generally have few prominent features. Many cracks, however, are located on low-angle walls where slab technique is essential. You're more likely to succeed on cracks if first you familiarize yourself with slab climbing.

Learning proper slab technique is probably the single most helpful thing a gym climber can do to ease the transition to real rock. The good news is that it's fairly easy to master. Initially, it will feel completely foreign; since most walls in gyms tend to be vertical to overhanging, there may be absolutely nothing familiar about it. But with a little practice, your comfort level will increase.

Good balance and proper body positioning is the secret to effective slab climbing. Relying on your lower body to do nearly all the work is also essential. Once you master these elements, the rest is in your head. It's a psychological game in which one part of your mind is negotiating with another part to initiate what appears to be an impossible move upward on improbable-looking holds. Once a deal is reached and the move successfully completed, you feel a temporary sense of confidence to do it all again. But if you linger too long on one set of holds, this internal battle will begin again and potentially sabotage your progress. Maintaining steady, consistent progress will quiet these voices.

Good slab technique requires your heels to be down, knees unbent, weight centered directly over your toes, and arms extended.

Smearing

The technique to master for effective slab climbing is the smear, which is essentially achieving as much rubber to rock contact as possible. To execute a smear, square your hips to the wall, bend and lift your knee waist-high, and press the ball of your foot against the rock. Now stand up, balancing to get your center of gravity over the front of your foot.

The key elements of smearing are proper body positioning, good balance, and commitment. Keep your center of gravity directly over your toes and maintain an upright position at all times. Imagine balancing a book on your head as you ascend. Hugging or leaning into the rock interferes with proper weight distribution. If you're not sure about your positioning, try monitoring the position of your heels. If they are at all elevated, try shifting them down an inch or two. This helps keep your weight centered over your toes.

Finesse and balance, not brute strength, are essential in getting up a slab. Since success in the gym often relies on upper-body strength, this balance and finesse business may seem foreign. With practice, it will come just as naturally as cranking on steep holds. Climbers new to slabs tend to focus too much on potential handholds. But in effective slab climbing, all the action takes place from the waist down. Instead of searching for handholds, try locating a good spot to smear, then initiate and execute the move. You cannot accomplish this without looking at your feet! Try to be as precise with your footwork as possible. Take small steps to conserve energy. Long reaches and high steps zap strength. Plus, if your hands and feet are too spread out, you can't keep your body weight centered over your toes. Don't make a move until you have a plan. Unlike the surface between holds at the gym, many types of real rock, especially granite, are highly textured. Search for subtle features on the wall that might increase your friction. Seams, edges, dishes, and nubbins all beg for your foot's attention when you're climbing slabs.

Finally, full commitment to each upward move will determine your success on slabs. This is not a psychological concept; it's a physical one. The amount of rubber-to-rock contact is maximized immediately when you stand up, without hesitation, on each smear. Your instinct may be telling you to ease onto each foot, but a more deliberate motion will help you accomplish the movement more effectively without compromising proper body position. When making a move, check your knees to assess your commitment level. Are they bent significantly? You can shift more of your body weight over your toes if you straighten your legs so that there's only a very slight bend in your knees, if that.

Hoisting yourself upward with the help of an inverted palm is the key to the low-angle mantling.

Mantling

Mantling is another helpful slab technique. It is similar to mantling in the gym but requires more balance and flexibility than strength. This technique involves inverting the heel of your open palm on a feature around chest level, shifting most of your weight over the top of your hand, and then pressing down while moving your chest up above the feature. Scoot one foot up simultaneously and then rock onto the feature to allow your second foot to join it. Stand up on the hold as soon as you can. Try to execute the movement dynamically—in one fell swoop. Otherwise you'll end up with your hands and feet in the same place—an awkward stance unless you're a yogi. The power of the slab mantle initiates in your

---

Troubleshooting Slabs

Problem: My feet keep slipping out from under me.
Solution: Use your hands only for balance, and focus solely on what's happening from the waist down. Shift your body weight over your toes by straightening your legs. Keep your heels down and your arms as straight out in front of you as possible.

Problem: When my mind tells me I can't do a move, I freak out and have to hang.
Solution: Climb (on top-rope) until you fall. Stop being a slave to the voices. Go for it! Use visualization techniques to imagine your lower body as a powerhouse of strength.

Problem: My feet and toes scream in pain when I climb slabs.
Solution: With more exposure to slab climbing, the muscles in your feet will become stronger and the pain will decrease.

---

upper body and culminates in your quads as you finish the move with what usually turns out to be a high step. Since the terrain isn't steep, you sometimes can use your feet to assist early on *(see photo, facing page)*. Mantling requires good balance and flawless commitment. If you hesitate mid-mantle, you might not be able to reverse your moves. Use this technique to surmount rounded holds and scoops. When you begin to excel at it, you'll discover you can use it on other smaller features.

BASIC CRACK CLIMBING

"Historical big walls and free routes of any honest length invariably follow crack systems, so to climb them you must be crack fluent," say authors John Long and Craig Luebben in *Advanced Rock Climbing*. While basic face climbing tends to be intuitive, crack climbing skills must be learned. If you're new to crack climbing, get inspired by watching a crack master in action: see Dale Bard finessing his way up Coyne Crack in the video *Moving Over Stone II* or Lisa Gnade on Ruby's Café in *Masters of Stone*. These climbers didn't learn crack technique overnight and neither will you, but as you devote season after season to perfecting your technique, it will begin to come naturally.

You are as unlikely to learn how to climb cracks from a book as you are to learn to ride a bike with this approach; reading does little for your crack climbing progress. What results in headway is groveling your way up cracks until you get it right. This kinesthetic process unfolds on the rock. And, like anything, some climbers initially have an easier time with cracks than others. Like learning skiing or snowboarding, you may find it difficult at first, but as you slowly become more competent you enjoy it more and more. Yet you should expect to experience discomfort and awkwardness throughout the learning process, plus you'll lose a lot of skin.

Crack climbing involves *jamming* techniques in which climbers wedge their appendages (hands, fingers, feet, legs, arms, or whatever works) into cracks to create enough purchase to make upward progress. More often than not, climbers supplement their jams with a combination of other techniques such as face climbing, smearing, and *stemming*.

Most climbers new to crack climbing experience a period in which they think they're not strong enough to climb cracks. By lifting weights in fitness facilities, they hope to build the strength they think crack routes require. Back at the crags though, they are met with yet another brutal and humiliating defeat. If they continue to practice outdoors on easy cracks though, they eventually discover they lacked cultivated technique not strength.

Developing Crack Technique

To develop basic crack technique, begin either by top-roping or by following low-angled crack routes with lots of features. Don't start on vertical or steeper routes unless they have a lot of face holds. Forget about how hard you can climb on bolted sport routes; cracks rated below 5.8 are recommended for first-timers. Difficulty ratings don't translate well between cracks and bolted clip-ups (see "Rating Translation & Style", pp. 235–236).

To initiate any jam, determine the best possible placement a particular section offers. The ideal jam might not be obvious, so experiment with different options until you find the right one. Initially, new crack climbers often make the mistake of rejecting *bomber* jams in favor of face holds outside the crack. Avoiding jams will only prolong the learning process and make the climbing more difficult than its rating. Since your motor memory needs to absorb the right information, focus primarily on taking advantage of the crack and give yourself over to the jamming action. The more cracks you climb, the more confidence you will gain in your jamming skills. And, as the cracks you climb become steeper with fewer hand- and footholds on the face, you will rely more and more upon pure crack technique. Eventually you'll discover the advantages (and sometimes the necessity) of using both your hands as well as both your feet simultaneously in the crack.

Hand jamming

Hand Jams

To initiate a hand jam, look for natural constrictions in the crack around head height that would facilitate wedging your hand in place like a Stopper. With your thumb tucked against your palm, insert your hand into the crack and locate that sweet spot that, when your hand is flexed, locks it in place *(see photo, top right)*. Don't be afraid to fish around for the best fit, and then gently rotate your elbow down and in toward your chest, torquing your hand securely in place. Jams can be executed with the thumbs facing up or down, depending on how much leverage you're going to need to reach the next jam.

Foot jamming

Foot Jams

The most efficient tool for establishing secure foot and toe jams is your eyesight. Blindly throwing a foot into a crack and expecting it to hold doesn't work. Look down and consciously decide exactly where you're going to place your jam. Find a location in the crack around knee level that is closest to the size of your foot and identify constrictions or knobs that may provide added security once your foot's wedged into place. Once you've got your target, gently lift and rotate your lower leg until the inside of your calf is perpendicular to the rock, pinkie toe down and parallel with the crack. Insert your foot *(see photo, second from top, left)*. If you've ever played Hacky Sack, you'll be familiar with this position. You keep the inside of your foot flattened the same way

Finger jamming—thumb up

Finger jamming—thumb down

Toe jamming

Fist jamming

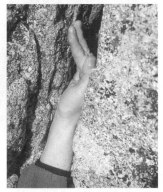

Cupped-hand jamming

you would in that game to keep the ball in flight. Now as deliberately as possible, transfer all of your weight to this foot by straightening your knee and allowing it to rotate inward until it is parallel with the crack.

Finger & Toe Jams

For good finger jams, again look for thin cracks with openings that constrict and form V-shaped slots. Insert your fingers, keeping your thumb free and pointed either up or down, into the crack *(see two photos, bottom of previous page)*, wedging them above the constriction to the best of your ability. It's not always necessary to get each of your fingers in all the way for the jam to be useful. Now rotate your elbow inward and downward, torquing the fingers in place. Toe jams work the same way foot jams do, except you may only be able to get the tip of your toe box into the crack resulting in a hybrid of a smear and a jam *(see photo, top left)*.

Fist & Cupped-Hand Jams

Fist jams *(see photo, middle left)* are reserved for cracks too wide for a secure hand jam. A fist jam can be executed with the thumb tucked inside your palm or outside, depending on the width of the crack. Wedge it in, and flex. If the crack's a tad too large for tight hand jamming, try a cupped-hand jam.

For a cupped-hand jam, start by making a C shape with your hand. Next, bring your thumb atop the first knuckle (where your finger meets your hand) of your first ("pointer") finger. Now straighten all of your other fingers while maintaining maximum curvature in your palm. The idea here is to make your hand as "big" as possible to achieve maximum rock-to-flesh contact. Place your hand inside the crack and flex it *(see photo, bottom left)*. As you flex, a camming action occurs as the ball of your hand presses against one side of the crack. These two styles tend to feel a lot less secure than good hand or finger jams, but with some practice you'll become comfortable trusting them.

Shuffling & Crossing Over

The best method for initiating each new finger, hand, or fist jam varies. Your options include crossing

Shuffling

Crossing Over

Hand Taping

Learning to crack climb is brutal on the hands. Skin loss and bruising can be prevented by a number of taping methods. This technique requires 1½ inches (3.75 centimeters) cloth medical tape and allows you to remove the tape from each hand in one piece to reuse it later. Unlike other methods, this technique purposely avoids taping across the palm of your hand, which is uncomfortable and unnecessary.

1. Stick 3–4 individual tape strips to the back of your hand lengthwise between wrist and fingers. (For added protection, double it.)
2. Create 3–4 wraps with the tape around your wrist.
3. Beginning at the wrist, pass the tape up and around each finger and down across the back of the hand several times. Each time you do so, angle the tape slightly to make one wrap around the wrist. Incorporate all your fingers, or eliminate the thumb or smallest finger, depending on the amount of protection you desire.

over or shuffling. Shuffling involves continuously using the same hand to reach for the next jam, and using the opposite hand jammed about chest high for leverage and stabilization *(see Shuffling, 1–5 clockwise, p. 65, top)*. This technique works well on cracks that lean or traverse. It is also ideal on straight-up cracks when you need to conserve energy and cover a long distance but do not necessarily have to reach high.

To reach higher, crossing over works better. This technique looks a little like the crawl stroke—you're going to be reaching for jams with alternating lead hands *(see Crossing Over, 1–4, p. 65, bottom)*. Crossing over on leaning cracks, though, is not ideal because it prevents you from keeping your weight directly on your feet. With experience your body will intuitively know whether to cross over or shuffle.

Taping Tips

- With the exception of the initial wrist wraps, this process can usually be done with one or two continuous pieces of tape. For a tidier result, cut the tape after each wrap, but make sure you tuck all ends away securely, and anchor your work with a few wrist wraps when finishing.

- A tape job that is too tight will restrict movement and cut off blood supply. To avoid this, periodically flex your fingers and hands as you wrap and keep your wrist wraps snug but not tight. If your skin bulges out from under the tape, it's probably too tight.

- Because all cloth medical tape isn't the same, try several brands until you find one that works well. I recommend Johnson & Johnson's. Plastic tape is not an option—it's too flimsy and doesn't adhere. Purchase cloth tape from either a pharmacy or a climbing retailer.

- Tincture of benzoin helps tape adhere better; apply a thin layer to the back of your hands before taping.

Reusing Tape

To remove a wrap, use scissors to clip the tape carefully on the underside of your wrist and peel or slide it off. To reuse a wrap, slide it on and add tape around your wrist to secure it. Apply tincture of benzoin for added security.

Chimneys

Chimneys have a bad rap, probably because they are often difficult to protect on lead. Yet standard, medium-width chimneys can be delightful; they often have protection options deep inside or along their sidewalls. Begin by wedging yourself between the chimney walls with your buttocks and back pressed against one and your feet pressed against the other. Create resistance by exerting pressure with the palms of your hands, buttocks, back, legs, and feet. To make upward progress, alternately walk your feet and scoot your butt up, with leverage from your palms pressed against either wall. Depending on the chimney's architecture, either keep both feet against the front wall or place them oppositionally against both walls (*see illustrations 1a and 1b*).

As you progress, avoid placing your feet too low—keep them as high as possible for optimal security. Use any face holds or cracks—no matter how small—for increased friction. Don't wedge yourself so deeply in the chimney that you miss easier climbing out toward the lip (where those new to chimney technique are afraid to go). In slightly wider chimneys, keep one foot on the front wall and the other on the rear wall, bridging the gap also with the palms of your hands, as you move upward one foot at a time (*see illustration 2, facing page*).

Expert Techniques for Advanced Cracks

Off-width cracks, squeeze chimneys, and flares involve advanced jamming techniques not covered in this book. Nevertheless, the basic skills you cultivate climbing standard cracks provide the foundation to master these more advanced techniques. When you've honed basic crack skills, check out Long and Luebben's *Advanced Rock Climbing* for tips on wide crack variants requiring advanced skills. Also view Peter Mortimer's DVD *Return2Sender* for fantastic Indian Creek footage of experts demonstrating off-width techniques on wide cracks.

BELAYING

If you're accustomed to using auto-cam belay devices (like a GriGri), you may need to change your belay

Climbing a standard chimney

method. Auto-cam belay devices are too heavy and lack versatility as they are not designed for rappelling. It's also my belief that the auto-lock capabilities instill a dangerous sense of passivity in a setting where lack of proactivity will get you killed. Learning the basic mechanics of operating a tube or plate device is easy but should be done under the watchful eye of an experienced belayer.

Top-roping requires that the belayer take in rope as the climber ascends; leading demands the paying out of rope. Although lead belaying requires a higher level of skill, both methods demand the same set of skills: preparedness, sensitive rope management, and proper body positioning.

Preparedness

Put on your jacket or eat an energy bar before you entrust your partner's life with the words "on belay." If chatting with friends at the base interferes with your concentration, wait to converse until your partner has safely finished. When lead belaying, situate the rope so that it feeds out easily—if you brake with your right hand, the rope feeds best if it is on your right, and vice versa. If you are lead-belaying and plan to follow the pitch, tie into the rope *before* the leader leaves the ground so that you're ready to climb immediately after the leader finishes.

Wide chimney technique

Positioning

Assume a firm and solid stance, and position yourself close to the base of the route. Belaying too far away from the rock puts your partner at risk, and the force of a fall could drag you into the wall. This movement results in your partner falling farther than he or she should. Lead belayers especially need to hug the rock. If they don't, the lateral force on the rope created by a fall could rip out the leader's gear, piece by piece (see "The Base Belay," pp. 127–130). Resolve to belay close to the wall, and you'll never have to experience these situations firsthand.

Rope Management

Always be prepared to take in or feed out rope without being forced to do so. Accomplishing this demands extreme sensitivity and the ability to visualize what's going on out of your sight. The more experience you obtain on the sharp end, the easier it will become. You will learn to read the movement of the rope to interpret your partner's needs. When top-rope belaying, you will always know when to reel in slack if you maintain a subtle but constant tension on the rope strand going up to the climber. In the trad realm, your partner may travel out of your sight and range of hearing. Because of this, visual and auditory cues are not always reliable. Be very careful to never put unnecessary tension on a lead rope, or you could pull the climber off the rock (every leader's biggest nightmare). Consequences for sloppy belaying are enormous in the trad environment. Trad leaders don't have the luxury of a bolt every body length, so not receiving immediate slack to clip a piece could cause a leader to lose his or her balance and take a long and possibly treacherous fall. Your goal is to master the tenuous balance of keeping slack out of the system and feeding out rope to the leader without him or her ever feeling you at the other end. Keep an arm's length of slack in the system at all times (except near the ground or above dangerous features). The disappearance of slack is your cue to feed out another arm's length of rope. This constant monitoring prevents the leader from ever feeling resistance on the rope.

COMMUNICATING OUTDOORS

Formality, volume, simplicity, and consistency are the watchwords for safe outdoor climbing communication. In gym settings, communication tends to be casual, as the needs of the climber are fairly predictable, and climbers are relatively close to one another. In the trad world, nothing is predictable, and communication must be consistently formal, whether you are near or far from one another. Commands should be as terse and simplistic as possible; requests given in lengthy detail are often misunderstood or not heard at all. Finally, it's important to aim your voice toward your partner and address him or her by name when giving (or confirming) a command. Outdoors, you compete with the sounds of wind, running water, airplanes, cars, and other climbers on nearby routes. A misunderstanding could be fatal. When belaying, consider all auditory interference you may have to contend with before your partner leaves the ground. Agree to communicate *only* before or after cars pass if you're near a road or as loudly as possible if it's windy or you're near a rushing stream.

I frequently notice that new outdoor climbers are uncomfortable formalizing and shouting their commands. Don't be shy. The repetition helps you carve out a habitual groove in your brain so that it becomes second nature. It will always contribute to your team's safety. I recognize it feels awkward or like overkill at times and often unnecessary. Imagine, however, a leader high up on a route, out of view, requesting "slack" with little or no amplification. The belayer misunderstands the message as "off belay." He removes his partner's lifeline from the belay device and waits patiently for the next command. Meanwhile, the leader is preparing for a delicate traverse and simply needed some slack to initiate the moves. I'll leave the result of this miscommunication mishap—with a shudder—to the imagination of the reader.

At the base, formal outdoor communication generally unfolds like this: "Belay on?" "On belay." "Climbing?" "Climb on." These commands basically translate into: "Are you ready?" "Yes, I'm ready." "Are you ready?" "Yes, I'm really ready." Each partner is given the opportunity to halt the progression with: "Hey, no—I'm not ready." Ditto high on the rock when the leader is out of view and difficult to hear. The majority of commands are answered by an affirmation of that command, whether the leader is close beside you, or high up on a route. For a complete list of trad commands, see "Verbal Commands," pp. 132–134.

ROPE HANDLING

Whether assuming the role of belayer or climber, each team member should know how to flake or coil the rope before and after use. In the gym, these tasks are not required. To engage responsibly as a full-fledged outdoor partner, learn to do both. Always keep the rope away from sharp objects and out of dirt and debris, and avoid stepping on it. See "Ropes," pp. 42–43, for more details regarding rope care.

The Backpacker's Coil

1. Locate the middle marker of the rope.

2. Beginning with a bight, or fold, and working with parallel strands, use one hand to drape multiple loops of identical lengths (creating what some refer to as "rabbit ears") on opposing sides of your other hand. Use all but 15 feet of the rope.

3. With the remaining rope, create several wraps around the bulk of the coil, working your way upward.

4. Create a bight and feed it through the top of the coil to create a girth hitch to secure it.

5. Done!

Coiling

Learning to coil a rope *(see photos, above and facing page)* is easy and is a shared task in the trad partnership. Coiling should be done with precision and care in anticipation of the next time the rope will be used.

How to Carry a Coiled Rope "Backpack"-Style

1. With a strand in each hand, drape the coil across your back.

2. Fashion "straps" from the remaining slack by wrapping the strands under your arms, around the back of the coil, and then back. Continue until you have just enough slack to tie a knot.

3. Done!

Rope bags are handy in climbing scenarios when the summit is less than a rope-length away. Unfortunately, bags rarely fit easily into a climbing pack (essential for carrying trad gear from route to route). The coiling process prepares the rope for transport and guarantees smooth flaking at the base of your next route.

Flake the rope by piling it in a neat mound out of the dirt, leaving both ends accessible.

Flaking

Flaking *(see photo, right)* is the process of preparing the rope for leading by carefully piling it by hand from end to end at the base of a route so that it feeds out without a snarl. The appropriate time to flake out the lead rope is when the leader is racking up in preparation to climb. For easy tie-in, leave both ends of the rope accessible when flaking. This is a good time to check your rope for evidence of wear and damage. For details about signs of wear and damage, see "Ropes," pp. 40–43.

TOP-ROPING

Learning to set up the yo-yo top-rope system will most likely be your first technical challenge outside. It's a simple process but not without risks. While the key elements are illustrated, and noted briefly on the facing page, step-by-step details are listed below.

Route Choice

Start on a route with bolted anchors on top that is no longer than half the length of your rope. The summit must be easily accessed via scrambling or walking. If you are not sure, ask a trusted local and/or consult a guidebook.

Gear

For a two-bolt anchor on a 90-foot route, you need:

✓ Two standard carabiners,

✓ Two locking carabiners,

✓ A cordelette or Web-o-lette (see pp. 52–53),

✓ A 200-foot (60-meter) rope, and

✓ Two extra slings and two standard carabiners to extend the anchor if necessary.

In addition, you might want to bring a locking carabiner and a sling for clipping in should your anchor need extending far below what you can comfortably reach.

Preparation

After getting your gear together, your next order of action is to put on your harness and shoes before heading up with your gear. You will be working very close to the edge of the cliff. If, for some reason, you get stranded in a precarious spot, you'll be prepared for assistance from another climber (or your partner).

The Anchor

Once you've walked up to the top of the climb and located the bolts, you'll need to establish an anchor (see pp. 94–102) with your gear. If this is your first time creating such an anchor, do so under the watchful eye of a trusted expert. Invite this person along your first few times out to check your work.

Usually, your anchor will need to be extended from each individual anchor component to prevent rope drag and unnecessary wear. Sometimes a cordelette is long enough, but you may have to add individual slings to each anchor component. The masterpoint (where the rope is threaded) must always be metal. Use locking carabiners and never, ever use webbing, slings, rope, or cord of any kind—friction from the rope will saw right through them. Make sure the halfway marker on your rope is resting in the cradle of the masterpoint before you leave the anchor area.

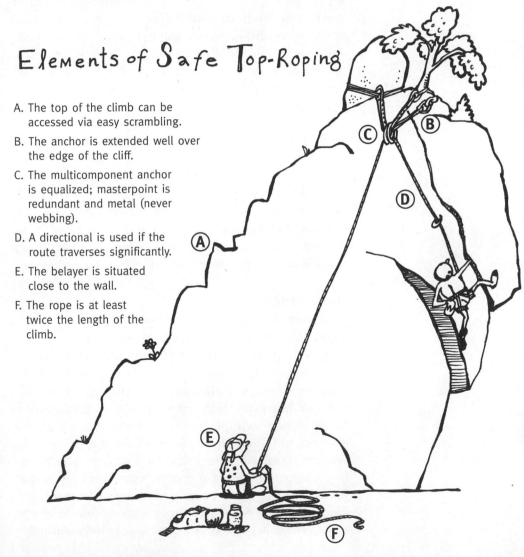

Elements of Safe Top-Roping

A. The top of the climb can be accessed via easy scrambling.

B. The anchor is extended well over the edge of the cliff.

C. The multicomponent anchor is equalized; masterpoint is redundant and metal (never webbing).

D. A directional is used if the route traverses significantly.

E. The belayer is situated close to the wall.

F. The rope is at least twice the length of the climb.

The Rope

Once the anchor has been created, you'll clip the halfway point of your rope into the masterpoint of the anchor, remembering to lock the carabiners. Now you are ready to toss the rope ends to the ground. To avoid tangles during this process, first split the rope into two carefully coiled sections. Next, make sure it is not wrapped around your leg or foot, and wait for any gusts of wind to subside. Finally, scan the wall for other climbers. If there is a possibility that the falling rope strands will hit other climbers, wait until they are out of range. Warn climbers at the base that a rope is on the way by shouting, "Rope!" Wait for their acknowledgment before you send it down. Toss one half of the rope, and then the other, in rapid succession, out and away from the cliff. Your goal is to get both ends to the ground without any tangles, first try. If you can't see the bottom, have your partner verify that both ends are at the base. If they're not, pull it up and do it again.

Once both ends have reached the ground, ask your partner to perform a test pull to make sure the rope runs smoothly and isn't running across any sharp surfaces. When you are satisfied with the arrangement, you can either walk or rappel down. Personally, I think rappelling down is a courteous way of demonstrating to your partners that they can trust your anchor because you're confident enough to test it first. Rappelling also gives you the opportunity to set up a directional if necessary.

Directionals

Directional placements are used to "direct" the rope where it otherwise won't hang. Directionals can keep a rope away from a sharp edge or prevent it from getting stuck in a crack. They are also used to prevent falling climbers from penduluming, or swinging, on routes that run diagonally. If the route traverses significantly, a falling climber will pendulum at points when the rope does not run plumb from his or her waist to the anchor. While a short swing on a smooth wall is usually harmless, climbers must be protected from pendulums that could result in them being dangerously slammed into *dihedrals* (corners) or other rock features (like knobs or chickenheads). The use of a directional placement helps solve the pendulum issue by creating an intermediate anchor that shares the burden of the primary anchor. It essentially "directs" the rope so it runs closer to plumb than it would without the piece, thereby eliminating the possibility of big swings.

Many top-rope accidents occur because the need for a directional is overlooked. Identifying when and exactly where to install a directional is a skill that requires significant forethought. With time and experience, you'll develop an intuitive sense about it. If the route traverses at any point, imagine where a pendulum might take a falling climber. Might he or she slam into an innocent looking dihedral off to the left or right? Will the climber be dragged across a sea of jagged knobs? Could an appendage get caught in a crack? How far will the climber swing? If it's a short distance on smooth, unfeatured rock, you might not need a directional as long as each climber is aware that they'll swing a short distance if they fall.

To establish a directional, rappel down with a friction hitch backup (see "Brake-Line Backup" on pp. 116–117), armed with an assortment of pieces (unless you know specifically what piece will fit). If the route diagonals significantly, ask your partner to grab both rope strands at the base to help pull you over to where you will place the directional piece. Once the piece is placed, clip your rope strand into it (careful not to cross the strands) and then continue rappelling to the ground. The climber ties into this strand and begins ascending the route. When the climber reaches the directional, he or she unclips the rope from the piece in order to climb past the directional. When the climber is being lowered, he or she should reclip the rope to the piece. The last person to climb the route removes the piece.

At the Base

Situate your belayer close to the base of the rock and have him or her assume a solid stance (see "Belaying," pp. 68–70) so he or she doesn't get dragged into the wall if you fall. Generally, there is no need to anchor your belayer to the base unless there is a huge weight discrepancy between the two of you. An anchored belayer cannot get out of the way of falling rock or debris.

Troubleshooting Problems with a Yo-Yo Top-Rope

Problem: The rope is difficult to pull when belaying.
Solution: Extend your anchors.

Problem: When in use, the rope keeps slipping into a crack and getting stuck.
Solution: Rappel down and place a directional piece to "direct" the rope away from the crack.

Problem: The rope is just barely long enough. Once the climber ties in, there's barely enough rope to thread the belay device.
Solution: This is a potentially dicey situation. The rope could zip through the device during the final stretch of lowering, causing the climber to plummet to the ground. Tie a stopper knot (see p. 115 for knot instructions) in the end of the rope before lowering the climber to prevent this from happening.

Problem: The rope runs over a sharp edge.
Solution: If you can't coax the rope away from it with a directional, find another climb.

The climber uses a figure-eight follow-through knot (see "Knots & Hitches," p. 217) to tie into the end of the rope strand that hangs closest to the majority of the route. If a directional is set, the climber ties into the rope strand leading directly to the piece.

MOUNTAIN SENSIBILITY

If you're new to human-powered outdoor sports, especially those of the mountain variety, it will behoove you to cultivate additional outdoor activities. Take up hiking, peak bagging, or, even better, backpacking. Trad leaders who enter the sport through the gateway of mountaineering and backpacking always have a significantly easier time adapting to the sport. Knowing how to walk on uneven surfaces, understanding dangers of rockfall, having previous experience feeling uncomfortable due to the elements, knowing how to behave around others in the mountains—all of these experiences affect the learning curve of the new trad leader. Your gym roots are nothing to be ashamed of, but they do mean you have a lot of catching up to do.

By devoting time to a variety of high-country activities, you will develop instincts that could one day save your life. Form a relationship with the elements, learn to read a map, and spend some time traveling on talus and third-class terrain (see "Class Ratings," pp. 232–233). Take a long, arduous dayhike with only a few provisions. Hike up a peak. Walk cross-country above tree line. Sleep outside in a tent, and sleep outside under the stars. Learn how to cook on a white gas stove. Go without a shower for several days and rinse off in a cold mountain lake. Ski in the backcountry and build a snow cave. Take an avalanche course or become a wilderness first responder. Carry a heavy pack. Travel above 10,000 feet. Learn the names of wildflowers, how the peaks and rocks were formed, and where the mountain streams originate.

Developing high-country sensibility will also help you fit in with fellow climbing peers at the crags. A certain degree of etiquette is expected at all outdoor climbing areas, especially those outside the cities and suburbs. Here are some general guidelines to keep you in favor with the locals while you're building your own outdoor foundation: Mountain savvy climbers don't bring boom boxes to the crags, throw or trundle rocks, or relieve themselves near the base of climbs. They try to stay on trails when possible, don't add unnecessary trail markers, and don't "manicure" the base of climbs or campsites. They are sensitive to local customs and land manager's rules, and they don't place any bolts without considering local tradition or consulting longtime locals. They come prepared for mountain terrain and weather, and don't expect to be rescued if they get into a pinch. The real courteous ones leave their cell phones off or at home. For more tips, see "Climbing Etiquette," pp. 236–240.

It's your job to adapt to the outdoors, particularly the mountains—not the other way around. Put effort into cultivating knowledge and appreciation for the high country through a variety of outdoor activities, and I guarantee your climbing will benefit, often in ways you might not even be aware of.

Chapter 5

Building a Solid Foundation

Pete Chasse

Once you're outfitted, the urge to start leading routes can be overwhelming. Take your time; the rock's not going anywhere and you have a lot to learn. Before leading, focus on building a solid foundation of trad skills with a mentor and a reliable partner in low-risk settings.

CLIMBING PARTNERSHIPS

Choose your traditional climbing partners with care. Find climbers with similar goals, interests, and abilities. When partners' skill levels are unbalanced, opportunities for individual growth are limited. The less experienced partner never steps into the leadership role, and the more skillful climber never learns from someone stronger.

Look for partners who are stable, responsible, and have their egos in check. Those with whom you choose to join forces on traditional routes—particularly long ones—must be honest about their limitations before leaving the ground. Beware of climbers who boast excessively about their accomplishments or disparage fellow climbers. While these folks generally have talent, their overconfidence, which sometimes masks insecurities, makes them more likely to overstep their true ability level. Likewise, humility and modesty often mask real strength.

Trust & Mutual Respect

Gear-leading requires continuous problem solving and decision making that can be harmonious with the right partner or a power struggle with the wrong one. Respect between partners is of utmost importance. Without trusting your partner's abilities, you soon find yourself at odds with one another. With mutual respect, trust is rarely an issue. Duties are shared intuitively, tasks are completed efficiently, and the climb unfolds naturally and safely. "The sum of two partners' energy, wisdom, and strength of will—when those partners are well adapted to each other after years of stress and adventure—is far greater than their individual power and spirit," says Marc Twight in *Extreme Alpinism.* He adds, "It's equally true that two partners who needle each other, who are not aligned in their ambitions or talents, are collectively weaker than they would be on their own."

Couple Partnerships

Climbing with spouses or partners *can* work, but those who try it should expect a few more psychological hurdles than they'd encounter with others. Partners in romance usually share a sense of comfort that encourages emotional vulnerability. While that's not necessarily a bad thing, sometimes—particularly when one climber is stronger than the other—couples find the emotional climate intensified on a climb. Distracting and counterproductive emotions may erupt. In climbing situations, many couples can end up arguing when, in reality, one partner is simply afraid.

Usually, conflicts between couples occur when the route is beyond one partner's abilities. I've been the weaker climber, scared out of my mind and scratching and clawing my way with my boyfriend up routes beyond my ability; I've also been the stronger climber, dragging a terrified, inexperienced boyfriend up tricky routes that I wouldn't have taken a client on. Before climbing with your romantic partner, be sure your goals are in sync. If you end up engaging in shouting matches mid-climb, devise a simple conflict-resolution process that, by acknowledging fear, works for both parties before you climb again. Drawn-out tensions rapidly overshadow the positive energy that fuels safe and successful ventures.

Even if you opt for a couple partnership, try climbing with others, too—particularly with members of the same sex. You'll experience a different dynamic that might help you recognize and dissolve any unhealthy pattern that develops by climbing exclusively with your spouse. For example, a woman who has learned everything from her more-experienced boyfriend may not feel comfortable taking on the leadership role. By climbing with another, equally skilled partner, she gets the opportunity. If this partner is another woman, she will probably feel even more empowered.

Climbing with Strangers

Whenever possible, obtain partner recommendations from climbers whom you trust. At some point, though, you may find yourself partnering with a complete stranger. By doing so, you risk climbing with those feigning a higher skill level than they actually possess. You don't want to find yourself hundreds of feet above the ground with some poser whose careless bumbling doesn't square with the grandiose picture he or she painted in the parking lot. Avoid partnering with anyone with a cavalier attitude—"Oh, it'll be easy" are famous last words. Also beware of the Jekyll and Hyde partners who are gentle as lambs on the ground but transform into seething hyenas on the rock. Because you may not have the skills to extricate yourself from such unfortunate situations as a beginner, assess potential partners on the ground as best you can before trusting them with your life.

Though it's always a gamble, climbing with a stranger can be a good experience. Perhaps because you feel comfortable exposing weaknesses to those you know best, in the presence of those you know least you can put your best foot forward. Work out any kinks in your partnership on a short route far below your ability levels, or at a top-rope site. Climbers from different regions often perform tasks slightly differently—be it a particular command, a belay method, or an anchoring technique. Before you commit to a route challenging your limits, assess a new partner's skills and methods, and, even at the last minute, don't be afraid to back out.

Mentors

Find a knowledgeable trad specialist willing to consistently spend time with you at the crags and make that person your mentor. Or hire a guide. In either case, express your interest in learning everything they're willing to teach you. If you find someone with the patience and tolerance to fill this role, be open to every learning opportunity as it occurs: observe carefully, ask questions, and then practice what you've learned with other climbers at your own level. In medical school, it's common practice for students to learn procedures by following these three steps: watch one, do one, and then teach one. This approach is also a terrific way for climbers to share knowledge.

PROTECTION PLACEMENT

The cornerstone of the trad leading experience is the slow but gratifying process of learning to place reliable protection. Take time to carefully study anchors and gear placement long before you take the sharp end, and pay close attention while following trad pitches. If you skimp on this phase of learning, you'll be doing yourself and future partners a great disservice. Be diligent and commit yourself to excellence.

Ground Work

The best place to learn protection placement is from the safety of the ground. Visit local climbing areas and practice placing hardware along the base of the crags. Take along an experienced gear-leader and ask for feedback. While this book provides basic guidelines, guidance from an experienced leader or a class will benefit you most.

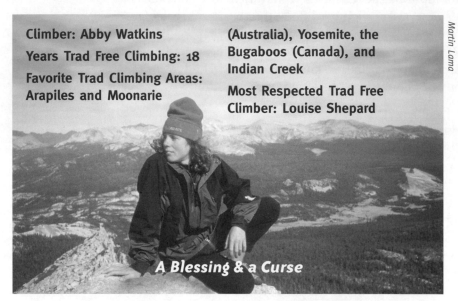

Climber: Abby Watkins

Years Trad Free Climbing: 18

Favorite Trad Climbing Areas: Arapiles and Moonarie

(Australia), Yosemite, the Bugaboos (Canada), and Indian Creek

Most Respected Trad Free Climber: Louise Shepard

A Blessing & a Curse

A woman alone on the road is fairly unusual in North America, yet we climbers often pack our cars to the gills and head off to some grand and beautiful mountain setting without a partner. For years I traveled North America in my Honda Accord hatchback, pulling into climbing areas and finding random partners whenever I could. It was a blessing and a curse. Though some of my best partners (now best friends) were among those strangers, I had some odd experiences, too—like backing off The Nose on El Cap after struggling up eight pitches, having led six myself and watching in woe while my partner took three hours to lead his. In my experience, men have often overstated their abilities when we talk in the parking lot. I became wary after that, and made sure I was prepared to do all of the leading if necessary. A few years later I ended up leading the whole of the Steck/ Salathe (also in Yosemite Valley) with another guy. He seemed to have credentials in the parking lot, but after the first pitch he said I should keep leading. To his credit he realized that to complete the climb before dark we needed to move fast, and that he wasn't up to it. It turned out to be an excellent day, and I really enjoyed leading pitch after pitch after pitch. But, if I hadn't possessed the skills to lead the remaining pitches, the situation would have had the makings of an epic.

These experiences didn't stop me from climbing with strangers though, and I'm grateful they didn't. Some years later I ran into a young guy who was climbing pretty well around Yosemite Valley. After he suggested we do Astroman, we racked up for this classic and flew up it in half a day, sharing responsibilities equally. A few days later we added the cream by cruising The Nose in a day. These are two of the most rewarding and memorable climbing experiences I've had in Yosemite.

Climbing puts you into very intense situations that depend on these partnerships. From rela- tionships coming together out of nowhere but making me trust another with my life, I've learned much about myself and gained new insights about others. I've also learned to be thoroughly self-suf- ficient in my climbing—something I might have missed if I hadn't struck out on my own.

Rock Integrity

A protection placement is only as stable as the integ- rity of the rock surrounding it. When considering each placement location, first evaluate the rock. Thump on the area with the palm of your hand and listen. If you hear a hollow sound, the rock is partially detached from the main wall, perhaps to the extent that the force of a fall would tear it completely off. In this unfortunate scenario, your protection is gone, and you, your partner, and the rope run the risk of being injured by rockfall.

Evaluate a crack by its depth and texture. If it looks shallow and feels particularly granular and crumbly, seek out another placement location; you don't want your piece too close to the opening, or resting on unsta- ble crystals or nubbins that could break under force. Be sure to choose a crack placement away from other inter- secting fractures. Even small fractures can undermine an otherwise stable crack's integrity.

Stoppers & Nuts

Stoppers and nuts are designed to slot or wedge into tapered cracks, with as much surface area touching the rock as possible. When force is applied, a Stopper's wedg- ing action is initiated. If the rock is strong enough to with- stand the force, the wedge will become more secure.

For an ideal Stopper placement, first locate a V-shaped narrowing constriction in the rock (see photo, right). With the wired stem of the Stopper in line with the anticipated load direction, slot your placement and give it a hearty tug.

A Stopper placement wedged securely into a bottleneck con- striction in the crack

The placement should resist a downward pull by wedging into the slot. If you have a choice, place a medium or large Stopper instead of a smaller micro-Stopper (less than 6 millimeters or ¼ inch). This is wise particularly at the beginning of a lead, where forces on your piece are generally greater. Tiny Stoppers are not as strong as the larger ones. When placing micros, also consider the type of rock you're climbing on. Steel nuts are stronger than some rocks, increasing the chance that the rock will shatter when force is applied (see "Stoppers," pp. 47–48).

Spring-Loaded Camming Devices (SLCDs)

"Life is good. As climbers, we now enjoy a wide variety of plug-and-go protection. Even better, the technology has been around long enough that the designs are thoroughly tweaked for the best performance, durability, and price,"[5] says climber, author, and former contributing editor to *Rock & Ice* Clyde Soles. While this is true, without the skills to place a cam correctly, you benefit little from the technology. Longtime climber and professional guide Scott Cosgrove warns, "Cams are not the cure-all or end-all. They are easily misused even by very experienced climbers. Get a guide or experienced climber with a long track record to show you placement guidelines early in your leading career."

This SLCD is placed dangerously close to the lip of the crack.

This cam placement is poor due to the debris and detached flake.

All SLCDs function according to the same basic mechanical principle: In short, each individual cam pushes against the sides of a crack when force is applied to the stem. With all their moving parts, SLCDs can dislodge or walk from a placement with relative ease. To correctly place an SLCD, orient its stem in the anticipated load-bearing direction. Place your thumb at the end of its stem and your middle and forefinger on the trigger like you would a syringe. Pull the trigger while pushing on the stem to simultaneously retract each individual cam. Insert the cam where the sides of the crack are most parallel to prevent one cam from being open more than another. Holding power is optimal if every cam on the device is retracted at mid-expansion range—no one cam more than another. If the cams of the unit you placed are more than halfway open, try the next larger size. An SLCD too small for a placement is prone to walking as a result of rope movement and to opening in an inverted (or tipped) position. Many new SLCDs, however, have cam stops designed to avoid the latter. Yet, if you overstuff an SLCD too large for a crack, your partner will have trouble removing it.

Because of their limited expansion range, micro-cams (under 1 inch) are usually placed beyond mid-expansion—up to 90 percent. These tiny units have less holding strength than most larger-sized cams, so save them for tricky placements where options are limited. Likewise, choose a 4-cam over a 3-cam unit for most applications; the 4-cam almost always offers superior holding power and tends to be more stable because it is wider and moves around less after placement.

Because of SLCDs' potential for walking, you must consider the morphology of the rock around a proposed placement. If a crack widens above or behind your placement, the device can walk due to rope friction, causing the cams to fully or partially open *(see photos 1 and 2, right)*. Look instead for a potential placement with constrictions above and behind to prevent the SLCD from walking *(see photo, next page, top left)*. While relatively simple in theory, SLCD placement can befuddle climbers new to cam-craft. When placing a cam, your focus often narrows such that you don't take in the surrounding area. Before making a placement, ask yourself where the device might walk.

This SLCD is precariously placed below a section that widens above it.

Here are a few special considerations for SLCD placement. A cam placed too close to the lip of a crack *(see photo, p. 86, top)* may pull out with force. A flared crack, wider at the lip and gradually narrower in its depths, is very difficult to protect with an SLCD, or any gear. Though offset SLCDs sometimes offer a solution, most new leaders don't own these specialty pieces. Often the only decent cam placement is deep inside where the crack is narrowest and possibly slightly more parallel. Horizontal cracks offer great placements for SLCDs with flexible stems. Though rigid-stem cams (like forged Friends) can be rigged with additional materials to work in horizontals, they are best reserved for placement in vertical cracks. Note that mud, dirt, ice, and snow, which reduce friction inside cracks, compromise the holding power of all SLCDs. On particularly soft rock, place each

The same SLCD after having "walked" into the space above it—this piece would definitely not hold a fall.

An ideally placed SLCD below a chockstone to prevent walking

A Hexcentric placement that utilizes its camming capability

cam beyond mid-expansion range but below 90 percent to help prevent the unit from "skating" out of the crack.

Hexcentrics & Tri-Cams

When loaded, Black Diamond Hexcentrics and Lowe Tri-Cams are designed to lock into place by a slight camming or rotational action. Tapered slots are excellent for using the cam action of a Hex *(see photo, bottom left)*. For optimal camming placement, the sling (or wire) should be off-center. These devices can also be wedged into cracks like Stoppers *(see photo, facing page, top right)*. Neither are exceptional for protection in a flared crack.

In a slightly irregular crack, secure a good Tri-Cam placement with the point resting in a slight depression or shelf and the rounded side against the opposite side of the crack. The sling is designed to run along the length of the curved side so that when the device is weighted downward, the sharp side cams into place *(see photo, facing page, bottom right)*.

Bolts

To many rock climbers, the fixed bolt represents security. In the sport climbing world, bolts are clipped thoughtlessly and often with great relief. Yet many of the bolts on traditional routes are not safe. Most older bolts *(see illustration, p. 90, top)*, which tend to be ¼-inch (6-millimeter) relics with low strength ratings, can shear with relative ease. These include ¼-inch Compression, Self-drill Expansion, Nail Star-Drive, Torque, and Zamac Nail-In bolts. You should back them up with a piece off your rack whenever possible. More trustworthy are an assortment of modern ⅜- to ½-inch (0.95- to 1.25-centimeter) stainless steel expansion bolts including the Fixe Wedge, Rawl 5-Piece, and Petzl Long-Life *(see illustrations, p. 90, bottom)*. The stainless steel Petzl Glue-In bolt is also a safe alternative. With strength ratings upward of 4000 pounds (8818 kilograms), all of these are safe in nonmarine environments if they're in good shape and have been placed correctly in compatible rock.

All bolts are subject to improper placement. A well-placed expansion bolt lies flush against solid rock. Any evidence of rock cratering (or chipping) around the base indicates a poor placement. Bolt hangers should be stationary and free from obvious damage or rust. Some internal errors specific to particular bolts include: overtightening the Wedge bolt, rock dust interfering with tightening of the Rawl bolt, and improper curing of the Petzl Glue-In. Besides curing time, the quality of the Glue-In is also affected by hole diameter, humidity levels, and temperatures. Bolts narrower than ½ inch (1.25 centimeters) are unreliable in soft rock such as sandstone. Unfortunately, these internal placement errors are undetectable by subsequent climbers. Nevertheless, understanding potential errors ensures that you don't worship the bolt as an infallible piece of equipment. Use your best judgment, trust gut feelings, and back up any bolts that you suspect won't provide optimal strength.

A Hexcentric wedged into a crack like a Stopper

Bolts at seaside climbing areas are another story. Stainless steel expansion bolts and one-piece glue-ins are no longer considered safe in marine climbing environments. These bolts are subject to corrosion caused by constant exposure to salt water and can fail without any visible external deterioration. Unfortunately, many of these bolts still exist in popular overseas climbing destinations like Thailand and Les Calanques. Because of its anticorrosive properties, titanium is now the recommended material for anchors or bolts at crags within three to four miles of the coast. Replacing existing bolts is a costly undertaking and will take years.

Natural Protection

Natural protection (pro) is my favorite. Whenever I come across a natural feature I can lasso for protection, I feel most in harmony with the environment and forces of nature. There's nothing like using the big, friendly girth of a Jeffrey pine as an anchor or slipping a runner over a flake on lead. Such features beg for your attention both on lead and at belays, and using them helps reinforce the trad leader's reliance on simplicity and ingenuity (see "Simplicity," pp. 24–25).

A small Tri-Cam placed in a crack

Though artificial climbing gadgets deserve high praise, don't miss the opportunities that natural pro affords. Always look out for sturdy horns, chicken heads, *huecos* (holes), tunnels, chockstones, trees, or flakes for use as protection. You won't have to use a piece off your rack—a plus if you're conserving gear on lead. To secure

Older Bolts with Low Strength Ratings

1) $\frac{1}{4}$-inch Compression ("buttonhead") , 2) $\frac{1}{4}$-inch Compression/nut, 3) Self-drill Expansion, 4) Nail Star-Drive, 5) Torque Bolt, 6) Zamac Nail-In

Modern Bolts with High (Upwards of 4000 lbs.) Strength Ratings

1) Fixe Wedge, 2) Rawl 5-Piece, 3) Petzl Long-Life, 4) Petzl Glue-In

Natural Protection

❶ chicken head

❷ huecos

❸ chockstone

❶ A rock tunnel secured with a threaded sling

❷ A small tree secured with a girthed sling

New and old bolts at Donner Summit. From left to right are the Fixe Wedge; the Compression ("buttonhead"); and the Rawl 5-Piece.

a sling through a small *hueco*, or around a small chicken head, tree, rock tunnel, or chockstone, use a girth hitch (see "Knots & Hitches," pp. 219–220). For examples of how to use these features, see illustrations 1–3 and photos 1 and 2, all on p. 91.

Avoid using the girth hitch on larger objects, which may result in a pulley effect and cause your runner to slip under force. Instead, drape a large runner over the object and join it at the base with a carabiner. Lacking these resources, untie one or two of your tied runners and retie them together around the object, completely encircling it. Either way, make sure your sling(s) are long enough to avoid dangerous load multiplication. If you're slinging a horn or a flake, be certain it has a stable connection to the main rock and loop your runner as close to the base as possible. Or, if your sling is long enough, secure it snugly with an overhand slipknot or an adjustable clove hitch that can be cinched around the feature (see "Knots & Hitches," pp. 216–222) and attach a carabiner. Slings made from standard webbing offer better-adhering, tackier surfaces than those made of slippery Spectra.

If your sling doesn't fit snugly around the rock feature you've runnered, it's bound to slip off from the movement of the rope, especially if there's any indication that your next placement is anywhere but directly above you or if your last piece isn't directly below you. If either is the case, your sling is at risk of jiggling off the feature. You're also at risk of this happening if the feature, such as a flake or horn, is shallow where it attaches to the wall. The sling could shimmy off even if your rope runs plumb to your placements. To solve these problems, simply add some weight to the runner to keep it securely on the feature. Get creative, and choose something heavy that you won't need until the follower cleans the pitch. A large cam is good; a full or near-full water bottle is better. Clip either to the runner you've placed around the feature, and allow the item to simply dangle. Remember, you're just using it for the purpose of adding weight to the sling, so pretend it's not there. Now with a carabiner, clip your lead line to the runner, like you would any runnered piece, and carry on.

Carabiner Use

Loads should always only weight a carabiner across its vertical axis (lengthwise). Never position a 'biner so that it could be loaded horizontally—across its gate and spine *(see photo, right)*. Known as "cross-loading," this practice reduces a carabiner's strength by 50 percent. Also avoid placing a carabiner in locations where it is resting upon a rock edge or shelf—if it is weighted while positioned over even the smallest of edges, under very low loads it could break.

An improperly placed carabiner at risk of being horizontally "cross-loaded"

"Of all the gear you use, carabiners suffer the most failures. . . . The problem isn't defective gear—it's because all of the things that can happen to a 'biner during a fall, resulting in an open gate . . . or accidental unclipping," say the editors of the June 1999 issue of *Rock & Ice*. If a load weights a carabiner at the moment its gate is open, the 'biner can fail. Collision with natural objects can force gates open, as can the vibration of a rope during a fall. Keep the gate openings of carabiners facing away from the rock, and prevent clothing and other equipment (particularly home-tied runner tails) from interfering with gate closure. Avoid linking two or more carabiners together because they can unclip from each other with ease. Instead, create extensions with slings whenever possible. Also, carabiners can easily come unclipped from the rope on lead protection, unless you avoid the practice of "back-clipping" (see "Rope Positioning & Clipping," pp. 143–144).

Locking carabiners are best reserved for primary links in your system, while standard non-lockers suffice for secondary links. A primary link doesn't have a backup; should it fail, you're a goner. Primary links include where your belay/rappel device attaches to your harness, your connection to anchors at belays and rappel anchors, and the masterpoint of top-rope anchors. Many self-rescue techniques also involve primary links where locking carabiners are a must. (For more about self-rescue, see Chapter 8.) Lockers might also be used on lead to clip critical pieces that could prevent a potentially devastating fall. In a pinch, two reversed and opposed 'biners will work in lieu of a locker *(see photo, right)*.

Two reversed and opposed 'biners

Multidirectional Placements

Join two unidirectional pieces with a sling and clove hitch to create an oppositional placement for multidirectional use.

Climbers new to trad climbing have little experience with multidirectional placements, which are set to withstand upward, lateral, and downward forces. Climbers use them most commonly as an anchor component on a multi-pitch route (see "Multidirectional Anchors," p. 103), although other circumstances (discussed in Chapter 6) may also require their use. Bolts or horizontal SLCD placements offer obvious multidirectional protection, as do some natural features (like a good-size tree). Since these placements aren't always available, you can create a multidirectional configuration by coupling two opposing unidirectional pieces. Place the upper one to accept a downward force, and the lower one to accept an upward force. Join the two pieces with a sling held in place with a snug clove hitch (see "Knots & Hitches," pp. 218–219). This is called an oppositional placement *(see photo, left).*

Many leaders rely on vertically placed SLCDs as multidirectionals, expecting them to rotate and accommodate other directional forces. They can and will sometimes. Since a cam is unstable when it rotates, failure is always a possibility. While you can't completely trust the unit during or after rotation, on the other hand, forces should be relatively low when a piece like this might be weighted—it's a judgment call.

ANCHORS

Once you've mastered the basics of gear placement, you can begin to learn how to create anchor systems. Anchor building involves creativity and ingenuity, and can be a lot of fun. During the learning process, remain at the base of the crags, under the watchful eye of your mentor or a qualified instructor.

The Pre-Equalized Anchor System

The ideal anchoring method for new leaders is what is known as a pre-equalized system using a tied corde-lette or sewn Web-o-lette. Introduced to the American

Climber: Doug Robinson

Years Trad Free Climbing: 48

Favorite Trad Climbing Area:
   High Sierra

Most Respected Trad Free Climber:
   Chuck Pratt

Jim Harrington

How Can I Trust My Placements?

You can't. Not at first. So don't expect to stake your life on them right away.

Trusting your placements is tough because it's a judgment of a technique. The technique is hard enough: take a few very simple tools, light alloy wedges, all sizes, and families of spring-open cams, and fit them into cracks in rock, infinitely varied in shape. Simple tools, complex and ever-changing application. And there's no practical way to spot-test placements, not for the tonnage of force you want, and may need, them to hold.

You need judgment. But how are you going to get it? Pro falls squarely into that danger zone where, as they say, "We get too soon good, and too late smart." It is far easier to learn to slot pieces into cracks than to decide how much they can be trusted.

Judging your pro is one of those cruxes in your climbing career where you need help, either from an experienced mentor or a professional instructor. As a guide,

protection and anchoring is one of my favorite subjects to teach. It's a big opportunity to help someone's climbing leap into new realms. The challenge is to go there while maintaining a margin of safety.

What I do is actually pretty simple. Students each take a rack and place all the pieces from the ground. Then the whole class goes over each placement, and I discuss what's good, where it could be better, and how I know. Then we do it again before going on to combining individual placements into a SERENE anchor.

—Doug Robinson

professional guiding community by their Canadian peers in the late 1980s, this comprehensive system has since become popular among recreational climbers.

The pre-equalized anchor system has many advantages not found in other systems. Best of all, it distributes the force of a load among all components, and prevents shock-loading should any one piece fail. These are two key features of the common SERENE mnemonic used in anchor craft.

This system is also ideal on lead because, relying on the cordelette, it doesn't eat up valuable rope (critical on multipitch routes involving long pitches); it eliminates the need to conserve multiple slings for the belay. Establishment is, however, time consuming and requires additional gear (the cordelette or Web-o-lette).

Three Piece Minimum

For climbers in their early years of anchor building a good rule of thumb is: *No matter how solid you think your pieces are, don't place less than three.* Obviously exceptions exist. If you can belay off a sturdy, sufficiently rooted,

---

SERENE Anchor Checklist

Use the SERENE mnemonic as a mental checklist to build bomber anchors. Ask yourself the following questions, and make sure the answer to each is affirmative:

S=Safe/Secure. Is your gear placed correctly in solid rock? Are fixed pieces (bolts and pitons) and natural features of excellent quality?

E=Equalized. When weighted, does each anchor component share the load equally?

R=Redundant. Is each component of the anchor backed up at least once?

E=Easy. Is your anchor simple? Does it avoid complicated arrangements and unnecessary gear?

NE=No Extension. If one component of the anchor fails, does your arrangement assure that no other component will be shock-loaded?

live tree, one piece is sufficient. Also, an anchor consisting of two bomber bolts is usually adequate.

Redundancy

Create additional redundancy in your anchor system by using more than one rock feature for protection whenever possible. For instance, when several cracks are available, use two. Then, if something happens to one feature to reduce its reliability, there's another anchor to protect you.

Force Multiplication

Anchor physics are such that the system load varies in proportion to the angle formed by any two components. The anchor system is safest when angles of the joined gear components are less than 60 degrees. Anything greater than 60 degrees exponentially multiplies the force bearing on your pieces, compromising the system *(see p. 98)*.

Think of the triangle formed between the masterpoint and any two anchor components as a slice of pizza: The larger the slice, the more load each piece must bear. A worst-case scenario would be loading the center of a taut horizontal sling between two level anchors. If one of your anchor pieces is far to the right or left, link it to the main system with extra slings to decrease the angle *(see photos 1 and 2, p. 99)*.

Climbers new to anchor craft are frequently confused about when and where to use a locking carabiner. Many overcompensate by using a locker at every link. Yet a carabiner linking a single piece of protection (or bolt) to a multicomponent anchoring system is generally a secondary link. Only the masterpoint—the primary link—on a Web-o-lette or cordelette anchor requires a locker. Although one locking carabiner is adequate here, use two at the masterpoint of any anchor you cannot monitor visually. Examples include the anchors of systems managed from below such as yo-yo top-ropes and rappels. When you can easily monitor the masterpoint, single lockers are sufficient.

81 lb pull ▸20°◂ angle 81 lb pull

50% of load   50% of load

160 lbs

85 lb pull ▸40°◂ angle 85 lb pull

54% of load   54% of load

160 lbs

Force Multiplication

Loads upon anchor components increase exponentially with increased angles between pieces. It is ideal to keep angles between each component 60° or lower to prevent unsafe load burdens.

104 lb pull ▸80°◂ angle 104 lb pull

70% of load   70% of load

160 lbs

160 lb pull ▸120°◂ angle 160 lb pull

100% of load   100% of load

160 lbs

Decrease Angles to Increase Safety

Angles created by cordelette between two pieces are too large, potentially requiring each piece to tolerate nearly 80 percent of the load.

Correct this dilemma by adding longer slings to the middle and highest pieces, decreasing the angle to around 50 percent.

The Cordelette

To assemble a pre-equalized anchor system using a cordelette, follow these steps:

1. Clip all three pieces of protection with single carabiners and attach your cordelette to form a giant circle connecting them all together.

2. Form two bights in the rope, one between each piece. Simultaneously pull these two bights down to join the bottom loop of the cordelette, ensuring that each strand meets precisely at the exact same point, thereby equalizing the future load among all three pieces.

3. Decide the exact direction of the anticipated load, and adjust the cordelette so that all anchor points will share the load. To easily accomplish this, place your thumb in the loops created by the gathered bights and, while pulling downward, slide it from side to side until you've accommodated the determined load direction. This must be done with absolute precision or the load will not be shared by all of your pieces.

4a. With your other hand, grasp all of the strands tightly above the gathered bights and, keeping your thumb in place, carefully slide this hand toward the anchors until you can tie an overhand knot. Be certain to keep all of the strands together as you tie the knot, and allow space in the loop for at least two locking carabiners.

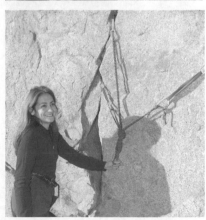

4b. The knot functions to prevent extension and shock-loading of any one piece in the system should any others fail. The loops below the knot are both clipped as your masterpoint, where you anchor at belay stations, or thread a rope to create a top-rope.

The Web-o-lette

To help beginners with the Web-o-lette assembly, Mountain Tools has created a simple equation: V + W + 8 = On Belay!

1. Clip all three pieces of protection with single carabiners, and clip each sewn loop end of the Web-o-lette into the carabiners on the two far ends forming a V.

2. Clip the center of the bight between the ends to your middle piece, forming a W.

3. Form two loops of equal length by gathering these bights together and tying a figure-eight, to create your masterpoint.

Anchors & Load Direction

Anchor systems are either multidirectional or unidirectional, depending on the anticipated load direction. New leaders should practice building both.

Unidirectional Anchors

Unidirectional anchors need only to accommodate a force in one direction and include the following types of applications:

- An anchor to resist a downward force on the top of a single-pitch route or atop the final pitch of a multipitch route.
- A base anchor established to accommodate an upward force on the first pitch of a route beginning from the ground. (This optional anchor is discussed in the "Base Belay" pp. 127–130.)
- A rappel anchor, almost always fixed (established by the first ascent party) usually needs to resist only a downward force. Fixed yo-yo top-rope anchors are also usually unidirectional.

Multidirectional Anchors

Where you need to accommodate upward, lateral, and downward forces, your anchor must be multidirectional. (At least one component must withstand upward and lateral forces.) The multidirectional anchor is used at all multipitch belays, with the exception of the final pitch and sometimes the first.

Upward and/or lateral forces in the multipitch scenario (described in Chapter 7) occur during standard leader falls where, because at least one of the leader's pieces holds, the belayer at the anchor below experiences upward and/or lateral tension while braking the fall (*see illustration, right*). A downward force occurs when the follower falls after having been belayed at the anchor above by the leader (*see illustration, p. 104*). A downward force also occurs if the leader falls before placing a piece of protection when climbing above the anchor, or if this piece or all lead pieces fail, resulting in a fall past the belayer (*see illustration, p. 104, top left*).

A multidirectional belay anchor withstanding upward and lateral forces

The component of a multidirectional anchor set to accommodate an upward and/or lateral force should be placed low in your cordelette or Web-o-lette *(see photo, bottom left)* configuration because lead fall forces could lift the belayer and, as a result, rip out the other anchor components. When a leader falls, the force of the fall is initially absorbed at the belay by the belayer. If the force is high enough, he or she is pulled upward until the multidirectional anchor component stops him or her. In falls generating high forces (see "The Physics of Falling," pp. 152–153), the distance the belayer is lifted could be significant. If the multidirectional component is placed too high in the arrangement, the belayer is not only lifted considerably, but worse, the lower anchor components, if unidirectional, will probably rip out. Without any multidirectional piece whatsoever, a high-force leader fall on a multipitch climb could generate enough force to tear out the entire anchor, and both climbers would fall to their deaths. If the multidirectional component is a unidirectional piece like a nut or Hex, consider securing it with an oppositional piece, or clipping it taut to the anchor system as shown *(see photo, bottom left)*.

Potential downward forces on multipitch anchors are always greater. The maximum upward force on a multidirectional anchor is subtler; it's determined by the amount of friction in the system. (Fall forces are discussed at length in Chapter 6.) Generally, the more rope in use and the more pieces placed by the leader, the less force on the belayer and anchor. Consequently, you need only one upward force placement as a component of most multidirectional anchors. If you don't have enough pieces on your rack to build a multidirectional anchor when you finish leading, you can always add on later once the second arrives at the belay with the rest of your rack.

A multidirectional belay anchor withstanding a downward force

Without the lowest piece in this configuration, this anchor would be considered unidirectional because all three upper pieces are Stoppers set to withstand only downward forces. Adding the lower component (a Stopper set to withstand an upward force) makes the anchor multidirectional. Its key placement *low in the configuration* will prevent the force of a leader fall from lifting the belayer and possibly ripping out the unidirectional placements.

Fixed Anchors

Although never guaranteed, you may encounter fixed belay anchors on a route. Expect fixed anchors only when they're mentioned in guidebooks. Rappel routes are always fixed, having been pre-established by first-ascent parties where walk-offs are not possible. The quality of a fixed anchor can vary—just because it's there doesn't mean it's safe. Bolts, pitons, and natural features are the most common components of fixed anchors. Before using one, evaluate the integrity of the placements and the rock. Avoid antiquated rusting pitons with broken eyeholes, and check natural features for stability. If a natural feature appears loose, do not use it. If any other component is questionable, back it up with a piece from your rack.

Many fixed anchor configurations exist, and some are better than others *(see illustrations 1–4, right)*. Use your knowledge regarding appropriate angles, equalizing and shock-loading possibilities to determine the quality of configuration. Chains or webbing link components of a fixed rappel anchor. Since some belay anchors double as rappel stations, you may encounter such anchors during your ascent. When belaying, don't clip into the masterpoint of such anchors. Instead, clip directly into each individual piece and create your own pre-equalized configuration with a cordelette or a Web-o-lette.

Never belay off open or closed cold shuts *(see photo, p. 106)*. These soft-metal hardware-store "anchors" rated poorly in unofficial 1997 strength tests and cannot withstand high loads. Primarily found on top of sport routes, most cold shuts are suited only for static, low-load tasks (like lowering a climber after a lead). Do not, however, use them as rappel anchors unless they have been

Fixed Anchor Configurations

The soft-metal cold shut rates poorly in strength tests.

hammered completely shut. Even then, I might back up a cold shut with a piece from my rack.

Rappel anchors are always fixed so climbers can retrieve ropes without leaving behind their own gear. Individual rappel anchor components are joined by either chain links or webbing. If necessary, cut away weathered nests of discolored, stiff, and/or abraded webbing and replace with webbing from one of your own tied runners. Check the masterpoint for redundancy, rust, and grooving, and replace or bolster with either a rappel ring or carabiner from your rack. Finally, check the anchor for appropriate equalization and make alterations with webbing (again, from tied runners from your rack) if necessary.

Other Anchoring Methods

Pre-equalizing with a cordelette is just one of many anchoring methods. Effective anchors can also be built without cordelettes or Web-o-lettes. One of these methods is described in Chapter 9, but several others exist. Many require more advanced protection placement skills and keener judgment than new leaders will likely possess. With more overall experience on the rock, you will benefit from learning more advanced techniques. Intermediate leaders should refer to *Anchors* by John Long and *More Anchors* by both Long and Bob Gaines.

NAVIGATION AIDS

Together with other resources, guidebooks and topographical (topo) drawings provide guidance for exploring new climbing areas and getting up and down routes. Beta is more specific information gleaned from other climbers.

Guidebooks

In a well-written guidebook, the introduction contains information about a particular area's human as well as its climbing history. It also lists optimal climbing seasons for that area, camping information, and hazards to be aware of (rattlesnakes, poison oak or ivy, loose rock, climbing on fragile rock shortly after rain, etc.). It describes any pertinent area rules and regulations and regional climbing ethics. A few examples include: Power drills are not allowed in national parks like Yosemite; most crags in North Carolina welcome only traditional, ground-up ascents; a voluntary climbing ban during the month of June exists at Devils Tower in Wyoming to honor sacred traditions of Native American Plains tribes including the Lakota, Sioux, Cheyenne, and Kiowa; and, many cliffs throughout the U.S. are closed for certain months to accommodate nesting raptors. By honoring requests like these in a cooperative spirit, climbers maintain favor with local nonclimbing communities, land managers, and conservationists, as well as local climbers.

The main section of a climbing guidebook usually features topo renderings of established area routes, and sometimes includes narrative descriptions and photographs. Though limited in use, photos can help you identify landmark features like roofs, corners, and ledge systems. Narratives provide fine complements to topos, but by themselves are vague and often confusing. Interestingly, when topos came onto the climbing scene in the 1970s, some viewed their use as "cheating."[6]

Topos

Topography is defined as the "detailed, graphic representation of the surface features of a place . . . indicating relative positions and elevations." Although climbing topos do not resemble maps with contour lines used for hiking and backpacking, they accomplish a similar task of guiding adventurers through vertiginous terrain.

Topo Literacy

One great drill for becoming topo literate is to study the legend of your local climbing area guidebook, head to the crags with paper and pencil, and then draw your own topo versions of a few routes. Then compare these to the topos of the same routes in the guidebook. Even better, sit down in front of a small boulder and draw a route that represents the miniature features on a short section as if they were full-sized.

Topo-Schmopo 5.8

Climbing guidebooks usually feature any combination of the following navigational data for each route: photo *(below left)*, topo *(below right)*, and narrative description *(on facing page)*. Familiarize yourself with a typical climbing topo by comparing information shown for the fictional route below and on the facing page.

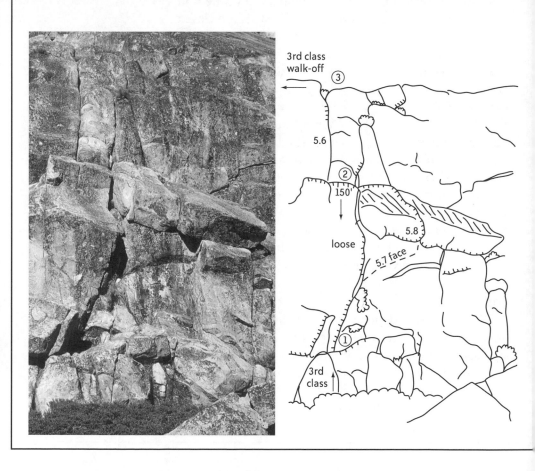

Guidebooks offer legends with fairly standardized symbols used to identify varied features of a rock face. Learning to read climbing topos is a little like learning a new language. To read them, you'll need to translate symbols for roofs and overhangs, ledges, corners (dihedrals), faces, straight-in cracks, flares, chimneys, and more. For more information, see sidebar on this page.

Narrative Description

PITCH 1: Scramble up third-class boulders to a ledge at the base of an obvious right-facing dihedral.

PITCH 2: Climb the corner past a large bush and surmount an oblong chockstone. Traversing right, face climb (5.7) below an overhang to the base of a short finger crack splitting a small roof. Proceed over the roof (5.8) and across a ramp leading to a ledge. Move 10 feet left and belay at the base of an obvious hand crack.

PITCH 3: Climb the hand crack (5.6) leading to the final belay ledge.

DESCENT: Scramble south to third-class ledge system leading back to the base.

Common Topo Legend

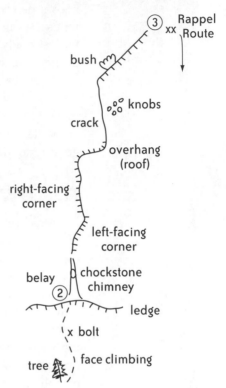

Gathering Beta

As a new leader, consider supplementing guidebook data with information from additional resources prior to your ascent. Such resources might include friends or acquaintances who have recently visited a particular climbing area or completed a specific route. Also check with qualified local climbing shop personnel. This supplemental information you gather is referred to as beta, which refers affectionately to the late climber Jack Mileski.[7] Obtaining beta for the approach and descent is also crucial. In this country, United States Geological Survey (USGS) maps can be helpful, particularly for backcountry routes with long and/or complex approaches and descents.

While guidebooks, topos, and beta are all valuable tools, only a portion of reality can be conveyed through maps, drawings, and friends' descriptions. No matter how detailed, these resources have limitations. Sometimes routes won't live up to the guidebook's description or your interpretation of it. Some topos are vague or even wrong. In other instances, you may strongly disagree with the published rating of a particular climb. To avoid frustration and disappointment, arrive prepared and don't be surprised when the route is something other than you expected. Equal in value to information gathered before any ascent are being flexible, thinking on your toes, and cultivating good route-finding abilities.

FOLLOWING & CLEANING

Mastering the skills of following and cleaning trad pitches is crucial if your sights are set on leading. Unless you can appreciate these as vital skills to learn, they can be trying tasks. Your ability to follow and clean with finesse, together with your overall attitude, makes good use of your time on the rock. A positive, competent follower always has more climbing invitations than an inexperienced, fumbling and grumbling, second. When instructing new lead climbers who are serious about the sport and want to climb as much as possible, I teach them first how to become good followers. Logging in lead climbing hours at the crags will follow. The climbers you follow before and during your initial trad leading experiences influence your abilities and style more than anyone (or anything) else. So, choose your partners carefully. Besides ensuring you get the most out of your experiences as follower, these tips help build the skills you need for leading.

At the Base

Make sure everything you need is within arm's reach before putting the leader on belay. Have your shoes on so you're prepared to climb. If the weather is chilly, put your fleece on before the leader begins.

On the ground, always tie into the end of the rope before the leader sets off. This way, when the leader finishes the pitch and pulls the rope up, you don't risk it going too far, if you're not paying attention. Now, you're ready to climb. For guidelines specific to belaying trad leaders, see "Belaying," pp. 68–70.

Climbing

As the follower, notice how each piece of protection is placed. Ask yourself why the leader chose that particular piece at that specific stance. Why is there a shoulder-length runner on it instead of a quickdraw? Assess the distances between pieces and think how and why they vary. Notice how certain placements protect the leader from hitting obstacles in case of a fall. If you find a piece of protection has walked or popped out, analyze how this occurred and what could have been done to prevent it. Imagine yourself in the leader's position placing each piece: Find the most energy-efficient stance, remove the piece, and then reset it yourself for practice. Climb smoothly as if you were on lead; move carefully and pretend that falling is not an option (but don't dawdle). Rerack gear neatly and orderly throughout the pitch; don't wait until you reach the belay anchor to get organized. Finally, do your utmost not to whine.

At the Belay Anchor

As your partner reracks, hand him or her one piece at a time—a quickdraw assembled with two carabiners is considered one piece, while a Stopper attached to a carabiner is two (if the leader racks Stoppers in groups). Because an SLCD without a 'biner is only half a piece, be sure each cam has one carabiner attached. In other words, offer pieces ready to clip onto the leader's rack. When you transfer more than one at a time, you both risk dropping something.

Particularly on a multipitch route, act efficiently at the belay and be as helpful as possible in preparing for the next pitch. Offer to reflake the rope and get water out of the pack. If you're not doing anything, ask your partner what you can do. This scenario is known as the *changeover* and is discussed in depth in Chapter 7.

Cleaning

As you remove protection, stay organized. Rack each piece individually in order by size, disassembling Stoppers on quickdraws and keeping all Stoppers on one carabiner. Not only will your partner appreciate it when you exchange gear at the belay, but climbing is easier if you're not disheveled with slings dangling down to your knees and hardware stacking up on the rope at your waist.

When approaching a piece of protection, leave it clipped to the rope. If it remains attached and you drop it, the piece will just slide down to your waist. For further security when removing the piece, clip it while still attached to the rope into your sling; then unclip it from the rope. Approach SLCD removal with finesse and delicacy and passive protection removal with gusto. Although yanking forcefully to remove Stoppers is a common method of removal, you can save your wireds from damaging kinks if you use your nut tool. If you do choose to yank, close your mouth prior to removal to protect your pearly whites. Don't give up easily. Persistency and determination usually prevail in extracting overcammed SLCDs or stubbornly wedged Stoppers.

In summary, the ideal follower climbs swiftly, cleans the pitch with efficiency and success, stays organized, and keeps the leader safe by providing an attentive belay and feeding rope out smoothly. He or she is always prepared to climb when the rope tightens, doesn't drop gear, and doesn't whine (too much). After acquiring these skills, you shouldn't have a problem finding climbing partners, and, once you start leading, your rope-handling and gear-management skills will be that much more developed.

RAPPEL OVERVIEW

Rappelling skills are necessary for anyone venturing into traditional climbing. Most climbers learning to trad lead already have basic rappelling skills. But if you were introduced to the sport through indoor gym climbing or sport cragging, your descent experience may have been limited to being lowered by a partner.

The hook on your nut tool can help extract large stoppers with eyeholes.

Stubborn Gear Removal Tips

Stoppers

- To dislodge a Stopper welded into place, tap with a carabiner or a rock on the bottom of your nut tool placed against the underside of the Stopper.

- The hook on your nut tool is invaluable for leveraging out larger Stoppers with eyeholes *(see photo above)*.

- Besides the use of your nut tool, don't underestimate the results of some finger maneuvering, especially on Stoppers that are partially loose.

- Look for wider sections above or below Stopper placements that indicate how a piece was slotted; reverse that action to retrieve it. Better yet, if you can hear your partner, ask him or her (likewise for difficult-to-remove SLCDs) how and exactly where the piece was inserted.

SLCDs

- Smaller SLCDs are often more difficult to extract because of their minimal camming range. If you're unable to extract a small cam on your first try, try gently rocking the stem while retracting the trigger as tightly as possible and pulling outward.

- For an SLCD that has walked so deeply into a crack you cannot reach it, use the hook on your nut tool and the loop on the end of a Stopper to retract its trigger bar.

- Use the hook on your nut tool to retract individually inverted cams on larger SLCDs without cam stops.

Gear Dependence

In trad free climbing, rappelling is one of the few scenarios where you rely completely upon your equipment and anchors. During an ascent, gear and anchors play the role of a safety net. Sometimes you can climb several pitches without ever weighting your harness, the rope, pieces of protection, or even the anchors. In altering your relationship with equipment, rappelling requires a leap of faith and a shift toward complete dependence. As long as climbers possess the appropriate skills and devote their complete attention to the task, rappelling can be relatively safe, but keep in mind that a small mistake can be fatal.

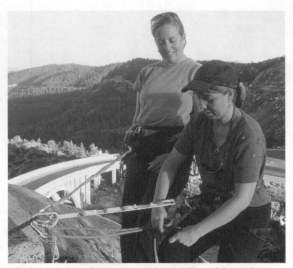

Climbers preparing to rappel are clipped in with a daisy chain (right) and a cow's tail.

Inexperienced rappellers should practice once or twice with an experienced guide or mentor in a controlled setting prior to rappelling on their own. Although elementary descriptions of how to rappel are not included in this text, a basic overview is. Tips are intended to supplement the newcomer's sessions with a mentor or a guide and reinforce several crucial concepts for those with more experience. Explanations assume climbers are clipped in safely at a reliable anchor with a locking carabiner and either a *cow's tail* (a sling that has been girth-hitched to your rappel/belay loop) or a *daisy chain* (specialty webbing with several sewn loops designed for adjustable, static clip-ins) *(see photo, top of page)*. The middle loops (or "pockets") on a daisy chain are designed only for static applications. Strength ratings for each loop are as low as 2 kilonewtons (kN), or 449 pounds, a force easily surpassed in dynamic loading.

The Rope(s)

Rappels are done on one rope or on two tied together. Before getting on any route with a rappel descent, determine the length of each rappel. To descend distances less than half the length of your rope, a single rope doubled at its center is sufficient. For longer rappels, use two ropes.

If you're unsure of a rappel's length, bring a second rope. Two ropes of similar diameter can be tied together for double-rope rappels by one of several knots. I recommend either the double fisherman's (grapevine) or the flat overhand (see Chapter 9). Use a triple fisherman's when connecting dissimilar diameter ropes. Because of the knot, only one rope can be pulled to retrieve your lines from below; note which one before heading down.

Avoiding Fatal Mistakes

Deadly rappel errors can result when a climber rappels off the ends of either two uneven strands *(see illustration, right)* or two equal-length rope strands *(see illustration, p. 116)*. If you accidentally rappel on uneven lines and the shorter strand's end passes through the rappel device, your weight suddenly shifts onto the longer strand and the rope(s) are pulled through the anchor. Avoid these mistakes by taking some simple precautions. First, tie secure individual "stopper" knots *(see photos 1 and 2, p. 115)* on the ends of each strand before tossing your rope(s) down the line of descent. (If the

Tying a "stopper" knot to the free end of each rappel line may prevent you from rappelling off the end of your rope(s). Effective "stopper" knots include the single figure eight *(photo 1)*; and half of a double fisherman's *(photo 2)*.

rappel is a "rope-stretcher"—if it requires every inch to reach the ground or next anchor—skip the stopper knots but be sure to use a brake-line backup.) After tossing each rope off separately (to avoid potential tangles), verify that each free end reaches the ground (or the next anchor). Don't accept ropes that are tangled midway or have landed short. Pull these lines up and take the time to toss them again. For added security, especially on descents where the ground or next anchor is not visible, clip a carabiner through each knot. Finally, before initiating the rappel, confirm that the center of your rope is at anchor level. (Bicolored and bipatterned ropes make identifying a rope's midpoint easy. But don't become complacent—an experienced and very competent fellow guide once rappelled off an uneven bicolored rope.)

Brake-Line Backup

To create a backup brake mechanism, attach a 28-inch (71-centimeter) tied loop of 6-millimeter nylon cord with a friction hitch onto both brake lines below your device. (To prepare a loop for this purpose, purchase 40 inches [101 centimeters] of nylon cord to have enough for knot and tails and then tie with a ring bend—see Chapter 9, p. 221—and trim as needed.) Clip it to your leg loop with a carabiner, and keep it loose with your brake hand on or slightly above it as you descend *(see photo 1, facing page)*. Most climbers I know prefer using the autoblock (see Chapter 9) for this purpose.

In the event you are hit by rockfall or pass out and lose control, the friction hitch will tighten *(see photo 2, facing page)* and prevent you from plummeting downward. The friction-hitch backup is a must for climbers rappelling with a heavy pack, and is a good idea for exhausted climbers facing multiple rappels. It's also helpful to free both hands when rappelling to establish a directional on a top-rope. Before descending, though, make sure the cord is short enough to avoid getting sucked into your rappel device. To prevent any likelihood of this happening, you can extend your braking device by adding a sling or quickdraw to your harness rappel loop as shown in photos 1 and 2 on facing page. Although your device is now farther away from you, the braking capabilities remain the same. This is common practice by European guides when descending with novice rappellers. Not only does it keep the braking device safely away from the backup friction hitch, it also keeps it away from loose clothing or hair.

Safety Check

Before you unclip from the anchors for any rappel descent, mentally review the following checklist:

❏ Are the anchor, slings, and masterpoint reliable? Are recently tied newer slings knotted tightly with adequate tails?

❏ Is my carabiner locked?

❏ Is the rope fed properly through my rappel device and locker?

❏ Is my harness doubled back?

❏ Are my hair and/or loose clothing secured away from the device? Getting hair caught in your device on rappel is extremely dangerous and, among other complications, can result in serious scalp injuries. Though easily prevented, it is surprisingly common.

❏ Is the center of the rope running through the masterpoint? Are the two rappel strands equal?

❏ Are the ropes tangle-free? Do they reach the ground or the next rappel station?

❏ If rope length is adequate to reach the next anchor or the ground, did I tie knots in each rope end?

❏ Is my backup hitch tied and attached correctly? Is it short enough to not get sucked into my device?

❏ On a double-rope rappel, is the knot secure and tied correctly? Which rope will I pull to retrieve the lines from below?

❏ Are the ropes running across any sharp terrain? If necessary, use slings to extend your masterpoint (see illustrations 1 and 2, p. 120) or pad the sharp area with duct tape or clothing.

In both photos a friction hitch is used to create a backup brake, and the rappel device is extended with a runner to prevent the cord from being sucked into the device. In photo 2 the safety feature is activated.

Rope Retrieval Tips

You risk rappel ropes getting stuck upon every retrieval. Since even the finest climbing day can be tainted by the ugly experience of dealing with a stuck rope, here are some tips to avoid it:

- After the first partner rappels, ask him or her to test pull the rope. If it appears the knot might get stuck on something within the first several feet of the anchor (which is usually the problem area), consider moving the knot below the suspect section and begin your rappel below it *(see illustration, right)*. Use extreme care as you begin the rappel, as you may have to down-climb a short distance while holding onto your brake-line. Do not attempt this if the rope is barely long enough to complete a full-length rappel as the ends will be uneven.

- If you're the last person to rappel, maintain control of the rope ends after removing your device to keep them from twisting upon your release. Before pulling your lines, be sure they're free of any twists or knots.

- When rappelling on two ropes of different diameters in windy conditions, arrange the knot so that you can pull the thinner rope during retrieval. Gusts are less likely to sweep the heftier rope into a nearby obstacle.

- On a single-rope rappel, you can choose to pull either end of the

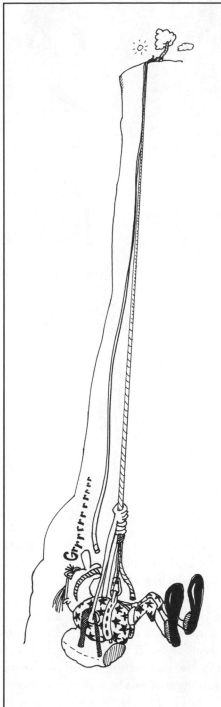

rope. Examine the rock and surrounding terrain to determine which side has less snag possibilities and pull from that side. For instance, if a tree is growing out of a crack halfway up the right side of the wall, opt to pull the left end.

• If you feel tension when retrieving the rope, try flipping it out of a potential snag to prevent it from possibly wedging in even tighter.

• Sometimes during retrieval, the knot of your rappel lines gets hung up on a lip. If you suspect this is the case with your ropes, have your partner hold onto the rope leading to the knot, then grab the other nonknotted side. With a firm whip of the rope, send a vertical wave up toward the anchor. Moments after—when the swell reaches the snag—have your partner pull the other end. The wave motion may create enough force to lift the knot from the rock, and, with the other end pulled, to free the rope.

• If your final resort is brute strength, make the most of your effort by attaching yourself to the stubborn side of the rope via a friction hitch to achieve maximum torque ability *(see illustration, left)*.

• In any difficult retrieval situation, prepare to take cover if loose rock is dislodged.

• Never try to retrieve ropes from a web of wet slings; the friction is tremendous. Sacrifice a couple carabiners from your rack; the replacement cost is minor compared to the grief avoided. Remember to reverse and oppose the gates.

Use slings to extend your masterpoint if the rappel rope is subject to a sharp edge.

Building the basic skill foundation a traditional leader needs takes time and patience. You must be confident and comfortable placing reliable gear, building solid anchors, tackling moderate cracks, and descending via rappelling before you can move on to the next learning phase. Mastering these skills will only occur with a lot of practice, as well as feedback from experts. As you gain experience in low-risk settings, scout for short routes with modest ratings that can be top-roped; there, you will eventually combine these skills with additional techniques described in the following chapter.

Chapter 6

The Single-Pitch Trad Lead

For your first trad lead, choose a single-pitch route with ample protection opportunities and good stances for resting and placing gear. Ideally, the climb is one you have previously followed or top-roped successfully. Choose a route of moderate difficulty so that the physical climb can be secondary in focus to gear placement and rope management—a few ratings below the level of ability at which you can easily follow is optimal. For example, if you've managed to eke up a few 5.9 top-ropes but feel completely solid following 5.7–5.8, then start on a 5.6 lead.

If your experience on traditional routes is minimal and your experience with ratings has been limited to those of sport routes, consider that you're no longer on common ground. The sport climber shifting to trad climbing initially finds that ratings rarely seem transferable (see "Rating Translation & Style," pp. 235–236). Pick something more moderate to ensure that your transition is gentle and then advance to more difficult routes at a modest pace.

Bill McChesney

121

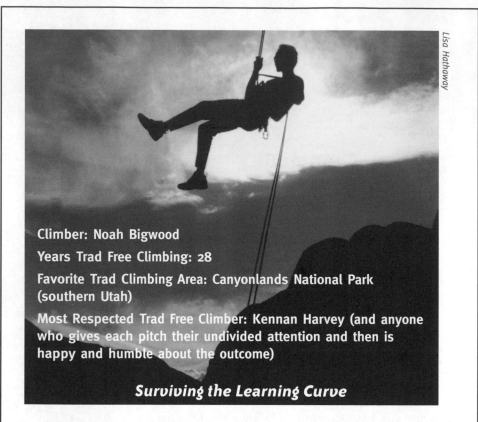

Lisa Hathaway

Climber: Noah Bigwood

Years Trad Free Climbing: 28

Favorite Trad Climbing Area: Canyonlands National Park
(southern Utah)

Most Respected Trad Free Climber: Kennan Harvey (and anyone
who gives each pitch their undivided attention and then is
happy and humble about the outcome)

Surviving the Learning Curve

Because they require that you hold your ambitions in check while maintaining self-confidence, beginnings are delicate times. In learning to lead traditional climbs, you face challenges and make decisions with your life (and often that of your partner) on the line. Because all climbing routes introduce different challenges, each climber must assess his or her own strengths and weaknesses, and reach beyond fear to gain confidence. Yet, some basic principles can help you survive the learning curve and emerge a safer, stronger, and more confident leader.

Know Your Limit—Everyone is limited by something: Some confront fears, others struggle with gear and knots, nearly all get pumped, and everyone has a physical limit to how hard they can climb. If you've spent some time bouldering, top-roping, and following others, you have a good idea where your limitations lie. Not to say you shouldn't be pushing yourself; in order to progress you'll have to move out of your comfort zone. Yet, good leaders look for challenges they can surmount and grow from, not ones that will shut them down.

Climb Carefully—The sheer excitement of climbing makes you hurry and feel rushed—slow down! Take time to do everything right the first time and then double-check it. Hurrying results in mistakes (especially when learning) and mistakes, if they don't kill you, will slow you down. Whatever has you hurrying, if you start making mistakes, can spiral out of control. Enjoy the journey as well as the destination by taking your time.

Savor Every Lead—Though when you're scared and pushing your limits climbing can feel more burdensome than pleasurable, accept both burdens and glory in the mantle of a traditional lead climber. To lead a route, step up to the rock with anticipation and confidence, not angst and dread. If you are not having fun, or simply not looking forward to every lead (whether you're nervous or not), take a step back. Regain your comfort level to rediscover the fun. When you're having fun, you climb better, learn more, and build confidence. Savor the experience of every lead.

—Noah Bigwood

LEADING ON TOP-ROPE

Lead climbing with a backup top-rope lets you assimilate the tools you've learned on the ground and work the kinks out of your system in a relatively safe setting. The stakes are lower with the security of a top-rope, so you can focus on technical tasks without agonizing over the consequences of falling. To accommodate a top-rope, routes must be half the length of your rope or shorter.

Expert Feedback

Ask your mentor to coach you and critique your performance. If you don't have one, be certain your partner has enough trad leading experience to analyze your lead discerningly, examine gear placements, and coach you along as needed. Without an expert's feedback, you may not be able to recognize a mistake. Take your time, ask for advice, and iron the wrinkles out of your technique before you consider eliminating the safety net of the top-rope. If you find yourself falling with frequency or avoiding gear placements because of awkward or strenuous stances, work on a less challenging route. Continue top-roping your leads until you can successfully coordinate their physical and mental demands with relative comfort and ease.

The Setup

You need two ropes for a simulated lead—one for your top-rope and the other for your lead rope. Set up a top-rope anchor, tie into one end of the top-rope, and have your partner put you on belay. Next, carefully uncoil your lead rope at the base so that it will feed out neatly, and tie into it. You are tied into both ropes but your partner need only belay you on the top-rope line. Protect any significant traverses with a pre-placed directional (see "Directionals," p. 176) to prevent a potential swinging fall.

AT THE BASE

If the tasks you need to accomplish at the base of the route are done thoroughly, when it's time to climb you can focus all of your energy on the actual act of lead climbing. Racking up ensures you have all the gear you need, and establishing a safe base belay with your partner creates confidence in a safety system you must trust. Finally, the checking and double checking of key safety elements should give you that final burst of confidence you need to get off the ground.

Racking Up

Every seasoned climber has developed a method of racking gear that best suits his or her physique and personal preferences. Most gear leaders use a combination of racking methods that use their harness loops, as well as a gear sling. On short routes, some climbers rack solely on their harness loops. Longer routes often require the additional use of a gear sling. Whatever the case, as a new leader, assembling your rack consistently on every lead lets you choose gear expeditiously; plus, it reduces the fumble factor.

Though consistency is your watchword, you should remain open to change. In multipitch climbing, climbers share the rack and, therefore, must be prepared for compromise when their partner's racking assembly differs from their own. Yet without some overlap, precious time is lost at belays (see "The Changeover," pp. 176–179). On the single-pitch front, flexibility is beneficial, too. For instance, if you've got a chimney to tackle, wearing gear on your harness loops, which increases friction against your hindquarters, can impede your progress. Or the route might dictate switching the gear sling from one shoulder to the other. An example is a crack that leans significantly to the right. In this scenario, if the rack is slung over your right shoulder, your gear will alternately be in the way (annoying) or completely out of view (unreachable). Whatever the case, be prepared to alter your primary racking system to accommodate the pitch. Get into the habit of scoping out the upcoming pitch and adjusting your rack accordingly before leaving the belay.

Examine the route description and topo in your guidebook and then view the route itself to determine which pieces you'll likely need. Even if the topo indicates "pro to 3 inches (7.5 centimeters)," don't be surprised if the opportunity to place something larger arises. If the topo doesn't indicate sizes or you can't get a visual of the entire route, take a couple pieces of each size up to 4 inches (10 centimeters) and, if you have one, bring a 5-inch (12.5-centimer) piece just to be safe. If you're new to trad climbing, you'll have more trouble contending with wide cracks until you gain more experience. So if there's any chance the route contains a wide section, bring appropriately sized pieces, even if you have to borrow gear. New trad leaders commonly flail on wide sections because they underestimate the severity of, say, a 5.8 wide crack—very different from a 5.8 face or a 5.8 hand crack. And, chances are, they aren't carrying the appropriate-sized gear for protection. During your first few years on trad terrain, it's safer to overestimate rather than underestimate the amount of gear you'll need, particularly when it comes to wide gear. While going light is often desirable, it's not recommended while you're learning.

Rack your SLCDs according to size, each with its own carabiner. I find that pieces are most easily removed if the carabiner gate is clipped facing my body, but I know a few longtime climbers who prefer the gates facing outward. On the gear sling, I keep the smallest cams closest to my navel and the largest cams toward my hip. Others may choose the opposite, but I find that bulkier pieces ride more comfortably the farther they are from my groin. Such details are personal choices and make no difference in the single-pitch arena.

You may choose to color code like-size SLCDs with similar colored webbing. SLCD sling colors (and in some cases anodized cam colors) for specific sizes from some manufacturers already correspond with other brands, but many do not and cannot because actual sizes differ too much. If you choose to color code cams, you have to remove the manufacturer's sewn runner on some pieces and replace them with your own hand-tied webbing. (Some suppliers offer sewn sling replacement for SLCDs, but webbing colors might be limited.) Eventually you will associate a specific crack size with a color. I did this for several years, and it definitely helped me find the right piece pronto. The drawback of color coding becomes apparent when you use someone else's gear (vice versa when another climber uses yours). You'll assess the crack size and then reach down for "yellow." What you find isn't always what you expect.

Rack a standard trad Stopper selection generally on two to three carabiners, preferably ovals where space is more plentiful. If you have too many nuts on one carabiner, you're more likely to risk dropping them when you're rifling through your selection on lead. Two schools exist regarding the racking of nuts. Some leaders carry their micro to small nuts on one carabiner and their medium to large nuts on one or two others. Some carry a mix of sizes on each carabiner, so that if they happen to drop one of the 'biners, they still have a decent range of nuts remaining to get them off the climb. You may select Stoppers for a particular trip or area based on the local guidebook's recommendation. Otherwise, I suggest you bring a full set with doubles in the ¼–½ inch (6–12 millimeter) range.

Hexes and Tri-Cams can either be racked separately or in groups. If you have few or no SLCDs, rack each on its own 'biner for quick and easy placement on lead. If Hexes and Tri-Cams supplement your standard rack, it might be easier to group several on an oval carabiner.

The total number of quickdraws, runners, and cara-biners you'll need depends upon your route length and any potential traversing. The most versatile quickdraw is a tripled 22- to 24-inch (50- to 60-centimeter) runner with a carabiner at each end (see Chapter 3). Unlike the shorter sewn quickdraws, these can be unraveled and used as longer runners. On straight-up, direct routes, carry most of your slings as quickdraws. On routes that wander and traverse, carry them as open shoulder-length slings over your head and across the opposite shoulder from the rack. Because you'll most likely also need a 'biner when you need a runner, rack each with a single carabiner. For quick and easy removal, make sure you put these on after you put on the rack. Double-length (44 inches or 110 centimeters) runners serve you well on meandering terrain, so bring at least one on indirect routes.

The majority of your remaining carabiners are con-sidered "free" or "single" ones. When deciding how many free 'biners to bring on a single pitch, consider that a cordelette belay anchor requires anywhere from three to six. So in addition to the carabiners attached to runners and quickdraws, plan to carry at least six single ones, and maybe a few more for unforeseen circum-stances. Some climbers carry free 'biners tripled or in pairs. Others prefer to link them together in a chain of five and to clip the middle 'biner to a harness loop.

If on lead you forget a crucial piece of gear in your pack on the ground, you can have your belayer send it up, provided you've got anchoring options and used less than half your rope's length. Set up a quick anchor, clip in, and pull up a loop of slack that can be lowered to the belayer to which the piece(s) can be clipped and raised. Since you're tied off to a piece now, it might be tempting for your belayer to take you off belay so he or she can have two hands to clip on the piece and feed out slack easier. However it's safer if the belayer completes the task one-handed while keeping you on belay just in case the piece you're clipped into fails.

The Base Belay

At the base, you must determine whether to estab-lish an anchor for your belayer. To decide, first consider your location. If the route starts from a small pedestal or outcropping, you need a base anchor that incorporates a piece that can withstand a downward force. This safeguards you (and your partner) from tumbling off the stance should you rip out all of your pieces on lead, or fall prior to placing your first piece *(see illustration, left)*. If the pitch begins from flat ground there's little need for an anchor. However, if you weigh significantly more than your belayer, an anchor that can withstand an upward force and prevent your fall force from lifting the belayer off the ground might be appreciated. If your belayer is not anchored and does get pulled up, you're going to fall that much farther. Still, this scenario allows the movement of the belayer's body to absorb some of the force generated in the fall, lessening the impact on other parts of the system. If the route is notorious for tricky placements and/or lots of smaller placements, you may want to forgo the anchor. Just make sure the belayer knows that he or she is being used as a fall-force reducer.

Many trad climbers, myself included, prefer to skip the initial (base) belay anchor when routes begin from the ground. Besides the benefit of using the belayer as a force-reducer, he or she can duck out of the way of potential rockfall. If you are concerned about a weight discrepancy, situate your belayer in a stable and secure position wedged between two features (trees, boulders, etc.) at the base of the climb. If this isn't possible, have the belayer brace one leg against the wall to act as a shock absorber.

Should have established a base anchor . . .

If you are using an anchor, have your belayer clip into the anchor point with the rope after tying in. The benefits of using the rope versus a sling are that:

1. You don't have to dedicate a sling to this task;

2. Your belayer is tied into the rope end and ready to climb; and

3. If your only anchor option is far from the base, you can still use it by creating a long, taut "leash" to secure the belayer at the base of the rock.

A clove hitch or figure-eight on a bight is equally appropriate for this purpose. I prefer a clove hitch because it is easily adjusted, although the figure-eight is slightly stronger. As long as the clove hitch is tightened after knotting and the load is on the appropriate strand (see "Knots & Hitches," pp. 219–220), it is perfectly suitable.

Improper belayer positioning can create unwanted lateral forces on lead protection.

As discussed briefly in Chapter 5, your belayer should be positioned directly below the first protectable moves of the pitch, and as close to the wall as possible. If he or she is belaying away from the wall and a lead fall occurs, the taut rope will create unwanted lateral force on your protection (*see illustration, above*). Depending on the anticipated load direction, it could rip out your first lead placement. In addition, an unanchored belayer far from the wall could be slammed against the rock if the fall force is great, and sudden slack in the system could result in a longer fall for the lead climber.

If your first piece cannot withstand an upward and/or lateral force and it fails, the torque may shift to the next highest piece, ripping it out, too. As momentum builds and each of your remaining pieces experiences force, it is possible that they all may fail—a hazardous scenario known as a *backward zipper*. (See pp. 136–137 for other potential backward-zipper scenarios).

Safety Check

Several years ago, after failing to complete her tie-in knot on a top-rope, world-class climber Lynn Hill leaned back to be lowered by her belayer and suffered a near ground fall. On my first climb after this incident, my partner suggested we check each other's knots and harnesses. News of Hill's accident traveled fast and, before long, most climbers I knew began doing safety checks before leaving the ground. No matter how often you climb or how hard you crank, you're not exempt from making a simple mistake. Why? Because you're human (although I sometimes wonder about Hill). Check each other's knots and buckles every time you leave the ground. Don't be embarrassed to check and don't be insulted when checked. If this warps your ego, take up a sport with fewer risks.

COMMUNICATION

When communicating with your partner on a climb, don't compete with the buzz of planes overhead, the roar of cars passing below, and other climbers hollering commands within the vicinity. Whenever possible, wait for a moment of silence and then give the command. When wind, rushing water, or other natural auditory phenomena could impede communication, face your partner and belt out your command.

Use your partner's name with each command. Essential when other climbing parties are nearby, using his or her name heightens your partner's awareness of the communication. Don't trust your or your partner's ability to differentiate each other's voices from those of

The Harness Ensemble

Each climber's harness ensemble should include the following:

- Large locking carabiner and belay/rappel device;

- Another locking carabiner for clipping into anchors;

- Cordelette or Web-o-lette for setting pre-equalized anchors;

- Nut tool; and

- A loop of nylon accessory cord for use as a rappel backup (see "Brake-Line Backup," p. 116).

The following are optional:

- Self-rescue tools (see Chapter 8)—strongly recommended, especially on long, multipitch routes;

- A small knife for removing old webbing from belay/rappel stations;

- Two rappel rings or sacrificial carabiners to augment a scrawny or antiquated rappel station (see Chapter 7); and

- A daisy chain for rappel-anchor clip-ins (a girthed runner also works).

the lads cranking up a route around the corner. If you're pulling some challenging moves on a dicey runout and your partner responds to another climber's request for "slack"—after your flash flood of terror subsides and the rope is adjusted—you will appreciate the value of using names with commands.

Verbal Commands

With each new partner, agree on which communication terms to use. The following are basic commands used predominately in the U.S.:

On belay: With the rope leading to the climber secured into the belay device, the belayer signals his or her readiness for the climber to begin.

Climbing: The climber reports that he or she is beginning.

Climb on: The belayer affirms a readiness for the climber to begin.

Slack: The climber requests some slack in the rope—about an arm's length, unless otherwise specified. Common reasons a climber might ask for slack include: needing the rope tension lessened to more effectively clean a piece of protection, needing slack to down-climb if he or she has gone off-route, wanting to rest at a lower stance, and wanting to try again after having botched a sequence. A climber might also request slack when preparing to follow a traverse where rope tension could hinder balance.

Tension/Take: The climber signals the belayer to take in any extra slack and lock off the belay device so he or she can hang on the rope.

Up-rope: The climber cues the belayer to pay closer attention and take in extra slack. As the climber, avoid the common mistake of asking your belayer to "Take up the slack." What the belayer might hear is just the word "Slack," and the result is obvious—a real bummer!

Watch me: The climber indicates a difficult move ahead and requests increased alertness from the belayer.

Falling: The climber alerts the belayer to take in slack and prepare to lock off the belay device.

Rock!: Not limited to rocks, use this command for all falling objects, whether it be a piece of gear, a camera, a water bottle, a sheet of ice, your helmet, a tiny pebble, a clod of dirt, or whatever else you lugged up.

Off belay: The leader communicates to the belayer that he or she has clipped into an established anchor and, therefore, no longer needs the belay-system security. If the belayer is absolutely certain this was the command given, he or she may disengage the belay device. (Climbers from other English-speaking countries might shout "Safe" instead.)

Belay off: The belayer alerts the climber that the device is disengaged and the belay done. By shouting "Belay off" you acknowledge the leader is indeed clipped to an anchor and no longer needs the security of the belay. If there was any miscommunication and the climber is not clipped securely, this gives him or her the opportunity to respond. For this reason, I like to shout this command seconds before disengaging my device—just in case. "Belay off" also tells the leader to pull up the rope to prepare the belay system that will eventually protect the follower. If you fail to affirm that the belay's off, the leader wastes precious time instead of moving on to the next task.

Avoid extra words whenever possible; by using basic commands you decrease the chance of miscommunication. If you say more, don't plan on being understood. I had a fairly regular partner one summer who liked to say "Gimme some" instead of "Slack." In response to "Slack," I'm like Pavlov's dog; the rope feeds through my device immediately without much thought. But it takes me several seconds to process, interpret, and verify any nonstandard command. Using commands that climbers aren't conditioned to expect wastes time and can result in further miscommunication.

Backup Tactile Commands

If there's a possibility that you won't be able to hear your partner once you've reached the belay anchor, discuss a backup plan for tactile communication. Three firm tugs can translate to "On belay." Although not optimal, it is better than no plan at all. Alternatively, partners could agree prior to the ascent that when the rope tightens, the leader has set up an anchor and engaged the belay. In this scenario, the leader mustn't pull the rope up until the anchor is fixed and he or she is ready to belay. The second keeps the leader on belay until the rope tightens. All commands are still shouted. If you're the following climber, you can be fairly certain that you're on belay if the rope is pulled tight with each move you make. The scenario where the leader accidentally climbs past the designated belay, and tugs the rope in attempting to move higher, unaware that there is no more rope left, is the obvious glitch in both of these plans. The same problem ensues if the pitch is a full rope length. Because these choices involve a lot of risk, they should only be used as last resorts.

Two-Way Radios

Once while I was instructing a beginning climbing class, the students were watching two men using two-way radios on a nearby route that is notorious for communication difficulties. Having traveled around a corner and over a roof, the leader was out of his belayer's sight. Each time he set a placement, he spoke to his belayer over the radio. One student asked what I thought of the system. Now, I very strongly oppose the use of radios for communicating on climbs. But preferring not to criticize the climbers as fervently as I would if I were talking to a friend in a nonprofessional setting, I held my tongue and, instead, asked what the students thought. Everyone agreed the system seemed ideal, but the students sensed that there must be a drawback.

From our vantage point, we could see both climbers and hear them both fairly well. The climber now at the belay was setting an anchor. He keyed his radio and we heard him tell his partner he was off belay. As he pulled the rope up, the belayer continued to sit there, feeding rope through his device, obviously unaware that the leader was off. When the rope tightened, the belayer seemed perplexed; he asked the leader through the radio if he was off but didn't receive a response. The follower sat and waited, occasionally talking into the radio but never receiving a response. By the time both realized the radios had failed, they began yelling furiously in long sentences without much volume or projection. Barely audible even to us, most of their words were lost in the wind.

With so much confusion, when the second climber finally realized he was on belay and began moving up the rock, the upper climber—adjusting his rope to move to a spot where he could lean out and see his partner—had taken him off belay. At that point we intervened, hollering frantically to the second to stay put, that he wasn't on belay anymore. Though my initial response to radio use was confirmed, the lesson allowed my students to make up their own minds. We all agreed that relying on radios prevented the climbers from having to be strong communicators and, when the system failed, they didn't have fully developed skills to fall back on. Radios are a personal choice, but they are fallible. If you use them, keep your communication skills sharp by not relying on the technology all of the time.

LEAD PROTECTION & ROPE MANAGEMENT

Placing protection takes on a whole new meaning on lead. As the leader, you must learn to identify good placements for your pieces and remain stable and focused enough to set, runner, and clip each piece correctly before moving on. To constantly shift between the physicality of climbing and the mental task of placing gear is a tremendous challenge. Practicing this juggling act on simulated leads with the added protection of a top-rope (see Chapter 5) will best prepare you for what's in store.

Runner Usage

Your protection is only useful if it remains stationary after placement. If the rope zigzags from one piece to the next, oblique forces can tweak pieces and sometimes pull them out. Runners and quickdraws help your gear stay in place by keeping the line of the rope running plumb between you and your belayer. It also prevents rope drag that makes it difficult (and sometimes impossible) for you to move easily on lead without feeling an unnecessary amount of tension on the rope.

To determine whether to sling your piece short or long, first consider your potential fall distance. If you use a long runner instead of a quickdraw, you're obviously going to fall that much farther. Unless you're facing a fall onto a ledge, into a dihedral, or to the ground, a few inches won't matter with a bomber piece. Next, consider the degree to which the rope could potentially zigzag, and the piece's innate susceptibility to movement. For extra security, I put shoulder-length runners on all pieces with rigid stems, even when the rope is running plumb between the belayer and myself. It doesn't take much rope movement to dislodge a wired Stopper or encourage a forged Friend to walk. On the other hand, a bendable shaft SLCD with its pre-sewn sling probably doesn't need an added runner on straight-up direct stretches, when the rope runs plumb between partners. Conserve your runners for use on meandering terrain and at the belay, or you'll run out long before the pitch ends.

Avoid girthing slings together as that reduces the material strength by 30 percent (see "Knots & Hitches," pp. 219–220). While insignificant in static loads, this decrease is formidable in dynamic, potentially high force lead falls. Instead, link runners with carabiners.

Multidirectional Protection

When runnering efforts or belayer positioning cannot keep the rope plumb between you and your belayer, set multidirectional protection (see "Multidirectional Placements," p. 94) that will withstand both lateral and downward forces. A common location where such a placement could be critical is the first piece placed preceding a traverse anywhere on a route. In addition, you can avoid the dreaded backward zipper if the first piece placed on any pitch is multidirectional, especially when your belayer is unable to belay directly below you.

Piece Selection

When choosing a piece to place on lead, you should consider two factors: the potential need for that particular piece higher on the pitch and the potential force factor in relation to that piece's holding power. Should a fall occur, the amount of force each lead placement must withstand depends on how the energy generated by the fall is dispersed throughout the system. The rope absorbs energy, as does each individual piece. So, lower on a pitch, when less rope is in use and fewer pieces have been placed, each piece must withstand more force than if you were higher up. How do these factors affect what pieces you place and where? Some pieces have better holding power than others. Reserve your tiny pieces and 3-cam units for placements higher on the route. Back up each piece you identify as marginal early in the pitch with another. Also, place protection often early in the pitch (see next section).

Depending on your gear selection, you may need to conserve pieces of a certain size for use up higher. Eyeballing the route from below and checking the guidebook might give you a clue. If not, avoid completely depleting one size or another early on the pitch. The belay anchor must also be considered. Try to reserve a few different sizes to create a belay, unless you're certain a bolted anchor awaits.

Placement Frequency

As a climber new to gear-leading, place protection frequently, particularly during the first 25 feet of the route to reduce the load of a potential fall. (Loads in relation to fall-severity ratings [fall factors] are detailed in a subsequent section on falling in this chapter.) If, purely from a fall-factor perspective, you established the optimal number of placements, the size of your required rack would anchor you to the ground. However, climber and metallurgist Steve Paterson of Los Gatos, California, has created a formula based on physics equations you can follow to keep potential fall factors reasonably low. His data suggests that placing protection approximately

What To Runner?

Make wise decisions about how and what to runner by always looking ahead. Clues that your protection needs to be runnered with long slings include:

- You're placing a piece in a significantly deep crack or corner (not illustrated)

- You're setting a piece off to the side of the route's main path

- The route travels around a corner, or you reach a traverse

- The route travels under and over a roof or overhang

every 5 inches (1.5 meters) for the first 25 feet (7.5 meters) and then every 10–20 feet (3–6 meters) for the remainder of the pitch significantly minimizes forces, assuming each piece is placed and runnered correctly. This requires approximately one to two dozen pieces per pitch. (This guideline should not prevent you from placing additional pieces to protect cruxes—difficult moves—and potential ground, or ledge, falls.)

Paterson recommends that new trad leaders follow this formula during their first 10,000 feet of gear-leading. "That really only amounts to several single-pitch routes and a handful of long free climbs in Yosemite Valley," says Paterson, AMGA-certified top-rope guide and trad climber for more than 30 years. By the end of your apprenticeship, you will have led around 100 pitches and placed about 1,000 pieces of protection. With this experience, you'll have the foundation to make your own judgments regarding when to place gear and when to run it out. As Paterson says, "During this time, climb routes well within your limits, and occasionally practice placing pro in spots that tax your static climbing and placement skills. Put in your mileage."

Stances

You place gear better when relaxed, so always look ahead for good stances from which to place protection. If possible, identify such locations before heading up, and plan your protection strategy accordingly. If there are few, have the pieces you anticipate needing most ready on the front of your rack. Don't stop in the middle of a crux to place gear unless absolutely necessary. Save your nuts for placement from good stances, and use SLCDs for more difficult sections, since they are generally easier and faster to place. Try to avoid clogging up a perfect finger lock or hand jam, although this may be impossible.

When I was learning, I was taught to place each piece as high as I could from each stance. Although I generally still do this for the first piece off the ground or a ledge, today I place most of my mid-lead pieces somewhere between neck and head high. The energy I save from not having to lift the rope so high is worth the few inches, and my shorter partners curse me less when cleaning.

If you are placing your first piece off the ground or off a ledge, consider bouldering up to place a high piece. Clip it and return to the stance or ground to rest before moving on. Or, if the section is particularly tricky, rest and then climb up past that piece to place another, before down-climbing to the stance again to rest up for harder moves. You've essentially created a top-rope to protect yourself on the first few moves of a difficult section. And having conserved energy, you might be able to climb smoothly and swiftly through the bottom section of the crux, building momentum and saving strength for higher up. This technique gives you the psychological and physical strength to place your next piece from a difficult stance or, possibly, climb through the hardest section without having to stop and place a piece (provided your lower ones can protect you from a dangerous fall).

Double Placements

Place two pieces in the following instances: if the section ahead looks difficult to protect or could be a run-out, if a piece is dicey, or if doing so provides necessary protection from a dangerous fall. Such situations might also warrant the use of a small locking 'biner and/or a load-limiter quickdraw (like a Yates' Screamer). Even when conditions are relatively safe ahead and your gear is solid, placing two pieces prior to a crux might give you the psychological boost to crank through the moves without hesitation.

Blind Placements

Never place gear blindly—you want to see your piece to determine its integrity. If this is not possible, test the piece with several meaningful yanks. Then place a second piece (if you can) and climb through the section with extreme care.

Fixed Gear

Clipping into any fixed gear is a gamble. While pitons offer temptingly quick and convenient protection (and anchor) options, many are so old that their strength is suspect—particularly if the eye of a piton is cracked. Any piton that protrudes more than ⅜ inch from the crack should be tied-off with a short webbing sling using a girth hitch. Back up any such placement whenever possible. Other fixed gear you might find include pieces that have gotten stuck and were left by other climbers. Assess the placement quality for each, as well the condition of the webbing (if it has any), before clipping it. Whenever possible, use your own runner on such pieces. Ultimately, backing them up with additional pieces best assures your safety.

Sometimes when you're leading, a piece you're trying to manipulate into a crack becomes stuck in a useless position. If this occurs and you're experiencing difficulty removing it, let the belayer extract it (if you can afford to forfeit the piece for the remainder of the pitch). The follower, with the security of a top-rope, can expend more energy getting the wedged piece out. Don't be tempted to clip a poorly established piece unless you're certain it's stable; it's not worth it. Instead, focus your energy on placing a different piece.

Protecting Traverses

Though rarely at risk of taking a dangerous fall, the second is in potential jeopardy following a traverse. When leading a traverse, establish placements adequate to protect your follower from a long pendulum fall, should he or she lose footing *(see illustrations, facing page)*. Following a traverse isn't much different from leading it, so leaders should place protection frequently, especially if the second's skill level is less than yours.

My partner once led a fairly easy pitch that involved a long but nontechnical traverse. Guessing it'd be as easy for me as it was for him, he decided to forgo placing much protection to save time—black clouds were forming, threatening rain. When it came my turn to climb, it poured buckets. With slippery rock underfoot, it took all the chutzpah I possessed to cross that unprotected traverse without having a complete meltdown. It remains one of my most frightening climbing memories.

Protect the follower on traverses with frequent placements.

Rope Positioning & Clipping

If you've led sport climbs, you've probably mastered these techniques. If you haven't, bolted sport routes provide the ideal setting to practice them. If properly clipped, your lead rope passes through the carabiner on your piece toward you from the direction of the wall, *(see illustration 1, top left)* leading directly to your tie-in knot. If you are about to traverse to the right, place the gate of the carabiner facing left *(see illustration 2, middle left)* and vice versa if you traverse left *(see illustration 3, bottom left)*. Remember, it's all about which way you're going—not where you came from. An improperly "back-clipped" rope could unclip from the carabiner during a fall.

During my first several years of trad leading I fell upside down a few times. I didn't understand why, and my partners were baffled, too. I eventually discovered that the rope had been positioned behind my leg and had flipped me upside down upon falling. Vigilantly monitoring the rope requires good judgment and helps prevent such mishaps. Pay attention to the rope's position as you continuously change yours relative to it *(see photos in sidebar on facing page)*. With the rope running straight down to your last piece, there's not much risk of getting it caught behind your leg and flipping you over; if the protection is directly below, it's safe to straddle the rope. If the rope angles even slightly to your last piece, keep the rope running between you and the rock; don't let it go between your legs and cross behind one of them.

Directionals

Trad routes occasionally travel over sharp or loose terrain and follow crack systems with an appetite for rope. Whenever possible, scout for locations where you can place a directional piece to divert your lead line away from loose debris *(see illustrations 1 and 2, p. 146)*, sharp edges, and rope-masticating cracks. Deep roof cracks are particularly notorious for eating lead lines, but this problem can usually be avoided by placing a piece at the lip.

Rope Positioning

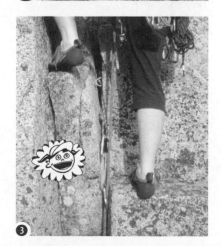

If your lead rope angles even slightly to your last placement, keep it running between you and the rock (1a and b) and not between your legs (2a and b). If the next move is directly above you, and the rope runs plumb between you and your last piece, it's safe to straddle the rope (3).

① Problem: Rope runs across loose terrain.

② Solution: Use directional placements to guide rope away from debris.

MOVEMENT

As you move up the rock on trad lead, your every movement must orchestrate several factors for an ultimately safe and enjoyable ascent. You'll need to find a climbing rhythm that best balances your need for protection with your need for smooth and continuous upward progress. You must pay close attention to the holds you grab and step onto because rock features are sometimes detached and can break. You'll make critical choices regarding when you are not prepared to fully commit to a series of moves and when retreating is a better idea than pushing onward. You'll also need to be energy-conscious and learn specific methods on how to rest throughout the pitch so you can successfully tackle cruxes and strenuous pro placement stances high up on the route, and still top-out with energy to spare.

Testing Holds

Trad rock can be loose and unstable. Before committing your entire weight to a suspect hold, test it first. Thump it with your palm and then ease onto it. This is a good practice particularly at climbing areas that are new to you. If you break off a hold because you didn't test it first, you'll probably fall. Worse, though, you've placed your belayer and other climbers below you at risk of being injured by the rockfall. Features that are frequently suspect include flakes, knobs, and chockstones.

Rhythm & Flow

Beginner leaders have a tendency to sew it up—that is, place a lot of lead protection. While that's good to a certain extent because of the harsh learning curve, excessive gear placement can interfere with the natural flow of climbing movement. When I was still sewing it up after 10 years of leading, a valued mentor suggested I make a few more moves between pieces, generating necessary momentum to launch my body more smoothly from hold to hold. I soon discovered the value of this advice and soon became able to lead harder and more technical routes on which overprotecting would have hindered me considerably. Your goal is to place gear thoughtfully and carefully while trying not to overprotect.

Climber: Mark Wilford

Years Trad Free Climbing: 33

Favorite Trad Climbing Area:
        Don't have one—I get
        most excited visiting
        an area I've never been
        before.

Most Respected Trad Free
        Climbers: John Bacher
        and Reinhold Messner

Photo by Barry Blanchard, Mark Wilford Collection

A Skill to Reduce Your Risk of Falling

When leading on trad climbs, make every attempt not to fall—make it your ethic and style. Learn when and how to rest on a pitch. Find stances where you can shake out and body positions that are conducive to resting (e.g., straight-arm hangs on crack sections). If you get out on a pitch and start getting tired, down-climb to the last stance and rest. If you do get to a point where you feel you're going to fall, still do your best to down-climb as far as you possibly can. Even if you can't reach the last good resting stance, you may be able to reduce the length of your fall. Don't grab the rope if you do fall—you'll only get burned. Down-climbing can be practiced on boulders close to the ground. This is an essential skill for trad leaders often overlooked by the novice in favor of techniques resulting directly in upward progress. Don't be fooled; if you fall and injure yourself, you're not going anywhere but down.

As a young climber I practiced down-climbing to get out of harm's way both on high boulder problems and on scary testpieces in Eldorado Canyon. Later I was able to apply these skills to alpine climbs. One instance that comes to mind is an experience on Mt. Alberta in the Canadian Rockies. This mountain forced me to down-climb hundreds of feet on my first failed attempt. Being able to safely retreat off a 4000-foot climb gave me the confidence to try again, and succeed on my second attempt.

—Mark Wilford

Energy Conservation

Energy conservation is an integral part of the climbing experience. Your success in this area relies on your ability to identify and maximize each rest opportunity. It's also contingent on how well you can "invent" a rest with some creative body positioning if a good stance isn't available. Royal Robbins expresses this ideal perfectly, "Often resting is an art requiring ingenuity and experience, and on many difficult routes discovering ways to rest is as much a part of the problem as the actual climbing."

Straight-arm hanging

When no obvious rest stances are available, you can often conserve energy by using one of the following positions: A straight-arm hang *(see photo, top right)* off a jam or handhold allows you to rest by shifting weight from your muscles to your skeletal system, and stemming *(see photo, middle right)* lets your legs share the weight burden with your lower body. On flaring cracks, try to relieve an overworked upper body by back-stepping (like you would in a chimney) *(see photo, bottom right)*. On overhanging terrain, try turning your hip perpendicular to the rock to better allow your feet to support your weight. The more climbing you do, the more intuitive your resting positions will become.

Down-Climbing

The value of honed down-climbing skills isn't obvious until you're up there on the sharp end. For instance, you've botched a sequence of moves and are too gassed to plug in a piece. Remembering that you're not on a sport route, you consider "letting go" an unfavorable option—especially having just placed a marginal microcam, with a ledge looming close below. After taking a deep breath, carefully reverse your moves one by one. When you've safely reached the ledge, you can rest while rethinking your moves and getting a piece ready to fire in on your second try. Save "letting go" as a tactic for sport climbing. At that point of despair where you know you're facing a fall, try to reverse your moves to the last stable stance before giving up. Although we protect ourselves as best we can on lead, falling is always risky.

Stemming

Back-stepping

Hanging

If you can't go on without a rest and decide to hang (take tension) on a piece, be certain that it's solid enough to hold your body weight. If it's the only piece between you and the ground or a ledge, quickly plug in another for backup. Although it's not a good habit to get into and some trad climbers even consider hanging "bad style," sometimes it's a safer choice than falling. Don't head up on lead with the mind-set that you can always hang on a piece when you tire; that option won't always exist. When protection is sparse or the climb is runout, a cavalier attitude won't serve you. Depend, instead, on your good down-climbing skills.

Backing Off

To retreat from, or back off, a single-pitch route, you can have your belayer lower you—only if the route is fairly direct, you haven't used more than half your rope, and you're at a solid piece of protection from which to be lowered. Unless your partner wants to finish the pitch, keep in mind that you must leave this piece, cleaning the others as you descend. Leaving a second piece is wise, so you're not trusting your life to just one. If you are more than halfway up the pitch or the route traverses in such a way that being lowered isn't an option, retreat becomes more complex. With adequate protection options, you might consider aiding your way to the top, or at least through the crux. To accomplish this, however, you may need more hardware and slings than you have. If you think you can make it, girth hitch several slings together to use as makeshift *étriers* and off you go. To best cope with this type of situation, become familiar with basic aid-climbing techniques before pushing your limits on trad free climbs. And on a difficult route, always consider how committed you are to the summit once you've used half the rope.

When retreat is necessary, climbers leading with double ropes (see Chapter 9) have less to worry about than those leading on a single line. No matter how long the pitch is, you can usually retreat with relative ease (unless the route traverses significantly) because you can tie the two ropes together to rappel.

FALLING

Several schools exist regarding falling on trad lead. When I learned in the early '80s in Yosemite, the motto was simply, "Don't fall." Because equipment technology was not as advanced then as it is today and many routes involved runouts, risks were greater then, so most climbers felt compelled by the "no fall" maxim. In addition, at that point in time—falling in Yosemite Valley was considered bad style by the majority of the locals. There was pressure to keep both your capabilities and limitations in check. Many trad free climbers still climb by the "no fall" adage (and may stay alive longer because of it).

The newer school of "If you're not falling, you're not progressing" was probably born out of the sport-climbing revolution that pushed free climbing standards. Climbers today who get their start in the gym or at sport crags learn that falling involves few risks and is an integral component of progressing. When these climbers cross over to trad climbing, this ideal, however tempered, remains a formative one in their consciousnesses.

My current philosophy lies somewhere between the two, with a tendency toward the "don't fall" school that probably reflects my climbing roots. Yet it also stems from a personal experience of a trad lead fall years ago in which I overreached my capabilities. My piece was good, as was my belayer, and I only fell a few feet. Still, my tailbone was dislocated skittering across a small bulge and today I live with arthritis in my coccyx. I am cautious about pushing my limits and recognize that a leader fall of any length can be dangerous.

Hazards

Falls happen regardless of your philosophy. As a new leader, it is your responsibility to understand the risks, learn to identify potential hazards, and do what you can to minimize them.

Place protection in key locations to avoid striking obstacles, even when climbing is easy. Never underestimate your potential to slip, break a hold, or lose your balance at any time on any climb. Look out for potential falls onto low-angle slabs and into dihedrals, and use

Highest fall factor—there are no placements between belayer and leader on a multipitch route.

caution when climbing directly above ledges and the ground.

As previously described, erroneous rope positioning increases your risk of being flipped upside-down during a lead fall. Maintain awareness of proper rope positioning to prevent such falls, and wear a helmet to reduce the risk of serious head injury should one occur.

If you know you're about to peel, quickly ascertain that the rope isn't wrapped around your leg and that your last piece (if you can see it) is stable and appropriately clipped. Warn your belayer, face the wall, and, catlike, cushion your fall with flexed legs. In some situations it may be advantageous to push yourself out and away from the rock, hopefully reducing the risk of catching an appendage on an obstacle during your flight.

Most instances of equipment failure on lead are due to user error. An improperly placed or poorly runnered piece of protection rips out, a rope running across a razor-sharp edge severs, the rope unclips from a quickdraw carabiner—all are preventable scenarios. Make the most of your equipment by understanding its limitations, cultivating keen protection placement skills, and paying attention on lead. In addition, study the fall force potentials explained in the following paragraphs and place pieces with the most holding power in high force scenarios.

The Physics of Falling

Your equipment is subject to differing degrees of force depending on the circumstances of each fall. Many variables exist, including the fall distance, the rope length in use, the lead climber's weight, and the amount of time during which energy generates and dissipates. Use this information to make safe choices on lead to help minimize forces whenever possible. Continue reading for a simplified discussion of how some of these forces are gauged.

Fall Factor

Because analyzing loads and forces in relation to falling is a complex process with many variables, a method was devised to calculate the relative severity of falls instead. This method determines fall factors, taking into account the fall distance and the length of the rope that absorbs its force. To calculate it, divide the length of a fall by the amount of rope out. The highest forces are gener-

ated most often on multipitch routes when a fall without protection between belayer and leader occurs; this worst-case scenario results in the maximum fall factor of 2 *(see illustration, facing page)*. Here's how the fall factor is calculated in this situation: If you fell shortly after leaving the belay with 10 feet of rope and no protection between you and the anchor, the fall would be 20 feet in length. Divide 20 by 10 and you get the fall factor, in this case 2. By placing gear as early as possible after leaving a multipitch belay, this can be avoided—the more protection you've placed and more rope that is out, the lower the potential fall factor. Ideally, you want to keep potential fall factors at 0.5 *(see illustration, right)*. Let's imagine the same scenario except that you managed to place one piece five feet from the belay, and fell five feet above it (still 10 feet from the belay). The result now though, is a 10-foot fall. So divide 10 by 10, the amount of rope in use (the distance you were away from your belayer) and the fall factor is 1. Still not ideal, but less force is generated than in a factor 2 fall. To achieve the desired fall factor of 0.5, you'd need to have placed two pieces within the first 10 feet. Although terrain and gear availability might dictate otherwise, make this your goal. If you predict that this is impossible, be sure the leader on a multipitch route clips the anchor as his or her first "piece" so that it will shoulder the burden of such an extreme force should a fall occur (see "The Changeover," pp. 176–179). A factor 2 fall directly onto the waist of a belayer can do some real damage. Review the formula on pp. 137 and 140 and do

Minimize the fall factor by placing protection early and often.

what you can to minimize fall factor potentials based on
this ideal. If you play with this equation and do some
more calculations, you'll discover that just because a fall
is long, the forces generated might not be anywhere near
the danger zone. Here's an example: You take a 50-foot
fall when 100 feet of rope is between you and the belayer;
50 divided by 100 is 0.5. Not bad, but the impact impulse
is greater (see "Impact Impulse," p. 155) and you still
have to deal with the possible carnage of scrapes and
abrasions that could easily occur during such a long fall,
especially if the terrain below is anything but vertical!

Impact Force

A lead climber's weight and acceleration in any given
fall determine the actual force exerted, and are together
termed the impact force. In theory and in research and
development tests in which the average laboratory lead
climber weighs 176 pounds, all falls of the same fall factor generate the same impact force. Impact forces in the
real world, however, vary according to the climber's
weight, the amount of friction in the system or between
the climber and the rock (terrain angle), the age of the
rope, and the rope elongation rating. Impact force is
buffered by the tightening of knots and lifting of unanchored belayers. Though impact force can affect other
aspects of the roped climbing system, most importantly
it affects your rope and protection.

Your rope's ability to stretch and absorb energy
allows it to greatly reduce impact forces. Prior to the
invention of the dynamic rope, pioneers of the sport
climbed on static lines without this important feature.
Modern climbing rope specifications allow a maximum
impact force of 12 kilonewtons (kN), or 2700 pounds,
with a fall factor of 1.78. A seven-fall rating indicates the
rope can withstand seven UIAA-rated falls[8] at this fall
factor before breaking. All ropes are tested to breaking,
so we know that they do. If your rope undergoes one
severe fall (with a fall factor approaching 2) or a few falls
with fall factors above 1, it may be time to retire it. After
any significant fall, let your rope recover 5–10 minutes
from its stretching and heating. If it can be done safely,
untie from the rope and retie into it, to restore your

knot's ability to absorb energy. (For more information on rope care and retirement, see Chapter 3.)

In relation to protection, impact force matters most when your pro is marginal and reducing the potential fall force could prevent your piece from failing. Although you have little control over impact force, you can attach a load-limiter to a dicey piece and request a dynamic belay (where the belayer deliberately allows slippage of some rope through the belay device—not recommended without the initial tutelage of an expert), or lead on a newer rope. As discussed previously, forgoing a base belay also reduces potential impact force by allowing the movement of the belayer to absorb some of the energy generated during a fall. Each of these options does, however, result in slightly longer falls. If you are facing a potentially injurious fall, use caution. Although using one of these tactics may prove a worthy trade-off, carefully analyze the situation first. Some lead climbers carry load-limiters exclusively for clipping manky bolts they might be forced to use. This is a great idea considering how many ancient bolts you're likely to come across if you climb in many different areas.

Impact Impulse

The length of time during which energy is generated and dissipated on the system—rope, belayer, climber, and the protection in place— is known as the impact impulse. The longer the fall, the greater it is. Though the impact force of a 10-foot fall with 10 feet of rope out (fall factor equals 1) generates the same peak impact force as a 100-foot fall with 100 feet of rope out, the impact forces last much longer with the 100-foot whipper, placing greater demands on climber, belayer, and protection. By placing gear frequently—even on easy ground, you can reduce the impact impulse in the event of a fall.

ESTABLISHING A BELAY ANCHOR

Once you're close to topping-out, you have many factors to consider regarding the anchor you must create. Questions you might ask yourself in anticipation of creating a belay anchor include: "How much rope do I

have left? Are there fixed anchors I should be looking
for? Are they safe and secure? How should I clip into
them? If I have to build one, where is the most suitable
location for a safe and secure anchor using the gear I
have remaining on my rack?

Location

On traditional routes, it's not always obvious at
the top of the pitch where to set up your belay anchor.
Sometimes the location is indicated on the topo, or on-
site by the presence of predrilled bolts, slings, and/or
other types of fixed protection. If it isn't obvious, find
out from your belayer how much rope is remaining so
you don't climb too high. There's nothing worse than
thinking the belay ledge is just 10 feet up and then
feeling an annoying tug on your waist and hearing
your partner yell, "That's it! There's no more rope!"
On long pitches, before leaving the ground, I request
my partner let me know when I'm down to 25 feet
(8–9 meters). If you're low on rope and have no idea
where the designated belay is, look for a location that
offers the best possible protection. While a fairly big
stance makes everyone more comfortable, what really
matters is your ability to set up a SERENE anchor (see
"The Pre-Equalized Anchor System," pp. 94–96 for
more details) with the pieces remaining on your rack.
If there's no nearby location where you can do that,
carefully down-climb to a place where you can. In this
case, you may have to do another short pitch to reach
the actual summit, but it will be worth it to have a
solid anchor.

Fixed Belay Anchors

Although it's tempting to hastily clip into a fixed
anchor (see "Fixed Anchors," pp. 105–106) after com-
pleting a demanding lead, first examine it carefully
and make sure it's as close to SERENE as possible. Set
up your own anchor if you don't like what you see.
If the fixed anchor doubles as a rappel station, avoid
clipping into the chains or the nest of nylon webbing

linking the bolts together. Rather, clip your carabiners directly into each bolt. If necessary, cut away old slings to make room for your 'biners; be sure to keep the blade far away from your climbing rope—especially if the rope is tensioned.

As you break into traditional leading, the basic principles and guidelines presented in this chapter will help you safely master the difficult learning curve. Although I've presented a lot of protocol, remember that when the going gets tough, what saves your butt is always going to be the result of your cumulative experience outside on the rock, and rarely memorized protocols from a book. I cannot emphasize the importance of hands-on experience for new trad leaders. With more overall experience, you'll realize the challenge is lifelong. With a few years of consistent practice—as your mind-body learns this unique language, trad leading can become second nature. But leave the crags for a season, and you'll experience a rapid decline in both mental and physical fluency that you can revive only with a return to basics.

As your comfort level increases on single-pitch trad leads, you'll probably experience a yearning for multi-pitch lead climbing. The next chapter discusses how to build on your single-pitch leading skills so that you can cope effectively with the challenges of long routes.

Bill McChesney

Chapter 7

The Multipitch Adventure

Reaching from a distant horizon, welcome beams of sunlight soften the bite of dawn's chill and beckon your muscles into action. Through misting breath, you peer up toward the steeple of white granite towering above. Your partner's groggy "On belay" initiates your ascent like a contractual agreement. Stepping onto the wall you make the first of thousands of moves that, with the grace of the mountain, will offer a moment of summit glory later in the day.

Several pitches up, high off the ground, the real adventure in trad free climbing begins. With your necessary lasting endurance and commitment, steep exposures, hanging belays, weather, and altitude create the thrill of the multipitch exploit. This chapter explores leading and belaying on long trad routes, as well as the tasks of preparation, the approach, objective hazards, anchors, organization, and the descent.

PREPARATION

Before a climber embarks on a long free route as a full-fledged leading partner, some groundwork is necessary. Many of the tasks are similar to basic prep for the single-pitch trad climb: route choice, partners, and gear.

But because of the complexity of multipitch routes, these issues require more forethought and energy.

Route Choice

Since retreat is complex on long climbs, the routes you choose must honestly reflect your team's collective lead-ability level—not just in terms of ratings but also of terrain. For instance, off-width cracks, even if moderately rated, are notorious enigmas for new leaders (see "Rating Translation & Style," pp. 235–236). A 5-inch-wide (12.5-centimeter) crack rated at 5.8 could be significantly more difficult than a hand crack of the same rating, if a climber's prior experience on wide terrain has been minimal. And it may be difficult to protect without a glut of large gear, which most new leaders do not have. Runouts also challenge new leaders—it often takes years to develop the mental capability to cope with them effectively. Many long routes involve off-width or chimney sections and even the most popular ones have short terrain sections that are difficult to protect. Before you commit to such a route, be absolutely certain one member of your team is up to the challenge.

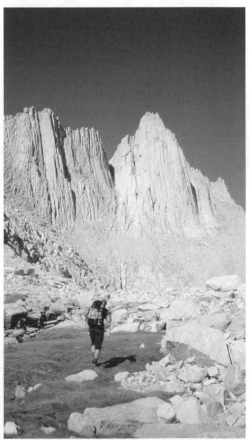

Also determine whether the number of available daylight hours is adequate to complete the proposed route. Schedule extremely long routes—particularly those involving long approaches or descents and higher difficulty levels—within a month or two of the summer solstice, and a few days prior to the full moon if you might end up walking out in the dark.

Although some long routes are located in popular climbing areas, where a shout for help might be heard easily by tourists or other climbers who can notify rescue personnel, many are not. These secluded backcountry settings, miles or even days from civilization, require that

Dave Nettle Collection

Typical Sierra Nevada backcountry approach

your team prepare for self-sufficiency and understand the ramifications of a mishap. You should be able to provide detailed answers to these questions:

- Am I prepared to take full responsibility for myself and my partner?

- Do I have a sound understanding of self-rescue techniques?

- Do I have the proper equipment and apparel?

- Am I trained in first aid?

- How will I initiate an evacuation if necessary?

Because backcountry climbers also commonly encounter loose rock, wear a helmet and move cautiously to prevent dislodging rocks. After climbing only popular easily-accessed routes, you'll find the backcountry is another world in terms of quality standards. Yet, what you give up in rock stability is a fair trade for the solitude and natural beauty you experience in wilderness climbing.

With a proposed route high in the mountains, consider the environmental implications and adjust your goals accordingly. An increase in altitude affects your endurance and strength because your body labors to compensate for lower concentrations of oxygen. Most people tire more easily at high altitudes. Since I regularly climb at 7400 feet (2312 meters), when I read a topo indicating a 5.8 pitch above 12,000 feet (3750 meters) I know it's going to feel more like 5.9. If you're a lowlander who regularly climbs at sea level, the difference will feel much greater. Altitude illnesses, which generally don't occur below 8000 feet (2500 meters), are discussed later in this chapter.

Partner Choice

Be selective when choosing partners for multipitch climbs. Partnerships must be cohesive—particularly where limited daylight or changeable weather requires a breakneck pace without sacrificing safety. In these situations, mastery in rope- and gear-handling skills is crucial, so look for someone experienced. If your partner isn't, choose a shorter and easier route. Choose a partner with whom you have done single pitches, have a good rapport, and whose abilities you know well and trust completely.

Don't be afraid of backing out of a multipitch climb at the last minute, if your intuition prompts you. I once drove four hours toward the trailhead of a Sierra Nevada backcountry route with a potential partner only to turn the car around and drive right back because a voice told me this person wasn't going to cut it. Our conversations during the drive had led me to conclude that I couldn't trust this fellow with my life. He was angry and I felt guilty, but I made the right choice.

Weather

Learned trad climbers study regional weather patterns and consult long-range forecasts prior to embarking upon any long route, especially if the adventure involves significant logistics and a time commitment. Climbers who don't might end up wasting precious free time and often put themselves in the position of making a difficult decision to retreat after a lot of time and effort has gone into the planning of an adventure. As a new leader, if the forecast is iffy, your best bet is to reschedule before you leave home. If I'm planning to climb in an unfamiliar area, I check the Internet for a local weather forecast and may even follow up with a call to a climbing shop in the nearest community. Locals can tell you about specific recent patterns (such as a progressive increase in thunderheads) or typical weather cycles (for instance, afternoon thundershowers are all but a given in the Rockies in June and July). Exercise caution when reports indicate a drop in barometric pressure. Learn to read the wind and sky to recognize when bad weather is approaching, so you can initiate a descent before it rains or snows. In the northern hemisphere, a shift in wind direction to the east or southeast may indicate an approaching low-pressure system. High-altitude cirrus clouds, typically identified by feathery narrow bands or thin wispy patches, are also common indicators of potential precipitation *(see photo, right)*. Be wary

High-altitude cirrus clouds indicate potential precipitation.

of cirrus clouds that form a tight halo around the moon or sun, or begin to lower and thicken.

Understanding thunderstorm cycles is also helpful—particularly in mountain and desert environments. Such cycles can last several days and are generally accompanied by a high-pressure system in surrounding areas. Although thunderstorms can occur without warning, they're generally preceded by a gradual buildup of cumulus clouds *(see photo, below)* a few days before. These billowy and bold clouds usually appear in the afternoon, but they occur earlier and earlier each day until a full-blown storm cuts loose.

In any mountain environment, be prepared for thunderstorms by always packing lightweight rain gear. For extra insurance, bring another rope (or climb with double ropes) in case retreat becomes inevitable. Some climbers carry an 8-millimeter rope religiously on long routes for this purpose. Because a rope this small tends to be unmanageable at its full length—because it is stiff and wirey, carry it in a pack. Another weather-beating tip is to get an early alpine start, giving you several hours to climb before most thunderstorms develop. One partner of mine insists on being off mountain routes by noon, no matter what the forecast. This is a smart philosophy, particularly for beginners.

Hot temperatures are as likely as rain or snow to put a glitch in your progress on long routes, particularly in temperatures above 90°F (32.2°C). With high humidity, the problem is worse. Not uncommon for long-route climbers in warmer climes, heat exhaustion quickly turns a capable partner into a tired, dizzy, vomiting mess. Although this condition is not particularly dangerous, if left untreated it can lead to deadly heat stroke. If your chosen route is in an area experiencing a hot spell, consider rescheduling your climb. If you decide to climb, don't forget sunscreen—particularly on highly reflective rock like limestone and granite—and copious amounts of water.

Cumulus clouds

The Pack

Although carrying a pack can be either helpful or a hindrance, the more water and clothing you need, the more you'll appreciate it. Only one pack is taken on multipitch climbs, and it is expected to be worn by whoever is following. It's traded off at belays whenever climbers switch roles. On routes shorter than 5 or 6 pitches, I often forgo a pack. I hang a water bottle and shoes on my harness loops and tie a lightweight rain jacket around my waist. Some outerwear manufacturers make lightweight jackets from waterproof but breathable fabrics that fold into themselves for tidy little packages you can clip to a harness loop. And if I can manage it, I also bring my light all-terrain sandals soled with sticky rubber for short, non-technical descents.

For climbs that take a full day, a pack is almost always a necessity. Choose one with minimal waist padding so it can ride above your waist belt and stay out of the way of your gear loops and chalk bag. Be aware, though, that a pack without waist padding can be uncomfortable on a long approach, when water bottles are full and the trail is generally uphill. A pack capacity of 1500–2000 cubic inches is adequate for most daylong routes although some climbers make due with smaller packs. Avoid a frame pack although a minimal internal stay might be okay. Choose one made of an abrasion-resistant fabric—particularly on the bottom—with sturdy stitching. Forget external mesh pouches, ski loops, and ice ax and crampon holders (although loops for a single tool are handy for approaches and descents in alpine settings). Since you may have to hand-haul the pack when negotiating a chimney, the fewer external features it has the less likely it is to get stuck. Some packs with gear loops on waist belts, which are mainly designed for ski mountaineering or moderate alpine climbing, can sometimes work well on long free-rock routes but might pose problems should hauling be necessary. Nonzippered top-loading packs are my personal choice; I particularly like them because if necessary I can sandwich in more gear between the top flap and the main compartment. Other climbers prefer zippered-loading packs because their lack of buckles makes them less likely to snag if hauled.

Be sure your pack has a sturdy haul loop for clipping off at belays and hauling.

Food & Water

Dehydration produces alarming dysfunction in an otherwise capable climber. Scientific studies indicate that as little as 5 percent dehydration can cause up to 30 percent reduction in athletic performance. Although you're rarely able to achieve optimal hydration on long routes, strive to meet healthy standards. Before a long route, drink a large volume of water. After your initial drink, the International Sportsmedicine Institute recommends ½–⅔ ounce of water per pound of body weight per day (around 3–4 quarts daily for the average-sized person). Though my rations rarely match these ideals— even when climbing in the frontcountry—I do my best. On hot, humid days I carry more. For mountain routes with long walk-offs, I carry iodine tablets to treat lake or stream water I'll likely stumble upon on the descent so I can drink all the water I bring up during the climb.

On my harness, I also carry a small half-liter water bottle when leading, which I refill from larger bottles and rig with a keeper loop from webbing secured with duct tape. I'm usually most parched after finishing a lead, and it's nice to take a drink before I begin to belay. Since the second almost always carries the pack (which contains heavy items like water) on long routes, I'd otherwise have to wait for him or her to clean the pitch and reach the belay before getting any water. Be considerate of your partner by not guzzling more than your share; it's hard to be forgiving, particularly on scorching days. Water rationing is essential on long days. Since hydration packs like CamelBaks make it difficult to monitor water consumption, I don't recommend using them.

Adding sports drink mixes to some of your water aids in electrolyte replacement on long climbs. Electrolytes help your body metabolize carbohydrates and boost muscle function, reducing muscle cramps and enhancing muscle cell contraction. Most important, sodium is lost via sweating during exercise, but electrolytes relieve dehydration by replacing it. For the most beneficial absorption rate, create these cocktails with no more than 8 percent drink mix. If you have a sensitive stomach, avoid straight glucose and sucrose mixes like Gatorade, and look for a brand such as Cytomax and Gookinaid in which the glucose comes from glucose polymers (malto-dextrins).

Calories provide the energy necessary for maximum performance. Eating a good breakfast is absolutely key for lasting endurance. Likewise, a hearty meal after your climb will aid in recovery. On the route, bring snacks that are high in complex carbohydrates with moderate amounts of fat and protein. Avoid foods extremely high in protein or fat that compromise performance by rerouting blood from the muscles to the digestive tract. This is why you may feel sluggish after gobbling a handful of nuts and a few slices of cheese and salami at the belay. Sugar alone is great for a quick burst of energy but won't sustain you for long, and neither will simple carbohydrates. Whole-wheat bagels, hummus, and whole-wheat fig bars are good choices.

As an alternative or supplement, bring along several energy gel packets and a few complex carbohydrate energy bars to consume en route. I prefer Clif Shots and Clif Bars. Clif Shots have added electrolytes and are easy to consume even if you're not feeling hungry. Some have a small amount of caffeine as well, proven by researchers to boost athletic performance. Clif Bars are a tasty form of complex carbohydrates that neither harden nor melt with varying temperatures. Wash them down with a few ounces of water to encourage digestion.

No matter what food choices you make, don't starve yourself on any long route or you'll reap fatigue as your reward. Says Marc Twight in *Extreme Alpinism*,

> . . . descending into calorie debt is counterproductive, no matter what the justification. Failing to maintain calorie intake may translate in the backcountry into hitting the wall. . . . Make sure your partner eats, too, because there's nothing worse than having one guy strong, and the other weak."[9]

Gear

Partners should review and be in agreement on equipment beforehand. On multipitch routes, only one rack is necessary. Take either partner's rack or a selection of pieces chosen from both. If your partner has a rack of Hexes and you're most familiar with SLCDs and your partner brings his or her rack for you to share, you'll be sorry when you discover this after hiking a distance to the base.

What if your partner is a more experienced leader, extremely familiar with the route, and comfortable with a rack composed of half the gear you usually bring on lead? A friend of mine had this very experience not long ago when a strong, longtime Yosemite Valley local invited him to climb the renowned Astroman with him one morning. After they hiked to the base, the local, who had lapped this Valley testpiece many times, pulled out the "rack"—a few nuts and a half-dozen cams. He set off on the familiar route, climbing swiftly and confidently, placing only a few pieces. When my friend attempted the notoriously long and difficult "Endurance Corner" with the scrawny rack, his confidence was shaken. Even though he had climbed the route once before, he realized the gear he had this time wasn't sufficient for him to lead with comfort. When the two reluctantly retreated, my friend cursed himself for not checking out his partner's gear, and the local felt awful. He wasn't trying to sandbag my friend but just had a skewed perception—because of his skill level and route familiarity—of what an adequate rack should be for that particular climb.

Information you glean from the topo, guidebook, and other resources help you determine what gear you'll need for lead protection. If the topo is vague, come prepared with two of each standard-sized piece up to 4–5 inches (10–12.5 centimeters) and a few extras to outfit belays (unless they're bolted). If your resources indicate that a long section requires one particular size, you might need to borrow gear from friends (common on desert routes where long, uniform, parallel cracks are the norm). If a wide section high on the route requires large pieces of protection, don't skimp because of their bulk; carry them in the pack until you need them.

Long trad routes, often linking several "weaknesses" on a rock face, tend to wander. For this reason, come prepared with several 22- to 24-inch (55- to 60-centimeter) runners. The number you carry will vary depending on the route's composition, as well as on individual pitch lengths. When you're learning, it's better to bring too many, since webbing weighs so little. I carry between 6 and 8 "shoulder-length" runners on the average multipitch route, and a few more if most of the pitches are rope stretchers—150 feet (50 meters) and up. If the route appears fairly direct, I carry them tripled as quickdraws (see "Recommended Runner Specs," pp. 51–52). If the route meanders significantly, I carry at least half of them extended to their full length over my shoulder opposite the rack. You should also bring along at least one 44-inch (110-centimeter) sling to protect traverses, runner natural protection, or tie in faraway anchor components to your other pieces. Two of these are optimal on wandering routes but, on blocky mountain routes, bring three or four.

Because many carabiners are required for belay anchors in the multipitch scenario, they aren't available for use on lead. So, rack accordingly by bringing along more than you would for a single-pitch climb.

You need a second rope (or "trail line") on a multipitch route if the descent involves rappels longer than half the length of your lead rope. Yet, regardless of the descent, bringing an extra rope on long climbs provides backup insurance if you run into trouble. If your primary lead rope becomes damaged, your trail line can be used for leading, provided it is of sufficient diameter (see "Ropes," p. 42). If you retreat by rappelling the line of ascent with two ropes, it will take half the time and require less gear loss for anchors. Two ropes or one—it's a personal decision that should be dictated by your experience and relative commitment to the route. Many teams forgo a second rope (unless necessary for the standard descent) in deference to speed and experience. But if you're new to the game, bring a second rope on all multipitch routes to increase your odds for a safe adventure.

Consider carrying unruly ropes narrower than 8 millimeters uncoiled inside the bottom of the pack until you need them. Although this increases the follower's burden, it helps keep rope-management problems to a minimum.

If you find yourself drawn to long, moderate backcountry routes, consider building a specialized rack with lightweight gear: asymmetrical featherweight carabiners, Friends (instead of Camalots) or, even lighter, Hexes and Tri-Cams (instead of SLCDs). Be sure your partner is agreeable to such equipment, and that both of you know how to use it properly. (Many climbers today are unfamiliar with placing Hexes and Tri-Cams.) Particularly at higher altitudes, you'll be grateful for the weight savings.

Cooperative Racking System

Before getting started, work out an agreeable racking scheme with your partner. If you are alternating (swinging) leads, an ideal arrangement is for both climbers to carry separate gear slings. As the second cleans each pitch, he or she can rerack equipment to his or her own specifications, in preparation for taking on the next lead. When you both reach the belay anchor, there's minimal gear swapping (unless the pitch was short or little protection was placed). If racking arrangements differ between partners, little time is lost reorganizing gear.

If you're the sole leader, you and your climbing partner will need to switch gear slings at the belay. In this case, make sure the follower is familiar with your racking preferences and can tolerate the same-sized gear sling if it's not easily adjusted.

Another option is to share one gear sling between two partners. If you choose this method, adapt to subtle differences in your partner's racking habits and strive for a uniform approach to carrying gear. If you're flexible in your willingness to tolerate a slightly different racking arrangement that your partner might prefer, sharing a gear sling will pose fewer problems and require less time at the belay. A final note to those who prefer racking only on harness loops: You're going to spend a lot of time swapping and rearranging gear at belays.

The Approach

Getting to the base of your route could be as simple as stumbling out of your tent or car and walking five minutes on a flat, manicured trail. In other cases, the approach might require miles of cross-country travel across talus and scree terrain, over snowfields, or up technically ambiguous Class 3 and 4 ledge systems.

Miles of seemingly flat, off-trail hiking in desert settings might require keen navigational skills to avoid steep gullies and ravines, often hidden by the one-dimensional mirage of desert from distant views. For long approaches that don't follow maintained hiking trails, obtain a good area topo map and bring a compass in case you lose your way.

For adequate time to complete the route and descend as soon as possible, hit the trail early. Though I hate getting up early, the words of a longtime mentor caution me against snoozing through the pre-dawn hours: "You should find yourself on the approach in the dark, not the descent." Always bring extra batteries and a bulb for your headlamp and, when you've finished using it, temporarily disconnect the battery so it won't turn on inside the pack.

If the approach takes hours longer than you planned, you may reach the base wondering whether to continue with your ascent or retreat and do the route another day. Use your best judgment: Realistically assess the weather and the daylight hours and think about the "what ifs," allowing time to get off-route or briefly lost on the descent. Try to sort out the tangled strands of ambition that tell you the summit must be attained at any cost.

MOVING UP

As your multipitch adventure unfolds, your team must accurately navigate its way up the wall, a process that begins long before you touch the rock. Another issue the team must consider is whether or not to bring a second rope, how it will be brought up, and who will be responsible for carrying it.

Route Finding

Finding your way on long trad climbs is a bit like the process a detective uses to piece together many clues to solve a great mystery. Depending on their traffic and terrain, some routes may pose greater puzzles. Climbs on remote or obscure crags present some navigational challenges that popular routes with mellow approaches do not. Unfortunately, misinformation is so common that

Climber: Scott Cosgrove

Years Trad Free Climbing: 28

**Favorite Trad Climbing Area:
    Yosemite**

**Most Respected Trad
    Free Climber: Silvo Karo**

Skillful Route Finding

Route finding is an art, especially on multipitch routes. Approach the task as if you were the first ascent team. They didn't have a topo. They had to look for the most natural line up the rock.

Think simply. Watch a dog run up a rocky hillside. It will intuitively find the most obvious natural weakness and follow that path. As a trad leader, you'll do just that. Look for the largest series of holds in sight, and the path most worn. Watch out for "sucker" holds (a series of holds that lead nowhere) known as traps. These are easy to identify on more popular climbs. Often you'll see slings at the ends of traps where others lured there have eventually bailed.

Scope out the climb from the ground before navigating long routes. The pros use telescopes and binoculars to closely scan their climbing routes, but a keen trained eye will suffice for most. Look closely at routes you've already climbed and learn to identify the correct line of ascent from below. First learn to identify the largest, most obvious features—huge dihedrals, roofs, ledges, and foliage—and work from there to locate smaller features. Eventually you'll develop the ability to read the rock, identifying distant lines with relative ease. Like getting used to contour lines on regular topo maps, with practice, you can distinguish hills and valleys at a single glance.

Remain close to reachable, solid protection to stay alive on nebulous terrain. Don't commit to a line of holds unless you're sure it goes.

Also, keep the pitch rating in mind and notice how it compares to that of lower climbing. Determine if the climbing is much too hard or easy for the grade. If so, stop and find the correct line. In addition to the largest holds, look for chalk and clean rock: On some types of rock, a subtle white streak is often present where traffic has worn lichen off popular routes; elsewhere you may notice black rubber streaks from climbing shoes.

Topos are only maps—don't be too dependent on them. Again, learn to spot your line from a distance. While on a route, always look ahead to identify the upper pitches. When in doubt, try to stay in control and coolheaded. Blindly surging forward off-route has resulted in many accidents. Always be ready to bail if you can't find a safe passage.

—Scott Cosgrove

a team must ultimately rely on good navigational skills and intuition to assemble the puzzle.

Longtime Colorado trad-specialist Mark Wilford recommends studying a long route first from a distance to get a basic understanding of where the climb goes. Once you're on the climb, he points out, you won't have a good perspective of the climbing above you. As he says, "After viewing the route, memorize features such as dihedrals, ledge systems, and overhangs so you will know what to look for as you work your way up the climb."

If all evidence of human traffic disappears or the rock takes on a loose and lichen-covered texture, you may be off-route. Sometimes climbers are lured astray by a fixed piece or a sling that turns out to be a retreat anchor from a previous off-route party. Before you're too committed to an unintentional remote, off-piste venture, be sure you don't make any moves that cannot be reversed. Use your down-climbing skills to return to the route or, if you have anchor options and enough rope, lower back to the belay. If you don't have enough rope, set up an anchor, bring your partner up, and put your heads together to determine the safest way for getting back on track.

Trail Line Management

Bringing along a second rope (for rappelling) is most often done by "trailing" it, uncoiled, and clipped with a carabiner to the haul loop of a climber's harness (see "Harness," p. 38). This rope is commonly referred to as the trail line and hangs freely from the climber chosen to trail it. The decision to bring a second rope (see "Gear," pp. 165–168) depends on a few factors. If the descent involves lengthy rappels, two ropes are a must. Climbers might also decide to trail a second rope if there's a chance that poor weather or route difficulty above and beyond the climber's ability level will force the team to retreat before summiting.

The trail line is generally but not always entrusted to the follower. There are benefits and liabilities to each course of action. If the follower trails the second line, the leader is free from the burden of the extra weight. However, if the rope becomes stubbornly wedged in a crack or hooked on a flake, the follower must down-climb or be lowered to retrieve the stuck line and reclimb the pitch. If the leader trails the second rope and it gets stuck below, he or she can simply clip it off onto a piece for the follower to retrieve. In this scenario, the rope should be tied in at the lower belay as a backup until the follower begins climbing.

Whenever you transfer a second line at the belay between partners, use extreme caution and recognize the cost of accidentally dropping it. Before unclipping it from your haul loop, first clip it off to the belay anchor. If you lose your second rope and the descent requires long rappels, you're in trouble.

THE BELAY

Anchors

Upon placing the first piece of an anchor system at the end of any pitch, immediately clip your lead line in temporarily. You will eventually tie into the masterpoint or *shelf* (see "Belaying the Second," p. 175) with a knot (and unclip the rope from this piece) once the anchor is fully constructed. This helps prevent a longer fall should you lose your balance before tying into the completed anchor. During this process, you must remain on-belay. Since you're still leading, don't tie off to and weight this one piece while finishing the rest of the anchor. To do so puts you at risk for a leader fall if the piece dislodges as the result of all the movement it's likely to incur as you build the anchor. If your last piece of pro is far below, which is often the case on long pitches, the fall could be a long one. Simply clip it for pro, and remain "on lead" until the anchor is completed and ready.

Aside from the first and last anchors on a multipitch route, your belay anchors must be multidirectional (see "Multidirectional Anchors," pp. 103–104). Although it can be time consuming, you can wait for the second to arrive to place the anchor component that will withstand an upward or oblique force. (Upward forces are not an issue until a climber begins leading the following pitch.) If you choose to wait, use a sling to clip it taut to either your harness or the masterpoint to avoid having to re-string your cordelette *(see photo, p. 104).*

Organization

Establishing an organized belay station is key to moving fast, and requires forethought. Before setting up the belay consider these factors:

- Where will you position yourself? What stance will provide the most comfortable belaying—the easiest stacking of the slack line as your partner ascends? How much of a leash will you need to be comfortable?

- Assess whether the rope to the second could run across loose pebbles or rocks presenting a potential hazard. If it could, give yourself a longer leash (more slack) so you'll be able, closer to the vertical relief, to keep the rope away from the debris.

- Will the masterpoint of your proposed anchor be at a sufficient height for use as a directional when belaying? (See next section, "Belaying the Second.") A masterpoint nose-high or above is ideal.

- Where will you pile, or flake, the slack rope as your partner ascends? Where will the follower clip into the anchor? If your belay brake is on your right, plan for the slack line from belaying to need to go on the right as well. Left-handers should pile their slack line on the left. If piling slack rope on a particular side is your only option, switch your brake hand to that side.

- Where will you place or hang the pack?

- If the second is trailing a rope, where will that line be stacked?

- Where will your partner sit, hang, or stand? Is this location good for exchanging gear easily? If you're swapping leads, can the next leader climb from the belay stance without becoming entangled in anchor components?

Consider each factor carefully and make appropriate decisions to ensure a rapid and smooth exchange at the belay. A messy belay station will delay the leader, and waste valuable time *(see illustration below)*.

Avoid annoying entanglements at multipitch belays by layering equipment properly.

Belaying the Second

When belaying the second, you can use the anchor as a directional to prevent your partner's weight from wrenching your body in a fall. Tie yourself in about an arm's length to the anchor, so that you'll be slightly below your masterpoint. Clipping yourself into the cordelette *shelf* (*see photo, top right*) prevents crowding at the loop where you clip your masterpoint carabiner. Put your partner on belay, then take a bight of the rope leading to him or her and clip it into your masterpoint carabiner (*see photo, middle right*). The drawback of this rig is a simple physics problem, known as an additive-pulley effect, in which loads on the directional are doubled when weighted. Another option is belaying with a Munter hitch and locking carabiner directly off the anchor (*see photo, bottom right*). This method makes belay escape a cinch and solves both the loading problem and the issue of additive-pulley effect. It does, however, tend to twist the rope if you don't manage it properly and cannot be used to belay a leader. If you have *any* question about the integrity of your anchor, skip the directional and belay your partner off your body (harness). By making your body part of the system, you provide an additional resource for energy absorption in a fall, relieving a sketchy anchor from the force. To do it comfortably, find a good stance wedged between two features for maximum stability; be certain the rope direction and your hand position is such that an unexpected weighting of the rope won't injure your hand or wrist.

As you belay the second up to the anchor, you have lots of slack line to manage. Rope management at the belay is crucial, not only for organizational purposes, but also to prevent the rope from getting stuck on features below. Keep the rope from dangling freely, unless the rock below is either overhanging or smooth (free of cracks or other features on which it could snag). If you're on a ledge, keep the rope in a neat pile beside you. At hanging belays, flake the rope butterfly-style on the taut rope between you and where you are tied into

To anchor yourself to the cordelette shelf: above the knot, clip one of every two strands that is leading to each anchor component.

Redirected belay

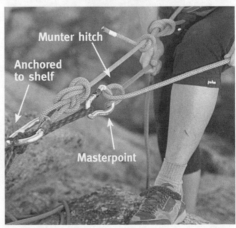

Munter belay off the masterpoint

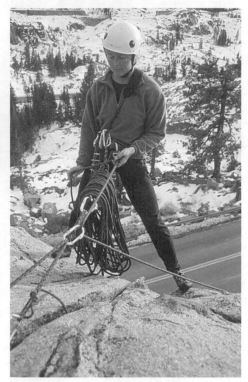

On hanging belays, flake the slack rope, butterfly-style on the taut rope.

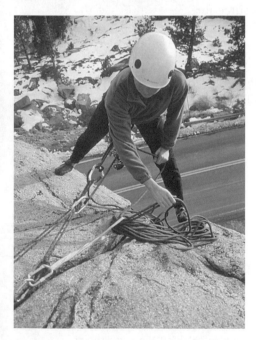

Or flake it in a sling.

the anchor *(see photo, top left)*. Alternatively, you could flake it butterfly-style in a sling off a piece of your anchor system *(see photo, bottom left)*. If you're not swinging leads, always restack the rope before setting off on the next lead.

The Changeover

All about gear management and organization, the changeover takes place at the top of each pitch after the second reaches the stance. If your team is committed to moving efficiently and fast, an effective changeover can save precious time. Yet, for obvious reasons, climbers often succumb to mental and physical weariness at belays on long routes. If you find yourself lagging during the changeover, snap out of your stupor; you'll have time to relax once your partner begins leading the next pitch (unless you're leading in blocks, see p. 179). According to the late climber Seth Shaw, "If you're not doing anything at the belay (changeover), you're being lame. Find a rope to flake, some gear to organize, or get your partner some water or food from the pack. Don't just stand there watching him do all the work." (Shaw was a talented climber from Utah who was tragically killed on a *serac* in Alaska during the writing of the first edition of this book.)

The following suggestions can make your changeovers smooth, efficient, and safe:

• John Hoffman, a retired Alpine Skills International (ASI) guide, says that when his partner reaches the belay he "goes verbal." An example might sound something like this: "Okay, I'm going to clip you in right here, and now you're off belay. All right, let me have the pack . . . here's the water—got it? I'm clipping the pack off over here—no, that'll be in the way of the lead line, but this works right here . . . okay, that's clipped off. Now, are you ready to give me some gear?" Verbalizing your actions reinforces your clarity and command of the system and lets your partner know what's going on at the belay. When climbers tire and errors are most likely to occur, it also helps keep things straight, according to Hoffman.

- When the second arrives at the anchor, the belayer should direct him or her to a stance best suited to that climber's next task (belaying or leading). If the climber will remain the follower, you should tie him or her into the masterpoint and disengage your device. If this climber is going to lead the next pitch, you should tie your partner off to the masterpoint but leave your belay device engaged. If you and your partner are alternating leads and are on a fairly large stance (eliminating the climber's need to weight the rope), you can skip tying your partner into the anchor by keeping your belay device engaged, passing a bight through your locking carabiner, and tying a mule knot (see "Basic Mule Knot," pp. 198–200) for temporary security. While the climber remains on belay, with the device secured by the knot, your hands are free for the changeover. When he or she is ready to climb, the mule knot can be released easily for an immediate belay.

- Use the rope to clip into belay anchors whenever possible. Both climbers should carry a locking carabiner strictly for this purpose. Although some climbers tout the daisy chain for use in multiple-pitch anchoring situations, it's unnecessary gear when you can use the rope. Plus, on hanging belays, the dynamic stretch of rope when weighted is far more comfortable than webbing. The quick adjustability rope offers when used with the clove hitch is lost if you use a daisy chain (unless you use two locking carabiners, thus having to carry more gear). A daisy chain might be useful in these situations: when rope ends need to be swapped at the belay, either because one partner is doing all the leading or your party is leading in blocks (see p. 179); or if you anticipate multiple rappels. Both scenarios require a method of remaining clipped to the anchors during transitions.

- Relieve the second of the pack, securing it temporarily into any component of the system, retrieve water and/or food as needed, and then secure it out of the way to one piece that accepts a downward force. Be sure it isn't lying against any part of the system that you need to access in the immediate future (such as the slack lead line). Never leave the pack unclipped from the anchor unless you're on a huge ledge.

- If you're swinging leads, the previous leader must transfer unused items quickly but carefully to the new one. If the former second has racked efficiently during cleaning, this step takes little time. When passing gear, hand your partner one piece at a time (see "At the Belay Anchor," p. 111). Don't let go unless you're certain he or she has a grip on the piece. Some climbers won't release their grip until they hear an affirmative "Got it."

- With the remaining rack available, now is the time to reinforce your anchor, if necessary. If your anchor is comprised of three pieces of the same size, consider that the lead rack is now void of that size—a potential handicap for the next leader. Swap pieces as necessary, and don't forget your upward pull component (see "Anchors," p. 103 and "The Belay," p. 173).

- If you led the prior pitch and will lead the next one, the rope must be restacked (so that the rope fed to you as you ascend is coming from the top of the pile rather than the bottom). If you skip this step, you'll regret it because untangling your partner's lead line single-handedly when he or she needs slack to move up or clip a piece is dangerous and unnerving. If one partner is leading every pitch on a long route, some teams prefer to switch tie-in points (see next section, "Leading in Blocks") rather than reflake the rope at every changeover.

- Before leaving the belay anchor, the leader should clip into the equalized anchor point as his or her first piece (as long as the anchor is absolutely bomber). I've seen belayer injuries ranging from dislocated wrists to severe rope burns resulting from Factor 2 falls (see "Fall Factor," pp. 153–154). In each case, the leader failed to clip the belay anchor as his or her first piece, and the belayer was poorly positioned. If, for any reason, you do not clip the anchor as you begin your lead, make certain your belayer is positioned so that a Factor 2 fall won't injure him or her.

- Finally, check that the leader has all necessary gear, including the topo, and that the second has the nut tool (if you're sharing). If you're belaying, check the rear loops of your harness for gear you might have missed, and be sure the new leader has all the slings. If you're hauling a second rope, make sure you transfer it to the appropriate partner's haul loop.

Leading in Blocks

An alternative to swapping (or swinging) leads on multipitch routes involves leading in blocks. In this system, each climber accepts leading responsibilities for several consecutive pitches. For example on a 10-pitch route, one climber agrees to lead pitches 1–5 and the other leads 6–10. Swinging leads requires the follower to jump directly into leading mode at each belay; whereas, this system gives each climber a chance to settle into his or her role. Though the pressure of continuous time on the sharp end can be exhaustive, some climbers prefer it over constant role changing. Be sure to consider beforehand, though, the burden of leading the final pitches after a tiring and possibly strenuous day.

To lead in blocks, climbers must either reflake the rope after each pitch, or clip in at belays with a daisy chain (or a cow's tail) and a locker so that rope ends can be swapped at each belay. To eliminate constant tying and untying, secure the rope to your harness with two locking carabiners and a figure-eight on a bight (see "Knots & Hitches," p. 218). It makes trading ends a cinch.

OBJECTIVE HAZARDS

Objective hazards tend to increase on longer climbs. These factors such as rain, snow, hail, lightning, rockfall, and high-altitude illness are generally beyond your control. You can, however, minimize their impact or the likelihood that you'll have to deal with them while climbing through prevention, preparedness, and sound judgment.

Poor Weather

Encounters with rain, sleet, hail, or snow are not uncommon on long routes, particularly those in mountain environments. Since they are a wild card that can instantly alter your progress on a long climb, climb prepared with appropriate clothing and an extra rope for a potential retreat.

In any area notorious for afternoon thundershowers, getting an early start helps ensure a safe and dry climbing experience. If there's a good trail to the base, use your headlamp and begin walking before sunrise; begin the route as the sun is rising. Your biggest concerns with rain or snow are exposure and potential hypothermia. If weather reports indicate a low-pressure system likely to bring precipitation, either choose a shorter climb with an easy escape route for a quick retreat or postpone climbing until another day. If risks are low but precipitation is still a possibility, carry a lightweight rain jacket, preferably made from a waterproof, breathable fabric. Forgo cotton and carry or wear a polyester-blend mid-layer. In colder climates and at higher altitudes, bring a fleece or wool hat. Balaclavas are great as the eyeholes provide ideal carabiner clip-in points. They can be rolled up and worn as a beanie or worn full-length for extra warmth.

If you're near the top of a long route and it begins to rain, your best choice might be to climb on through to the summit. However unpleasant, climbing in the rain is possible (but not recommended for extended periods or after downpours on some types of soft rock). Yet, consider that a rope loses significant strength and stretch capabilities when soaked, and although dry-treated ropes prolong absorption, most treatments wear off. In prolonged or extreme cold, unprotected hands lose dexterity and become useless for gripping holds and handling gear. If necessary, use a combination of aid and free-climbing techniques (a.k.a. *French free* climbing) to get off the route as quickly as possible. Belay your partner up and find temporary shelter until the rain lets up and then descend. If the descent involves technical, Class 3 and 4 scrambling and the rock is still wet, consider roping up and belaying each other down, or rappelling if that's a possibility. On exposed descents, wet, slippery rock has caused many fatal accidents.

A better decision for unprepared climbers or those farther from the summit is to retreat to the nearest escape route or the ground via rappel. The reduced strength of a wet rope is not as crucial on a static rappel as it is for a potential lead fall. You're in luck if the route has fixed anchors from which to rappel, especially if you have two ropes. If not, you'll have to sacrifice a lot of gear for anchors. When it comes to your life, don't be a cheapskate: never trust a single piece of old webbing. Though some climbers trust a single rap ring when rappelling, I prefer an additional backup. Yet, if you're being lowered, never, ever thread the rope directly through slings or runners; the moving rope can saw right through the webbing. If necessary, leave two reversed and opposed carabiners.

If it appears the rain might let up and you're prepared with rainwear and a dry rope in good condition, another option is to hunker down in the most protected area available, wait out the storm, and continue to the top when conditions improve. Just beware of wishful thinking.

Lightning

Lightning kills more people in the U.S. every year than almost all other natural disasters combined. Most of those hit by lightning are either working or playing outdoors. Injuries caused by lightning strikes are also common, ranging from mild to severe. Most serious lightning-related injuries involve cardiac or respiratory arrest caused when the brain "shorts out" from the electrical charge. The good news is that 80 percent of all pulseless, breathless, lightning victims are resuscitated with cardiopulmonary resuscitation when it's performed correctly, so keep your skills sharpened.

Avoid lightning-prone areas when storms are likely. In general, be down and off a summit before early afternoon whenever possible. If weather reports indicate the area is in the middle of a cycle in which storms occur regularly each day, reschedule your long climb in favor of a morning bouldering session or some single-pitch routes. Otherwise, begin your route in the pre-dawn hours armed with rainwear and an extra rope.

If you are caught in a thunderstorm, thoughtful positioning can reduce your susceptibility to being struck by lightning. Electricity travels most efficiently in terrain offering courses of less resistance. Obvious potential targets are positioned in wide-open spaces. Water is an excellent conductor of electricity and, unfortunately for climbers, so is metal. The most dangerous location for climbers during thunderstorms is on an exposed ridge. Another hazardous position is at the base of a crack system or an exposed face, since this terrain quickly turns into a water course through which electricity easily travels. Because broken terrain and talus stymies the efficiency of electric flow, these locations are preferable.

While your alternatives may be limited if you are mid-climb, by acting quickly you may have time to reposition yourself in a less dangerous location. Heed the first sound of distant thunder and count the seconds between it and the lightning crack to determine its proximity. (Yes, the old "one-one-thousand, two-one-thousand" count is effective in determining how far away lightning is striking. This rule of thumb roughly equates one second of time with one mile.) Take as many of the following precautions as you can until the lightning has passed:

- Make yourself as small as possible by assuming the lightning-protection position—squat or sit, head down, with knees drawn up to your chest and both arms wrapped around your knees.

- Huddle in a dry, deep cave—crouch in the middle without leaning back against its walls (keep your contact with the rock as limited as possible). Avoid small, wet caves.

- Sit on the nonconductive closed-cell foam pad on your pack (if it has one). Otherwise, sit on your coiled rope.

- Move away from your partner and your climbing hardware.

If you're hiking along the approach or descent and lightning occurs, temporarily abandon your hardware, move away from your partner(s), and huddle in broken terrain, such as a large talus field, or in a flat forested area. Avoid such open areas as alpine meadows or large bodies of water, and towering, isolated objects like lone trees or snags.

Rockfall

Rockfall occurs on single or multipitch routes alike and can be attributed to various factors. Natural rockfall is commonly caused by snow and ice melt—particularly in spring—but can result from animal activity. Probably the most frequent rockfall occurs because of climbers above you. And falling gear can be as hazardous as rockfall.

Although a climbing helmet can reduce the impact of falling objects, it can't completely eliminate the possibility of harm. Many people won't climb a multiple-pitch route if other climbers are already on it. Other prevention tips include: on warm spring days avoid routes with snow still present in cracks, on ledges, or on the summit; find overhangs and sheltered locations for belay stances; and rise early, so that your party is first in line at the base of popular long climbs.

Prevent rockfall onto others by testing each hold before committing to it completely. Move cautiously across ledges strewn with loose rock, dirt, and gravel, and place directionals to guide the rope away from such terrain. Even a tiny falling pebble, once it accelerates, could injure or kill someone below.

High-Altitude Illnesses

Although physiological changes from increased altitude (barometric pressure) begin occurring as low as 4000 feet (1250 meters), most altitude-related illnesses affect people above 8000 feet (2500 meters). Generally the higher you go, the more serious the effects will be.

Unfortunately, science has yet to determine what makes one person more susceptible to an altitude-related illness than another. Fitness doesn't even play a role; people in better physical shape may actually be more susceptible because they tend to climb faster.

Acute mountain sickness (AMS) is the most common form of altitude sickness and tends to occur within 6 to 72 hours after high-altitude exposure. Symptoms of mild to moderate AMS include headache, loss of appetite, nausea, insomnia, fatigue, and shortness of breath (relieved immediately with rest). Not a life-threatening condition, AMS can be relieved with rest combined with light exercise.

If AMS symptoms are accompanied by a staggering gait (ataxia), they may indicate a progression toward life-threatening high-altitude pulmonary edema (HAPE) and/or high-altitude cerebral edema (HACE). If you're not sure, have your partner stand steadily with his or her feet together on level ground. If he or she cannot do this for 10 seconds without shifting a foot, start descending. Symptoms of HAPE include: all those for AMS except that shortness of breath is not relieved with rest; a cough producing a pink, frothy mucous; chest pain; increased heart rate; and crackling or gurgling sounds with breathing. HACE symptoms include severe headache, extreme ataxia, and personality changes progressing to disorientation and combative behavior. While both HACE and HAPE can occur simultaneously, HAPE tends to come on gradually while HACE is rapid. Climbers with ataxia, or HACE or HAPE symptoms, *must descend immediately*, as these conditions are life-threatening and will not resolve at altitude. Generally, symptoms begin to vanish immediately upon descent, so it is imperative to identify symptoms early on before the patient becomes too disabled, physically and or mentally, to move on their own accord. Neither of these conditions are common below 14,000 feet (4375 meters), particularly HACE. Nevertheless, if you're prepared to identify either condition, you may be able to save a life.

To prevent altitude-related illnesses, climbers should stay hydrated, drinking enough water to keep urine clear. In addition, climbers should gradually acclimatize before climbing at elevations significantly higher than where they reside. For instance, if you're at sea level and ascending about 14,000 feet (4375 meters) to climb Mt. Whitney in the Sierra Nevada, consider arriving three or four days early to acclimatize. Above 10,000 feet (3125 meters), the Wilderness Medicine Institute (WMI) recommends you gain no more altitude than 1000 feet (312 meters) per 24 hours. If this isn't possible, know the signs of HAPE and HACE and be prepared to descend should they appear. Diamox (acetazolamide) is a prescription medication used as a prophylactic against AMS, which can also reduce symptoms from mild to severe. Because Diamox is a diuretic, be prepared for excessive urination and drink a lot of water.

Interestingly enough, since altitude illnesses don't develop within the first six hours of reaching higher altitudes, an extremely fast team able to approach, climb, and descend a route within this period can actually avoid altitude-related illnesses altogether. Buck Tilton of WMI and author of several texts on wilderness medicine cautions, "This does not exclude the possibility of unusual breathlessness and fatigue or the possibility of a debilitating injury that prevents the descent." As a new leader you should save such a time frame for a short route with a simple approach and an easy descent.

THE DESCENT

Descents from long routes involve walk-offs and/or rappels. The complexity and danger factor of a descent is measured in terms of length and terrain. For instance, two short rappels down a loose gully with several hundred feet of Class 3 scrambling might be far more dangerous than 10 rappels down the ascent line of a clean, steep route. Climbers must stay alert and resist the urge to relax simply because the summit has been attained. Ringing especially true for the multipitch descent is the adage *It's not over until it's over*.

Multipitch Rappelling

As long as you stay focused on multiple rappels, and follow the guidelines listed in Chapter 5, the following suggestions will help you avoid epics:

- After each rappel, clip into the next rappel anchor with your daisy chain or cow's tail before removing your device from the rope.

- If you're last to rappel, don't let go of the lines after clipping into the next anchor and disengaging your device.

- Make sure at least one rope end is threaded through rap rings at each intermediate rappel station before pulling your lines. Continue threading the rope as you retrieve them and, when both ends come down, the rope(s) will almost be ready for the next rappel. Make any small adjustments as needed to keep the center point or knot at masterpoint level.

- In windy conditions, don't lose control of your rope(s). If necessary, consider lowering the first person in line to rappel, and have him or her tie in the loose ends at the anchor below before you follow on rappel.

- If you're exhausted or injured, have your partner rappel first and give you a "fireman's belay" from below. This simply involves the "belayer" holding both lines loosely, but pulling tightly to halt the rappeller's progress should he or she lose control.

- As suggested in Chapter 5, check and double-check all primary links, tie knots on the ends of each rappel line, and use a friction hitch backup.

Class 3 & 4 Terrain

Trad climbers often forgo ropes and protection when scrambling on Class 3 and 4 terrain (see Chapter 9), though a slip can be fatal. While seasoned mountaineers have little trouble covering such ground, climbers without much backcountry experience can have difficulties, particularly if they are tired from a long climb. Without honed backcountry skills, don't attempt Class 3 and 4 descents after nightfall, and be prepared to rope up on uncomfortably exposed or loose sections. Absorb advice from your resources before the climb, and bring any available maps. Until you're walking safely on a well-maintained trail, stay alert.

Potential Problems & Solutions on Multipitch Rappels

There are many issues that can arise on rappel, particularly during multiple rappels. Some common problems and their solutions are provided below:

- **You have accidentally passed the next rappel anchor and are now below it.** Tie into *both* ropes and then ascend the lines with friction hitches (see "Rope Ascent," p. 201). It is critical that you wrap each cord around *both* rope strands.

- **You drop your rappel device.** If you're carrying at least four standard D or oval carabiners (the latter are better), you can set up a carabiner brake system (see Chapter 9). Otherwise have your partner tie them onto one end of the rope and you can haul them up.

- **You've just completed a slightly traversing rappel, with several more to go before reaching the ground.** When your partner joins you at the stance, he or she disengages the rope from the device and lets go of both ends. You watch helplessly as the rope lines fly across the rock face and stop several feet (or more) from your reach. If any other parties are rappelling above you, ask for their assistance. Or get creative: Extend a chain of gear to reach the rope end you need to pull (either end if you're using a single rope). Athletic tape might help you join

the gear. Use longer rigid, yet fairly light pieces such as nut tools and wired Stoppers. If you're on a ledge, look for useful sticks and branches. Now, extend your tie-in point to the anchor with cordelettes and/or several girth-hitched slings, and move out onto the face closest to the ropes and reach. . . . Good luck!

- **Upon attempted retrieval the rope becomes stuck; no amount of pulling will disengage it.** Like in the first scenario, tie into *both* ropes, and ascend the lines with friction hitches. Again, be sure to wrap each cord around *both* rope strands. Attempt *only* if you have access to *both* rope ends, and the strands are of equal length and still threaded through the anchors. Never ascend on a single rope strand. Disengage the stuck line when you reach it and then rappel back down. With only one line available, don't think you'll ascend the rope hand over hand up the fixed line without a belay. After considering your fate, if the rope shimmies loose and/or you fall, tie in and get a belay. If you're lucky, the terrain is moderate and you'll have enough rope available to lead up (belayed) and free the stuck line. If not, combine aid moves with free moves to ascend. Without enough rope to do this you're in trouble if you haven't reached the ground.

Scree & Talus

Scree are tiny shards of rock and dirt covering slopes of varying degrees of steepness in backcountry settings. Ranging in size from a breadbox to a small passenger car, talus consists of larger versions of scree. Scree and talus slopes can result from glacial debris in moraines or from long-term erosion or rockfall. Wear your helmet when climbing or descending these slopes. Be careful not to dislodge loose rock and avoid traveling directly above or below your partner. How long ago the debris was deposited determines the slope's stability; left recently, it will be very loose. When you descend over steep scree, take deliberate steps, letting yourself slide a bit. With hesitant, unsure steps the going is slower and probably more harrowing. Relax and get a rhythm going, but, if you're overly worried, ask your partner for a belay.

Snow & Ice

In mountain environments, snow and ice travel on approaches and descents might require an ice ax. If you bring one, know how to use it. Practice self-arrest beforehand with an experienced guide or mentor on high-angle snow patches with long runouts. To cross short sections of snow or ice, two partners can share one ax. The lead can chop footholds for the second and then send the ax down to the second for his or her ascent. If you forgo an ax but come upon unexpected snow or ice, substitute two hand-size sharp rocks.

In late spring when you're crossing large talus covered in snow, travel early in the day when the snow is frozen and still relatively solid. Under softer conditions, you're at high risk for breaking through boulder gaps and incurring a significant injury.

If an approach or descent involves glacial travel, become familiar with glacier rescue techniques and the basics of moving over such terrain. This includes coping with seracs, crevasses, *bergschrunds* (caverns created when ice melts away from a rock wall), avalanches, and other alpine hazards. If you're not, then choose a route with an easier approach or descent, take a basic mountaineering course, or learn these skills from an experienced mentor.

Epics

Every longtime trad climber has a good tale about a climbing foray turned epic. Sharing misfortunes increases climbers' awareness of their own vulnerability. But don't bolster your own ego by critiquing another climber's accident—it could have easily been you. Understand what went wrong and when, and use this information to prevent mistakes of your own.

An epic often results from one poor decision or careless action. Getting a late start, not bringing enough water, climbing off-route, climbing regardless of threatening weather, dropping critical gear, discovering the route is too difficult for the team's collective ability, getting a rope stuck—these are all grist for the epic mill and all preventable. Regardless of best intentions and preparations, though, epics occur. Once a mistake is made, do whatever you can to prevent the situation from worsening. Every epic has a turning point at which you can either resolve it safely through teamwork, or it balloons into a serious accident. When facing the consequences of an error, gather your respective wits before the situation spirals out of control.

Retreat

As noteworthy as summiting is making the difficult decision to retreat. Success has more to do with style and staying alive than reaching the top. Facing climbing peers after a retreat, as well as coping with feelings of failure, can take more courage than undergoing dangerous maneuvers to reach the top. Go with your gut feeling about retreat, without letting your ego interfere.

THE UNPLANNED BIVOUAC

Though an unplanned bivouac is uncomfortable at best and utter misery at worst, if, having summitted, you doubt your ability to descend—either because of imminent darkness or other changing conditions (such as a snowfield refreezing)—wait until morning. Lightweight items that make an unplanned "bivy" more tolerable include:

- **Fire Starters**—a lighter or matches (preferably waterproof) and kindling material such as steel

Mike Pennings Collection

Climber: Mike Pennings

Years Trad Free Climbing: 23

**Favorite Trad Climbing Areas:
Black Canyon (Colorado)
& Patagonia**

**Most Respected Trad Free Climber:
Charlie Porter**

Retreat Factors

The little voice inside me says when to throw in the towel on an ascent—no formula governs when to retreat and when to push farther. My decision is affected by weather conditions, route conditions, difficulty of the climb ahead, time of day, partner psyche and desire, personal psyche and desire, other climbers on the route, when my girlfriend expects me home, etc. Yet the most important factor influencing the decision is intuition.

Jeff Hollenbaugh and I went to the Kitchatnas in Alaska to attempt the first ascent of the southeast face of Mt. Nevermore. An avalanche that occurred near the base of the route buried a haul bag containing most of our gear.

Approaching the wall to search for the lost bag, we both experienced an eerie feeling—the mountain didn't want us to be there. Without a very thorough search—despite our pilot not returning for three and a half weeks—we abandoned our effort.

In a situation where you want to climb but your partner wants to retreat, you must respect your partner's reasons. Whether they're just being lazy or truly believe they'll die if they continue isn't really for you to decide. By continuing upward with a begrudging partner, you potentially compromise the safety of both team members.

—Mike Pennings

wool, a small amount of paper, or a few cotton balls previously soaked in Vasoline (petroleum jelly);

- **Extra Clothing**—wool or fleece hat (or balaclava), wool- or polyester-blend socks, a fleece pullover, and a wind/rain jacket; and

- **SPACE Emergency Blanket**—super lightweight Mylar "blanket" that retains 80 percent of radiated body heat.

Build a fire in a contained space if you can find dry timber, and try to keep it burning through the night. Use extreme caution to prevent it from getting out of control and clean up in the morning (see "Leave No Trace," pp. 237–239). Assume the heat-saving fetal position and stay close to your partner to help keep each other warm. Use the rope and pack (or leaves and pine needles) as insulation from the cold ground. A removable closed-cell pad that forms the back panel of some packs makes excellent insulation. In addition, extension flaps at the mouth can transform your pack into a waist-high bivy bag. If it begins to rain or snow, seek shelter under an overhang or in a cave. Some outdoor enthusiasts carry extra-large plastic garbage bags for such a situation.

What if I don't make it to the summit? Don't wait until the last minute to find a good bivy ledge. As twilight fades, many deluded teams forge ahead frantically, passing spacious ledges that would soften the blow of an unplanned bivy. When halted by complete darkness, these climbers often have no other option but to endure the night dangling from the anchors of a hanging belay. If you can't locate a ledge, situate yourself under an overhang, if possible. If the weather is threatening, avoid perches at the base of obvious water paths (grooves, crack systems, or areas with black streaks).

Certainly not for everyone, the multipitch trad adventure does offer memorable experiences. If you long to try it, you could get hooked—it happens. Stay safe by maintaining realistic goals, partnering with competent people, and never shedding your beginner's mind. Also take responsibility for the risks you shoulder by learning self-rescue skills and encourage your regular partners to do the same. Basic self-rescue techniques are discussed in the next chapter.

Chapter 8

Introduction to Self-Rescue

The climbing experience can often seem like an amusement park ride in which thrills are safely guaranteed. Each successful and safe ascent reinforces this illusion until one day an injury or mishap harshly dispels your false sense of invulnerability. There are no guarantees in trad climbing; you work toward reducing risks but can never eliminate them. Since routes typically lure climbers to heights well above the possibility of a simple retreat, knowing how to extricate your team from a mishap is essential. "Self-rescue" refers broadly to taking responsibility for your team without relying on outside help; it is a specific elaboration of self-reliance. By studying and practicing self-rescue skills and techniques, you prepare yourself for action should your team's "what ifs" become all too real.

After prevention, self-rescue skills are your best insurance against rescuers having to pluck you from a wall when you run into trouble. Outside assistance can be costly and undependable. In remote areas, professional rescues are often unavailable. In regions where they are, you might have to pick up the tab for your rescue or, worse, find your team at the mercy of an incompetent rescue crew. Although climbing areas such as Yosemite National Park rely on a well-trained Search and Rescue (SAR) team, others may not. Your rescue may fall into the hands of a group of well-meaning but inexperienced sheriff deputies generally better equipped to fight crime than perform high-angle rescue.

Complex self-rescue scenarios require techniques, materials, and/or skills beyond the scope of this book, but this chapter introduces the basics. Hands-on practice is indispensable when learning and is the only realistic way to understand basic concepts. Don't try to learn these skills solely from reading this or any other book or article. Taking a class will help. Contact your local guide service to enroll in one. You can prepare yourself for the class and improve your level of understanding by studying this chapter. Once you receive professional instruction, begin practicing these techniques in low-risk settings. As your leading skills increase, add techniques to your repertoire, learn how to use a variety of tools, and share what you've learned with fellow climbers.

A clear head is essential for safe and successful self-rescue. In his book *Self-Rescue*, David Fasulo says, "The most important tool in any self-rescue is your brain. Carefully survey the scene to prevent further difficulties and ensure safety. Plan your course of action safely, and if necessary locate assistance."[10]

At first, self-rescue techniques may seem very complex, yet most operations combine a few, fundamental techniques. With your mind open, absorb the information in small doses and practice a lot. Once these fundamentals become second nature, your self-sufficiency on the rock is within sight.

PREVENTION & RESPONSIBILITY

Most trad climbers racking up mileage on long technical routes know little about self-rescue. Because confidence soars with success, these climbers sometimes get stricken with a case of *It can't happen to me* or *If it happens to me, I'll figure it out on the spot*. Winging it may be possible for a longtime climber with keen tech skills, but it's wishful thinking for most. Mastering self-rescue skills empowers you to take on adventures confident that you'll be capable of handling almost any unexpected situation without outside help.

Self-rescue is less likely to be necessary if you use sound judgment to prevent errors. Climb within your honest ability level and make realistic choices with regard to route length, weather, and daylight. Analyze the mistakes of other climbers. Don't feel bad discussing their accidents; a real-life close call of someone you know is highly affecting, and you can really learn from their experience. Valuable insight can also be gained from reading. Check out the American Alpine Club's annual *Accidents in North American Mountaineering*, as well as my personal favorite, *Close Calls* written by John Long and illustrated by Tami Knight.

FIRST AID

All climbers should know basic first aid and cardiopulmonary resuscitation (CPR). If you're climbing in backcountry settings, advanced first-aid skills are highly recommended. If, while climbing in a remote area, your partner hits his or her head during a leader fall, could you distinguish a minor goose egg from a head injury that requires immediate evacuation? Could you monitor your partner for signs of increasing intracranial pressure that is life threatening? If your partner dislocates a shoulder or wrist, what would you do? Using what you have on hand, could you splint a fractured bone to stabilize an injured partner for evacuation? For climbers who frequently venture into remote areas, a Wilderness First Responder (WFR) certification provides a very comprehensive set of lay medical skills. A WFR course prepares students to distinguish between conditions that require immediate evacuation and those that do not. Curriculum includes how to treat, stabilize, and evacuate victims using improvised equipment. WFR courses address the scenarios and conditions mentioned above, as well as numerous others, including wound management, hypothermia, altitude illness, heat exhaustion, heat stroke, frostbite, dehydration, shock, and lightning injuries. Ten-day training sessions are held throughout the U.S. and in some locations abroad. Locate companies offering WFR courses in your area by searching the Internet.

A victim's physical and mental condition plays a large role in determining which method of self-rescue you employ. For instance, if a climber has sustained serious injuries, lowering or raising the climber might compound his or her injuries. In this case, you may have to ascend or descend to the victim first, assess his or her condition and provide assistance, and then perform an assisted rappel. The severity of your partner's injuries might also determine whether you can safely execute all or part of the rescue without outside assistance.

Conditions posing an immediate threat to life take priority over rescue efforts. Always initiate first aid if your partner isn't breathing, doesn't have a pulse, is bleeding, has a potential cervical spine injury, or is exposed to environmental hazards (rockfall, extreme heat or cold, etc.). Learning to conduct a primary survey of the victim's condition allows you to identify and treat immediate threats to life. This skill is taught thoroughly in WFR and other first-aid courses, while CPR courses cover the basics.

EQUIPMENT

The following equipment composes a basic kit for performing the introductory self-rescue techniques outlined in this chapter:

- A cordelette reserved specifically for rescue scenarios;
- Two locking carabiners (two reversed and opposed standard 'biners can be substituted for each but are awkward to use in some applications);
- Four standard carabiners;
- Two 24-inch (70-centimeter) loops of nylon cord (purchase 80 inches, or 202 centimeters)—this should be enough material to create two loops and accommodate a ring bend (see Chapter 9) and adequate tails[11]; and
- Three %16-inch (1.4-centimeter) shoulder-length runners made from tubular nylon webbing (not Spectra).

While you're gaining lead climbing experience, carry these items with you every time you rope up, and don't hand them over to the leader at changeovers on multi-pitch routes. With greater experience, you can explore alternate self-rescue methods that enable one material or tool to be substituted for another. Fasulo's *Self-Rescue*, listed in the "Resources" section, is an excellent resource on such methods.

KNOTS & HITCHES

Knowing a handful of knots and hitches will prepare you for learning the self-rescue methods described in this chapter. Use a basic mule knot to lock off the belay and free up your hands as rescuer, and the Munter mule knot to let you release a knot under tension and transfer loads. Friction hitches grip the rope. You can use them as brake-line backups or to transfer loads and ascend fixed ropes.

Friction Hitches

The prusik is the most common of many friction hitches, all of which can be slid up or down a rope when unweighted but will grip it under load. Some other friction hitches include the Klemheist, the Bachman, and the autoblock. Prusik and autoblock friction hitches are described below.

Most friction hitches (with the exception of the prusik) can be tied with either an accessory cord or a ⁹⁄₁₆-inch (1.4-centimeter) tubular nylon sling. Do not use slings made from Spectra because they are too slippery to grip the rope adequately. Cord that is 6 millimeters in diameter is ideal for use with the average 9.4- to 10.5-millimeter climbing rope. For ropes of lesser diameter, use 5-millimeter cord. Cord narrower than 5 millimeters is too weak and wider than 6 millimeters won't grip. Since any hitch with too few wraps can slip on loaded ropes and burn from friction heat, always test each hitch prior to use. If it slips, add more wraps.

Prusik

The prusik works effectively only with cord, but unlike other friction hitches, you can tie it easily with one hand—a

Prusik

Prusik hitch start (a loose girth hitch) on a 10 millimeter rope

Autoblock

To tie an autoblock on a 10 millimeter line, wrap your cord or webbing three or four times around the rope depending on the amount of friction desired.

Wrapped twice

With one final wrap (3 total), the weighted prusik will "bite" the rope. (Add another wrap for added friction if desired.)

Complete by clipping both loop ends to your carabiner.

huge benefit in some scenarios. It is multidirectional (able to hold loads from either end) but difficult to loosen after being loaded. To tie a prusik, make a girth hitch (see "Knots & Hitches," p. 219) around the rope *(see photos 1, 2, and 3, left on p. 197).* Keep this initial hitch loose and tie two to three more girth hitches with the free loop, adding each new wrap to the center. Three loops are usually sufficient to get the hitch to "bite" the rope.

Autoblock (a.k.a. French Prusik)

Also multidirectional, the autoblock releases with relative ease after being loaded. Because of this, it works great both as a brake-line backup for rappelling (see "Brake-Line Backup," p. 116), and for ascending a fixed line. Another advantage over the prusik is that it can be tied with either cord or non-Spectra webbing. The major drawback is that it's difficult to tie with one hand. To tie an autoblock, wrap your loop of cord or webbing candy-cane fashion at least three times around the rope *(see photos 1 and 2, right on p. 197).* Complete the hitch by clipping both loop ends to a locking carabiner.

Basic Mule Knot

Use the basic mule knot to tie off a loaded belay rope and free your hands, the first step in escaping the belay. Use it also in combination with the Munter hitch to transfer loads (see "Munter Mule," p. 200 and "Belay Escape," p. 204). Say you have caught a fall, are holding your partner on tension, and want to free your hands to begin a self-rescue task. If you are braking with your right hand[12], take a fairly large loop of your slack brake line and feed it through the locking carabiner from right to left *(see illustrations on facing page).* Feed a bight of slack from this loop under the loaded rope from left to right, and make a twist (clockwise) in the rope. Using a bight from the remaining loose portion of the loop, form another coil to the left of the loaded strand with another twist (counterclockwise). Feed the left coil through the right coil over the loaded rope strand. Tighten and cinch the knot closely to your device. With the protruding bight, tie an overhand knot to the loaded strand. For extra security, clip a carabiner to the final tail. *It is absolutely essential to*

Basic Mule Knot

1. to climber

bight of rope through 'biner

2. pass this loop.. ...through this loop!

3. tie an overhand with this bight.

4. Set & dressed.

complete the mule knot with an overhand; all subsequent references to the mule knot assume that you have done this.

Munter Mule

The Munter mule is a combination of a Munter hitch and a mule knot. Because this knot can be released easily when weighted, it is ideal for transferring loads in self-rescue scenarios. Tie a Munter hitch onto a locking carabiner, then tie a mule knot as described previously but without passing a loop through the locking carabiner *(see illustration below).*

This illustration depicts the Munter mule tied with a *single* strand of climbing rope—an application used to free your hands when belaying with a Munter hitch. In some applications, however, you will tie the Munter mule with your cordelette loop, so the strands you are working with are *doubled*.

FUNDAMENTAL TECHNIQUES

Self-rescue scenarios vary from simple to complex, but no matter whether you're assisting an immobilized leader or helping your second pass a difficult section on a route beyond his/her capabilities, you'll use one or a combination of four basic techniques: rope ascent, belay escape, assisted raise, and/or assisted descent.

Don't attempt any technique presented here without first practicing it in a low-risk setting under the watchful eye of an experienced mentor. These methods require an absolutely reliable anchor, as most result in a tremendous multiplication of forces. It is a good idea to reinforce your belay anchor before proceeding. Backing up your work is also important, especially during training. Create a backup with a figure-eight on a bight clipped to your anchor. Also, remember to use locking carabiners (or two reversed and opposed standard 'biners) on all your backups and primary links.

Rope Ascent

The rope ascent is the most basic of all self-rescue skills *(see illustrations, p. 202)*. The following instructions outline the "Texas-style" method:

Step 1: Attach a friction hitch to the taut rope. Using a locking carabiner, connect yourself with the appropriate-length sling (no more than the distance between your waist and forehead when standing).

Step 2: Add a second friction hitch to the rope below the first one. Make a foot sling for this hitch by attaching either two slings girthed together or one long sling (measuring no more than the distance between your feet and waist when standing). Different body types may require fine tuning of the sling length. Your cordelette can be used in lieu of the sling(s).

Step 3: Alternately weight each hitch to ascend, making progress by sliding the unweighted hitch up the rope. Begin by standing up in the lower loop. Without weighting the upper loop, push it up the rope as high as possible. Now weight it and,

1.

Rope Ascent

Weight lower friction hitch by
standing up on this leg . . .

2.

. . . slide upper fric-
tion hitch up as high
as possible . . .

3.

. . . hang by upper
hitch while you slide
the lower hitch up, then
repeat the process!

reaching down, slide the lower hitch up the rope until it is near the upper one.

Step 4: Repeat Step 3 until you have reached your destination, tying backup figure-eights into a large locking carabiner attached to your harness every 15 feet (more often above ledges or close to the ground). For an additional backup, link the lower hitch to your harness loosely with a long sling. (For clarity, neither backup method is shown in the illustration.)

Tips

- Ascending a fixed rope can be strenuous, especially on overhanging terrain. Make sure you fully weight the upper loop at each opportunity, as this is your only chance to rest. Bend one leg and tuck it under your torso, resting your butt on the heel of your foot; you can stretch your other leg straight out in front of you.
- For optimal efficiency, adjust the slings to a length that minimizes effort and maximizes the distance you can cover with each slide. If your upper sling is too short, progress will be slow and you'll tire faster. If it is too long, you'll find it difficult to rest and won't be able to cover as much distance. Before setting off, test your system by ascending a short distance. Then take the time to adjust the sling lengths correctly. Reduce a sling's length by tying an overhand knot onto it. This knot simply takes up space thereby shortening the runner.

Common Scenarios

Instances when you need to ascend the rope include, but aren't limited to, the following scenarios:

- After taking a leader fall from above an overhang, you might end up below the ceiling, dangling helplessly in space too far from the rock wall to be able to climb back. Lowering might not be an option, especially if you have used more than half the rope or the route traverses significantly. Ascending the rope as your belayer maintains tension will get you back to your last piece.

• When seconding a multipitch route, you might encounter a section too difficult for you to free climb. Since lowering to the ground isn't an option and you don't want your lead climber to have to set up an assisted raise, you might ask your partner to lock you off on tension and let you ascend the "fixed" line past the difficult section.

• If you accidentally rappel past an anchor when executing multiple rappels, you might have to ascend two lines together to reach the stance above. Since you attach your friction hitch to both lines, you should add additional wraps for optimal security.

• If you are belaying and the leader takes a fall, becoming immobilized and requiring assistance, you may need to ascend the rope. In this scenario, the anchored rope won't let you tie backups. Instead, use a third hitch as a backup (see "Leader Rescue Overview" on p. 215).

Belay Escape

Escaping a loaded belay is the first step in many self-rescue efforts. Briefly, it involves freeing your hands and transferring the weight of the loaded rope off your body, so you can disengage from your belay mechanism. This method uses the Munter mule to shift the load first onto a friction hitch so you can disengage your belay device and then directly onto the anchor *(see illustrations, pp. 206–207)*. This provides the opportunity to either transfer the load again, or resume belaying. Use this method any time you are belaying off your harness with the rope redirected through the anchor to the climber.

Step 1: Tie a mule knot onto the loaded rope strand to free your hands. Tie a backup on the loose brake line, leaving two arm's length of slack between your device and the anchor.

Step 2: Using a bight of your cordelette, attach a friction hitch onto the taut line leading to the climber, then, with the double strand of the other end of the cordelette, tie a Munter mule on a locking 'biner attached to the anchor. (This Munter mule will let you ease the load onto another Munter mule you tie with the rope in Step 4.)

Step 3: Now transfer the load onto the friction knot by releasing the original mule knot that you tied to free your hands. (You have now officially escaped the belay. The friction knot set-up is backed up by your Step 1 tie-off. The next two steps allow you to transfer the load directly onto the anchors.)

Step 4: Using the brake line between the load and your backup, attach a Munter mule to the anchors with a locking carabiner.

Step 5: Release the mule knot at the Munter mule you tied with the cordelette, then let the Munter slide, transferring the load directly onto the anchor (now secured by the Munter mule you just tied with the rope). To resume belaying, pop the mule knot free and belay off the anchor with the remaining Munter.

Comments

If you are belaying the second directly off the anchor with a Munter hitch, his or her weight is already on the anchor, simplifying the belay escape. All that's required is to tie a mule knot (and back up) to free the hands. This is why rock guides prefer this belay method for clients who are following.

Common Scenarios

Almost all self-rescue attempts require belay escape. Whether you are going to initiate an assisted raise, rescue the leader, or rescue the second via rappelling, a belay escape frees you to take action.

Assisted Raise

Few climbers—even the strongest— could hoist their partner hand-over-hand on a rope. Raising a climber requires some sort of mechanical-advantage system. The most versatile and widely used raising method in climbing is the Z-rig *(see illustration, right).* The 3:1 Z-rig is an improvised pulley system that provides approximately twice your unassisted strength.

Assisted Raise

ANCHOR

MASTER POINT

MUNTER MULE in CORDELETTE

the 'Z'

PULL!

FRICTION HITCH

FRICTION HITCH (RATCHET)

To VICTIM

Belay Escape

STEPS ①–②

ANCHOR

BACK UP

MUNTER MULE
~tied with cordelette

TIE IN TO CLIMBER

FRICTION HITCH

STEP ③

BACK UP

TIE IN to climber

LOAD HAS BEEN TRANSFERRED TO THE FRICTION HITCH

Munter Mule untied

STEP
④

BACK UP

TIE ANOTHER MUNTER MULE

TIE IN to CLIMBER

FREE YOUR BELAY DEVICE

STEP
⑤

CLIP TO ANCHOR WITH GIRTHED SLING before removing TIE IN.

BACK UP

UNTIE

(Theoretically the advantage is 3:1, but in practice it ranges from 1½–2, depending on the degree of friction.) It employs two friction hitches: The locking or "tractor" hitch helps you pull rope up, and the ratcheting hitch prevents back-slippage of the rope pulled up. Once the stretch is out of the rope, for every 3 feet you pull up, the victim will rise 1 foot.

Step 1: Follow Steps 1 through 3 in "Belay Escape" (see pp. 204–205). You have transferred the load to a friction hitch (which will serve as the ratchet for your Z-rig) and to the anchor, via a Munter Mule tied with your cordelette. Your hands are now free to work.

Step 2: Using a short loop of cord or webbing, attach a second friction hitch on the loaded rope above the existing ratchet hitch. This will serve as the locking hitch.

Step 3: Clip a locking carabiner into the anchor, and run the slack side of the rope through this carabiner, and down and through another 'biner attached to the locking (upper) hitch. Now you have your Z.

Step 4: To raise a victim, pull upward on the slack rope until the upper (locking) hitch almost meets the anchor. Now slide the lower (ratchet) hitch back down the rope (toward the victim) and ease the load onto it. Now slide the locking hitch back down and repeat the process. As you make progress, clip backups every 15 feet alternately into two, pre-placed carabiners at the anchor.

Tips & Comments

- The locking hitch can be established below the ratchet instead of above it. This allows hauling in longer increments but requires careful monitoring of the ratchet to prevent it from slipping through the locking carabiner at the anchor.

- A Z-rig assisted raise requires the victim to remove lead protection, or at least unclip the rope from protection. If the victim is unable to do this, you must rappel down to provide assistance.

- Even though mechanical advantages help make it easier, raising a climber is still a difficult and strenuous procedure. Excess friction in the system (e.g., raising a victim up low-angle terrain) makes the process even more difficult. Before launching into an extended Z-rig raise, consider other options. If you have enough rope and your partner will not likely be able to continue, rappel down to him or her, establish another anchor, and perform an assisted rappel to the ground.

Common Scenarios

Trad free climbing scenarios requiring the use of an assisted raise include, but aren't limited to, the following:

- The second can't get past a difficult section and doesn't know how to ascend the rope.

- The second, though conscious enough to unclip or clean protection, has been injured and is unable to physically or mentally make the moves required to reach the belay.

- The second, having fallen on an unprotected traverse, is now off-route and dangling in space too far from the rock to climb again, and he or she is not carrying the equipment necessary to ascend the rope.

Assisted Descent

If your partner's condition is such that he or she is incapable of rappelling solo or being lowered, the simplest descent option is the tandem rappel. The description below assumes that both climbers are clipped into a secure and reliable anchor with a daisy chain or cow's tail before beginning. It also assumes you have tied a safety knot in appropriate rope end(s) to prevent rappelling off the end of the rope.

Tandem Rappel

In a tandem rappel, two climbers descend on the same rope, attached to the same device, with one partner in command of braking. First, prepare the rope(s) in the same manner as with any standard rappel (see "Rappel Overview," pp. 112–120).

Step 1: Thread the descent rope into a rappel device attached to a locking carabiner. Girth-hitch a single-length runner to your harness and a double-length to the victim's. Clip both into the locker.

Step 2: Take control of the brake line, assemble a backup friction hitch attached to your leg loops, and descend with your partner *(see illustration below)*.

Common Scenarios

Instances when you use the tandem rappel include but aren't limited to the following scenarios:

- When beginners experience severe apprehension over an impending rappel descent;
- When at any time during a descent you suspect your partner's consciousness level is deteriorating, due to extreme fatigue, altitude illness, hypothermia, or heat stroke/ exhaustion; and

Tandem Rappel

brake hand

autoblock backup to harness

- When rescuing the leader. (Note that learning the more advanced counterweight rappel simplifies the leader-rescue procedure, and though it's beyond the scope of this book, I recommend the counterweight method of assisted descent for intermediate self-rescue students.)

Passing a Knot

If you are fortunate enough to have two ropes, you can sometimes tie them together to reach the ground faster, either via standard rappelling or lowering. One drawback of this tactic is that you'll need to get past the knot joining the ropes together. The two methods described below require advance rigging.

Rappel Knot Pass

Step 1: Pre-rig a friction hitch above the rappel device and clip it into your rappel/belay loop on your harness. Keep the hitch loose through your initial descent and make sure it doesn't get sucked into your rappel device. I suggest you use the autoblock because, of all the friction hitches, it is the most easily released when weighted. *(See illustration, p. 212.)*

Step 2: Rappel until you approach the knot and then engage the hitch when it is within an arm's length of the knot. Now your device is unweighted.

Step 3: Between 3 and 4 feet below the knot joining the ropes, tie a backup figure-eight and clip it to your harness with a locking carabiner.

Step 4: Remove your rappel device and reattach it below the knot. *(See illustration, p. 212, bottom.)*

Step 5: Establish a rappel backup below your device.

Step 6: Now loosen the friction hitch and transfer your weight from the upper hitch back to your rappel device. Finally, untie the figure-eight backup.

On overhanging terrain, it may be difficult or impossible to loosen and remove the loaded hitch as instructed in step 6. If this is the case, you must first unweight the hitch. You have two options to accomplish this:

A. Loop a section of the unloaded rope strand around one foot. Then, grasping a bight of the rope taut at your chest, stand up and loosen the now unweighted hitch with your other hand (not shown).

B. Attach another friction hitch onto the loaded rope and extend (with girthed runners) a loop of webbing into which you can stand to unweight the hitch. Then loosen and remove the hitch. (*See lower illustration below.*)

Rappel Knot Pass

STEPS
① – ③

Weight and engage pre-rigged autoblock, then tie your backup well below the knot you are passing.

STEPS
④ – ⑥

Reattach the device BELOW the knot. Then, establish your rappel backup hitch below your device. Finally, remove the pre-rigged auto-block using a girth-hitched sling and a friction hitch to create a foot sling if necessary.

Lowering Knot Pass

Lowering Knot Pass

The lowering knot pass *(see illustrations, above, right, and top of p. 214)* requires the following pre-rigging *(see A–C in Step 1 illustration)*:

A. With a cordelette, tie a friction hitch onto rope #1 between the victim and your belay device.

B. Attach to the anchor with a Munter mule.

C. Using rope #2, tie a Munter mule opposite the knot joining the two ropes and attach directly to the anchor with a locking carabiner.

ANCHOR

Knot is passed now.

Before you begin lowering the victim, consider the overall picture—to pass the knot, you've got to release your initial belay/lowering device. Engaging the hitch when you reach the knot will allow you to do this. Next, you need to transfer the load from the hitch to the Munter mule on the second rope (opposite the knot) so that you can continue lowering the victim. You can make this initial transition because the Munter mule tied with the cordelette can be released under load, and you can ease the load onto the second rope with the remaining Munter on the cordelette. Releasing the mule knot on the second rope leaves a Munter for continued lowering.

Step 1:   After pre-rigging your system (see A–C), lower the victim with your belay device, tending the pre-rigged friction hitch so it won't bind.

Step 2:   Just before the knot reaches your belay device, allow the hitch to load. Then remove the rope from the device. (The pre-rigged Munter mule tied with rope #2 is your backup.) Prepare to release the Munter mule tied with the cordelette to transfer the load to the Munter mule tied with rope #2.

Step 3:   Release the Munter mule on the loaded friction hitch, maintaining control of the free end of the cordelette. Let the Munter slide, transferring the weight of the victim onto rope #2 above the knot. Establish control of the brake line and release the mule knot tied with the rope. With your free hand, remove the friction hitch from the rope to prevent it from snagging later on the rock. Continue lowering with the remaining Munter. As a backup, attach a friction hitch to the brake strand and clip to your harness (not illustrated).

LEADER RESCUE OVERVIEW

Rescuing the leader is, not only complex and risky, but it also requires thorough knowledge of the aforementioned techniques. As with other self-rescue methods, don't attempt it for the first time on the fly. Practice it beforehand in a class and then later in a low-risk, controlled setting with a top-rope backup. The steps described below assume a scenario in which the pitch is fairly direct (without major traverses) and adequate rope is available for the descent. They also assume you have only one rope and have confirmed the reliability of the high piece anchoring the victim. (If you as rescuer have any misgivings about this piece, don't try ascending to the victim.) Here is a condensed overview of the procedure:

Step 1: Rearrange and reinforce your anchor to securely hold an upward force. (If you are on the first pitch, you may need to build an anchor with several upward-force components.) Escape the belay.

Step 2: Ascend to the victim. Since the rope strand will be anchored taut, preventing you from tying figure-eight backups, you will use a third friction hitch as your backup as you make upward progress. (*This ascent is hazardous, with potentially dire consequences should the leader's top piece fail.*)

Step 3: Reinforce the piece holding you and the leader to form a solid anchor. Attach the victim to this anchor with a load-releasing knot.

Step 4: Attach yourself to the anchor and descend back to the original anchor (using appropriate backups) and disassemble it.

Step 5: Reascend to victim, cleaning the pitch as you go.

Step 6: Lower the victim or perform an assisted rappel.

Because of the complexity and potential hazards of leader rescue, it's an advanced self-rescue skill. This brief introduction is meant to provide a general explanation of how it uses techniques described earlier in this chapter. May the description inspire you to learn this skill from an experienced mentor or professional.

Chapter 9

Knot Craft & Gear Tricks

KNOTS & HITCHES

Understanding the application of knots is as important as knowing how to tie them. Though basic guidelines exist, you have choices in many situations. You will have to choose the best knot for the task at hand. As with other climbing decisions, weigh the pros and cons before making your choice.

By paying close attention to your task and avoiding distractions, you can ensure the integrity of every knot you tie. Cinch each knot down tightly, tying it neatly so your partner can evaluate it easily from a distance. Whenever applicable, leave a minimum of a 4-inch (10.2-centimeter) tail. Tighten newly-tied permanent knots with extra gusto and monitor them closely. Use extra care with new ropes and webbing, which are prone to slippage.

Basic knots and hitches commonly used by trad climbers include a figure-eight follow-through, figure-eight on a bight, clove hitch, overhand on a bight, girth hitch, double fisherman's, ring bend, double bowline, and flat overhand.

Figure-Eight Follow-Through
(a.k.a. Rewoven Figure-Eight)

Since it's very strong and hard to untie, the figure-eight follow-through makes an ideal tie-in knot (and is the *only* tie-in knot I recommend for trad climbing). Allow approximately 8 inches (25.5 centimeters) to finish it with half of a double fisherman's knot. *(See photos 1–5, right and below.)*

Figure-Eight on a Bight

The strongest knot for clipping into the anchor is the figure-eight on a bight *(see photos 1–3 below)*; in this application, it's not adjustable and requires a significant amount of rope to tie. This knot can also be used to clip into the rope with a locking carabiner when you're leading in blocks (see "Leading in Blocks," p. 179).

Clove Hitch

The clove hitch *(see photos 1–2 below)* can also be used to clip into anchors. What it lacks in security as a hitch and strength (it's about 10 percent weaker than the figure-eight), it sometimes makes up for in static clip-ins because of its adjustability. When rope availability is an issue, it is also useful since it requires

To load

very little. For it to be effective, though, you must tighten each strand after creating the hitch, with the load strand in line with the carabiner spine. Otherwise its strength is compromised by up to 30 percent.

Overhand on a Bight

Although it provides slightly less strength than the figure-eight on a bight, the overhand on a bight *(see photo, right)* is another secure knot for tying into an anchor. It requires less rope than the figure-eight but more than the clove hitch. Once weighted, however, it is more difficult to untie than the figure-eight on a bight.

Overhand on a bight

Girth Hitch

The girth hitch *(see photos 1–3, right)* is best reserved for use in securing natural features, and   static tie-ins at anchors (e.g., attaching a cow's tail or daisy chain at rappel anchors). It's also been used without scrutiny for decades as the best way to join two runners when one is not long enough. Climbers are now, however, beginning to rethink their reliance on the hitch for this purpose based on the findings of 2006 strength-tests[13] prompted by reports of girthed runners breaking in the field. After reviewing results of his tests and comparing them to other unofficial tests, Black Diamond's Quality Assurance Manager and mechanical engineer Kolin Powick suggests climbers consider the following before girthing slings:

- Using a longer sling altogether is always preferable.

- If you must join two runners, using a carabiner is stronger.

- If you must join two slings via girthing, use (runners of) the same width and (made from) the same materials.

Powick also observed included that in general, the narrower the material of the runner used, the greater the reduction of strength. The highest strength values resulted when girthing two ¹¹⁄₁₆-inch nylon runners. Says Powick, "More testing is required in order to come to any firm conclusions."

Double Fisherman's (a.k.a. Grapevine)

The double fisherman's is one of the most common knots used to tie two ropes together for rappelling (*see photos 1-6, below*). Because of its bulky profile, use it on rappels where terrain is steep or overhanging. Because it is difficult to untie once weighted, it is also a good choice for tying permanent knots in cord and webbing (e.g., making runners and tying cordelettes). For tying together two ropes of different diameters or for extra security, add another wrap on each side to make a triple fisherman's.

Ring Bend (a.k.a. Water or Tape Knot)

The ring bend *(see photos 1–4, below)* is a good choice when tying together webbing that is a diameter of at least 1 inch (10 centimeters). Although particularly good for a permanent knot, the ring bend can be more easily loosened than the fisherman's knots when freshly tied, so monitor it carefully until the force of several loads has tightened it. One bonus is that the ring bend requires less material to tie than the double or triple fisherman's do. Also, because of its bulky profile, it wedges nicely into constricting cracks—if needed in a pinch for protection.

Double Bowline

The double bowline is sometimes the preferred tie-in knot for sport climbers because it unties easier than the figure-eight follow through. But, because it is so easily

Ring Bend

untied, it has resulted in several injuries and deaths. For this reason it is neither recommended nor illustrated in this text. It is, however, useful for anchoring the ends of ropes around trees or other natural features. For a description of how to create a double bowline, refer to Luebben's *Knots for Climbers*, which is listed in "Resources."

Flat Overhand

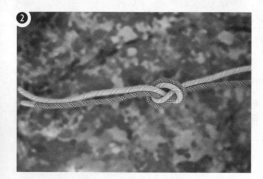

The flat overhand *(see photos 1 and 2, left)* is appropriate for joining ropes of similar diameter that are likely to receive low-load forces (as in rappelling). Although not as strong as the double fisherman's, this knot runs far more smoothly over rope-snagging terrain. Because of this feature, it has been popular in Europe for years, and is finally catching on in the U.S., where it was once unknowingly called the "death knot," seeming too simple for such a responsibility! For those still doubtful of the flat overhand's performance for connecting rappel ropes, tests conducted in the late 1990s found it safe and effective for tying similar-diameter rope and cord ends together, provided the person tying the knot allow an adequate tail on each end—enough to allow it to invert one time. The flat overhand is, however, difficult to untie once weighted.

IMPROVISATION TECHNIQUES

Trad adventures hold many surprises, requiring adaptability on the part of climbers. Although the "Keep it simple" adage often applies, enhancing your repertoire of tools and methods increases your ability to handle tricky scenarios. You'll have to improvise in situations where conventional gear and solutions are unavailable, but at other times it's comforting to have a choice. Prepare yourself to think on your toes with these simple alternatives that can come into play on lead, at the belay, or on rappel.

Carabiner Brake Rappel

The carabiner brake can provide a smooth rappel ride for climbers who have either forgotten or dropped their rappel device. While ovals are best suited for this configuration, standard Ds also work.

Attach two carabiners with the gates reversed and opposed (see "Carabiner Use," p. 93) to a locking 'biner that you clipped to your harness belay/rappel loop *(see photos 1–4, below)*. Next, feed two equal bights of the rappel line into these two carabiners so that the line leading to the anchor is at the top, and the line leading to the ground is at the bottom. Now take two additional 'biners and clip them perpendicular to the first two underneath the rope bights, gates reversed and facing down (away from you). This is crucial: Carabiners with gates facing up can unclip from the weight of the rope. If you want more friction (for a steeper rappel or when using a smaller diameter rope), add another 'biner.

Rope goes to anchor

Brakeline

Climber: **Dave Nettle**

Years Trad Free Climbing: **30**

Favorite Trad Climbing Area:
Sierra backcountry

Most Respected Trad Free
Climber: **Peter Croft**

Dave Nettle Collection

Advanced Techniques for Backcountry Efficiency

Efficiency is the most valuable skill you can learn as a trad climbing newcomer, especially on long rock routes in the backcountry. Efficiency is often translated as climbing fast and placing gear quickly. But these are skills that time will usually teach. For now, follow experienced leaders on backcountry routes and observe how belays are set up and rope is managed.

If you pay close attention to your backcountry mentors, you might also be fortunate enough to pick up a handful of key trad "tricks" that support efficiency, namely walking pro, back-cleaning, and simul-climbing. These are advanced and often risky techniques, but nonetheless essential if you have your sights set on climbing difficult backcountry routes fast and efficiently with a lean rack.

Walking Pro

When climbing a crack of the same size for a long distance, a light rack might dictate that you choose between a long runout or "walking" a single piece upward every few moves. Always try to situate yourself in the most solid stance possible before sliding the piece up. The obvious danger is that you place increasing distance between you and your last stationary piece, and if you fall while sliding your piece up, you could take a real screamer. Keep your eyes peeled for protection possibilities in surrounding features—be sure to sling these.

Back-Cleaning

Not as risky is back-cleaning a similar section with two pieces. Set the first one, climb slightly past it (but not so far that you can't reach it) then set your second piece. Once the rope is clipped, reach down and remove and unclip the first piece, move up and repeat. This technique is known as leap-frogging and employs the art of back-cleaning. Back-cleaning is also helpful on a long pitch when you need to conserve gear, or on a route that you know requires the exact piece of protection you placed previously on a difficult section higher up.

It pays to look ahead on pitches to see which pieces may be needed again. There is no need to back-clean if a piece won't be needed higher. Generally when I find an opportunity for a bomber Stopper placement, I'll set it and leave it for pro, back-cleaning more versatile cams for later. Back-cleaning is also a great way to reduce rope drag which is exactly that—a drag! If you ever get to a point where you must lower off a piece to back-clean several lower placements, lower to the last (furthest) piece first and clean on the way up. This keeps multiple pieces protecting your "top-rope" while you're fiddling around.

Simul-Climbing

Finally, simul-climbing is handy on terrain that is relatively easy for both leader and follower and allows rapid coverage of long stretches of your route. Begin with the usual belay-leader roles, and when the rope comes tight, the second begins climbing simultaneously, cleaning pieces along the way. Try your best to climb at a similar pace, and always keep at least three pieces of solid gear between partners. If your rope is longer than 165 feet (50 meters) or this practice is new to you, use more. Try not to let slack rope pile up between you, and be careful not to pull your partner off the rock by unnecessarily tightening the rope. Note that you need to take every precaution to not fall, so don't attempt this on difficult terrain, or when conditions prevent partners from communicating with one another. Simul-climbing inadvertently may be necessary when a leader is combining two pitches and needs more rope to reach a belay, or has accidentally passed a belay ledge and needs a few extra feet to reach a stance with adequate anchor options.

On easier ground when a team knows it will be simul-climbing for a distance, it's best for the second to shoulder coil half the rope then clip into the middle (with a locking carabiner). This eliminates rope drag, makes it easier to manage slack, and helps communication. A good trick is for the second to leave the rope in his belay device so that if the leader calls for a belay, the follower simply places a few pieces of gear, clips in, and resumes a safe and timely belay.

—Dave Nettle

Munter Belay

The Munter hitch *(see photos 1–3, left)* has numerous applications including use as a belay mechanism. Because the longest leader fall I have ever held was a 50-foot (16.6-meter) screamer that was halted by this simple hitch, I'm a big fan of the Munter belay. Use it on your harness to belay leaders or followers; or directly off the anchor to belay followers.

When you belay with a Munter, the hitch will shift (or "pop") from one side of the carabiner to the other, depending on whether you're feeding rope out or taking it in. To lock it, bring your brake line parallel with the strand leading to the climber.

A Munter belay directly off the anchor *(see photo, facing page, top)* is ideal for belaying the second when you are absolutely positive your anchor is bomber. Not only does this system provide a built-in directional to keep the weight off your waist when your partner falls, it also eliminates the need to escape the belay during self-rescue. Because of this, it is the preferred belay method for professional guides with seconding clients. Belaying with a Munter directly off the anchor is not appropriate when belaying a leader. Climbers new to gear placement should consider getting a few years experience building anchors before using this method. (Do not use friction belay devices to belay in this manner.)

Hip Belay

Using the body as friction for belaying was standard practice for decades before the introduction of today's belay devices. Virtually outmoded by modern technology, the hip belay remains practical when you do not have time to prepare a standard belay or lack gear. Keep in mind that it can be extremely dangerous; it's never recommended for belaying a leader.

Face the climber requiring the belay and take in any slack as you would before any other belay. Now wrap the rope around the backside of your lower torso, positioning your hands alongside each hip. The hand grasping the strand leading directly to the slack line is your brake hand (*see illustration, bottom right*). As your partner climbs, use the same rope-handling technique you use with your device to take in slack, without letting go with your brake hand. If a fall occurs, wrap the rope across your pelvis with your brake hand, creating as much friction as possible. Be careful how you position yourself between the climber and your anchor; if you are positioned improperly, the weight of the climber could cause the rope to "unwind." If this occurs, you will lose control of the rope and probably drop your partner. Use this belay method only on low-angle terrain with a solid stance or anchor, when you don't have the time or gear to belay with a device.

Munter belay off the masterpoint

Bowline on a Coil

Picture this: You're hiking to the base of a climb or walking off its summit, and the terrain briefly becomes technical and exposed for a short section (see "The Approach," p. 168, and "The Descent," p. 185). You wish you had a belay, but your harness is tucked away in the bottom of your pack. Forget the harness, tie directly into the rope with a bowline on a coil, and ask your partner to wedge him or herself between two rocks and give you a quick belay from above.

Wrap the end of the rope around your waist four times, leaving about an arm's length of slack as a tail.

Now take a bight of the line leading to the belayer and bring it up and under the coils level with your belly button. Give it a twist so that the line closest to your body leads down and out to the remainder of the rope. Now bend the loop down and over the four wrapped coils and push a small bight of the rope leading to the belayer up from underneath into the loop. Finally, take the short rope tail and slide it through this bight. Tighten by tugging firmly on the rope leading to the belayer. Use half a double fisherman's knot to tie the tail off around the coils. *(See illustrations 1–6, left and on facing page).* Climb on.

The bowline on a coil should only be used when you have no other immediate options and should be avoided by anyone leading. Before using this tie-in alternative, consider that a fall with enough force could break your ribs.

Rope-Equalized Anchoring

If you don't have your cordelette or Web-o-lette, it's possible to create an equalized anchor system using only the rope. Although this method *(shown on p. 230)* requires a lot of rope and is harder to escape from in a self-rescue scenario, it provides a valuable anchoring option without sacrificing equalization. Before using it, be sure your next pitch isn't a rope stretcher, requiring every available inch.

3 turns around body

Double-Rope Lead Technique

Leading with two ropes, which is more common in Great Britain and a few other countries than in the U.S., involves clipping alternate ropes into protection. The ropes used for this system are (confusingly) known as "half ropes;" while smaller in diameter, they are the same length as standard single ropes.

Double Figure-Eight Equalization

Tie a figure-eight on a bight with an extra-large loop of rope. Now feed the loop through the strands forming the top of the figure-eight to create three loops to equalize each of your three anchor components. (Use the three loops you created to clip into your pieces.)

Best reserved for expert leaders, double-rope lead-ing *(see illustration, right)* has both benefits and draw-backs (with many do's and don'ts, most of which are not described in this overview). It's most advantageous on an indirect route zigzagging its way up the rock. By alternately clipping each line, the leader experiences less rope drag and relies less on runners and slings. Always carrying two ropes can also benefit you during planned and unplanned descents. That extra rope can save the day when one gets stuck or dam-aged.

The major system draw-back relates to your alter-nately clipping each line into lead protection—at any one time you are trusting a single half rope alone. (Though you could clip both ropes, there are times when this is inad-visable.) Because carrying two lines increases the chance of confusion and rope tangles, it requires advanced rope-man-agement skills for both leader and belayer. Belaying with half ropes takes practice, and requires only certain tubes and plates advertised as such by manufacturers. Figure-eight devices are not an option. A belayer must master feeding out and taking in one rope at a time, while monitoring appro-priate tension or slack in both lines.

Half ropes are advertised as such by manufacturers, and should be purchased as a pair. Using two ropes of different diameters results in uneven wear and is dangerous.

Dave Nettle Collection

Chapter 10

Common Know-How

Becoming knowledgeable about climbing can take a considerable amount of time. This process happens over years, as climbers gain experience and learn all that the sport involves. At the very least, you should develop an understanding of ratings and etiquette early on. This is the foundation upon which all your more specialized knowledge will rest.

RATINGS

There are several free climbing rating systems in use today. Americans and Canadians rely on the Yosemite Decimal System, an elaboration of Class Ratings, which was developed by the Sierra Club in the 1930s.

Class Ratings

In Class Ratings, a class is assigned to terrain depending on its physical and technical difficulty. Because assessing difficulty tends to be fairly subjective, I've added risk factors and the consequences of an unroped fall to differentiate Classes 1–5.

Classes 1–6

Class 1—Hiking. Minimal risk.

Class 2—Simple scrambling on minimally exposed boulders and rocks, with the occasional need to use your hands for balance. Low risk.

Class 3—Moderate scrambling (with hands and feet) on rock in an often exposed environment. A rope should be considered for beginner climbers. An unroped fall could be fatal or result in serious injuries.

Class 4—Technical and exposed scrambling in which a rope should be considered, particularly for beginners. An unroped fall far from the ground would most likely be fatal.

Class 5—Technical climbing requiring a rope, belay, and equipment. An unroped fall far from the ground would be fatal.

Class 6—Direct-Aid Climbing.

Yosemite Decimal System

The Yosemite Decimal System (YDS) extends from the Class 5 rating, numbering from 5.1 to 5.15, with "a" and "b" (or "-") and "c" and "d" (or "+") increments for 5.10 and above. Objectively and in theory, the lower the number, the easier the route. But since, in reality, ratings are highly subjective, depending on physical differences (height, etc.) and terrain familiarity, each route will feel a little different to each climber. Because of this, ratings are not the final authority on route difficulty. Use them in combination with other analysis and research in determining which routes you're capable of climbing.

Guidebook authors aren't responsible for rating climbs; they simply collect and compile data from local resources. Routes are most often rated initially by first-ascent parties. Many parties encourage feedback from subsequent teams to develop a rating by group consensus. Although rare, some routes are later either down-rated or up-rated based on collective agreement, usually among local climbers. This is likely particularly if a key hold breaks, altering the climb's anatomy and therefore its difficulty level.

YDS ratings traditionally reflect the single most difficult move on a route or pitch. That means that a pitch with several 5.11 moves receives a 5.11 rating, while the same rating is given to a route with 165 feet of continuous 5.7 with only one 5.11 move. Obviously, climbing continuous 5.11 requires a stronger, more skilled climber than accomplishing one move of 5.11. Nevertheless, the ratings are the same. Yet, depending on the area, climbers should factor in other considerations when rating climbs. If a pitch is strenuous, sustained, or very exposed, it might receive one rating higher than its most difficult move.

Protection Severity Ratings

An additional rating system of G, PG, R, and X, which is becoming more common, indicates that protection is good, pretty good, seriously runout, or extremely runout with severe consequences, respectively. This system alerts climbers to protection issues that help them choose the appropriate climb not just for their physical abilities but also for their technical skill levels.

Grades

Multipitch rock routes are assigned a YDS rating (based on the most difficult pitch), as well as a grade. Grades were first used in the 1950s in Yosemite, and later codified under the National Climbing Classification System (NCCS). This system generally describes the length of a route, the time needed to ascend it, and the general technical difficulty—for an average experienced climber (assuming competence for the expected level of climbing).

Grades I–VI

I—A few pitches, requiring approximately 1–3 hours.

II—Several pitches, requiring roughly a half day.

III—Several pitches, requiring a full day.

IV—Several pitches of moderate climbing difficulty, requiring a full day.

V—Multiple pitches of moderate to advanced climbing, requiring 1–2 days. Can involve a bivouac, but may be done by experts in a day.

VI—Multiple pitches involving difficult climbing and requiring two or more days.

The grade system, clearly very subjective, can serve only as a general benchmark. Talented and fast free climbers are constantly challenging this system. For instance, The Nose on El Capitan, probably the world's most famous Grade VI, was first climbed in a total of 47 (nonconsecutive) days in 1957. Two years later, its first continuous ascent was completed in six days. Many climbers now complete The Nose in fewer than 24 hours; the record is a mere 2 hours and 48 minutes. Recently, a team climbed *two* Grade VI routes—the northwest face of Half Dome *and* The Nose—in a day. While these extremely talented athletes are no doubt exceptional, NCCS grades are becoming less meaningful in light of such endeavors.

Rating Translation & Style

When exploring a new style of climbing, people often assume that their capabilities in one style will transfer directly over. This happens frequently when sport climbers are breaking into traditional climbing, or when frontcountry trad climbers get on backcountry terrain. In the sport realm, a 5.9 rating is generally considered "easy." Some sport enthusiasts may have climbed a 5.9 on their first day at the crags and never again; their idea of "hard" is most likely 5.11 and above. Yet, for new trad climbers 5.9 is usually difficult. So difficult, in fact, that even a 5.11-capable sport-climbing specialist may experience a significant struggle on a 5.9 crack.

More often than not, rating differences are due to a climber's concentration on a particular climbing style. If a climber has basic crack technique wired, a 5.9 crack isn't going to challenge him or her as much as if he or she had focused largely on mastering the delicate and balanced moves required on steep, bolted faces. Because the mental and physical demands of sport climbing and trad climbing are quite different, those who enjoy both styles can take days—and sometimes weeks or months—to train muscles and mind to succeed at both styles.

Relying on ratings as your sole barometer of progress is a huge pitfall. There are many ways to improve that have little to do with the numbers game. For years I couldn't lead anything rated higher than 5.10a/b—a common plateau for many trad leaders. So I focused on doing as many climbs as I could within the 5.8–5.9 range, and doing them well. I had a lot of fun once I let go of my attachment to high numbers. After several years, I noticed a huge improvement in my overall intuition and comfort on the rock. I built anchors with proficiency and speed, and improved my rope-management skills tenfold. As a result, I became more comfortable on-sighting routes, ascending various rock types in new and different areas, climbing in the backcountry, and doing longer routes. When I felt capable of attempting climbs with higher ratings, my core experience had expanded such that I had a better chance of succeeding, and of succeeding safely. When you recognize that improvement often comes in small but significant increments, you'll no longer be a slave to ratings.

CLIMBING ETIQUETTE

The "my beach, my wave" philosophy of surfing is rarely tolerated in climbing. Most climbers welcome the opportunity to share their local crags with others, and in the process meet new people from different areas. Nevertheless, awkward moments occur when someone's personal space is encroached upon, or climbers new to the trad arena misunderstand local etiquette.

Common Cragging Courtesy

You'll easily resolve, if not completely avoid, possible conflicts at U.S. crags by adhering to these basic guidelines of climbing etiquette:

- Though some negotiations may occur, generally climbers who reach the base of a route before you have dibs on starting first. A team that gets up early and packs its gear the night beforehand usually is the first party at the base—and they've earned the right to start the route.

- If you find yourself behind a slow team on a long route and are considering passing them, obtain their consent first, and then pass at an appropriate location like a belay with a large stance. Be absolutely certain your team will move quickly enough to stay ahead of them. If they refuse to allow a pass, accept their prerogative. Get up earlier next time.

- On crowded multipitch routes, wait for the follower of the team ahead to reach the next belay stance before you start leading that same pitch. This courtesy prevents crowding at small belay ledges.

- When top-roping several climbs side-by-side at popular locales, consider that other climbers may wish to lead those climbs. Avoid tying up many routes at one time and, when your group has finished, remove your ropes as soon as possible. If one of the climbs you've set up isn't in use and other climbers indicate a desire to lead it, move your rope aside to allow them to pass.

- Don't top-rope off rappel rings. This creates unnecessary wear and tear. Use your gear to create your own anchor and reserve the rings for their intended uses—lowering or rappelling.

- Never clip into any protection or anchors already in use without permission.

- Don't throw your rope near someone who is climbing without ample warning, especially if he or she is leading.

Leave No Trace

Future use of many climbing areas depends largely on how well climbers practice minimum-impact principles. Although generally an environmentally conscious group, climbers can be careless, lazy, and sometimes uninformed. Besides being a great ethical concept, Leave No Trace (LNT) is a national program devoted to educating outdoor enthusiasts on these principles. Begun as a government program, LNT was run for awhile by the National Outdoor Leadership School (NOLS), and is now is an independent nonprofit organization based in Boulder, Colorado. LNT hopes to change behavior through education, basing their guidelines on "abiding respect for and appreciation of wild and unique places and their inhabitants." Many suggestions in this section derive from LNT guidelines.

Inappropriate disposal of human waste, litter, and erosion are the three major ways climbers impact the environment. Cutting established trails in haste creates erosion. In populated regions, follow the most obvious trail up to the base of crags as well as when descending. When traversing where no trails exist, spread your party out on stable ground to avoid creating new paths. Avoid fragile areas like meadows, steep hillsides, and the delicate black cryptogam you encounter in desert regions. Respect flora at the base of routes by not removing or trimming bushes or plants.

Camp in existing sites (if possible) at least 200 feet from water. Resist the temptation to "improve" a campsite by moving natural features, and don't dig drainage ditches around your tent. Build fires, where allowed, only in established fire rings. Burn wood from home, or collect small dead pieces from the ground well away from trails and camp to diffuse your impact. Don't make fires in fragile alpine regions, or directly at rock bases, where they leave scars lasting decades. If you're going to sleep at the base of a route, don't build a fire.

An unplanned bivy in cold nighttime temperatures may dictate a fire for comfort or survival. In this case, build a fire ring in dirt or sand, away from dry leaves or timber. Dispose of ash when cold by dispersing it widely. Deconstruct the ring and return the site to its original state.

Energy bar wrappers, climbing tape, spilled chalk, cigarette butts, toilet paper, and feces are all evidence of careless climbers. Although most climbers pack out bulky food wrappers, they're often careless with wrapper corners and gel packets torn off and tossed (with great intention) into packs and pockets. Yet, when a jacket or topo is hastily retrieved, trash can fall out as well. I keep a small resealable plastic bag on hand to contain my trash within my pack.

And then there are land mines—piles of feces coiled carelessly behind a bush or a crag, when the pressure of leading hits us in the gut and we gotta go. Bury human feces at least 6 inches (15 centimeters) below ground 200 feet (60 meters) from trails, campsites, water sources, and drainage areas. Because this may not be possible in alpine environments, find a sunny location and smear feces in thin layers on a rock. However gross and unsanitary, it dries quickly and disintegrates. For sanitizing your hands afterward carry antibacterial handy-wipes, which reduce the risk of passing fecal-borne bacteria to your partner. Pack your toilet paper out, or, better yet, use natural objects such as rocks, leaves, or sticks for wiping.

Should you need to urinate mid-climb, avoid the wall and pee off into space—in a direction other than where climbers will likely approach from below! Recently a friend returned from climbing the crowded Nose route on El Capitan. As she was leading, she felt a few droplets of moisture, which she thought oddly must be rain, but it was a stellar bluebird day. When she glanced up and realized it was urine, she was horrified. A climber on a ledge above her had urinated while waiting his turn for the next pitch. Hearing her story temporarily curbed my interest in that climb. If on a ledge, always urinate (or defecate) as far from the most obvious belay location as possible. In remote areas, find a flat rock, deposit your feces upon it, and toss it off the route. Never do this, however, if there is the slightest chance you could clobber a climber or hiker below.

Access

Though access to climbing areas is always threatened, thanks to a few nonprofit climbing organizations, climbers have the representation of a group of dedicated individuals working throughout the U.S. for continued access. These groups help reduce climber impact by organizing crag-cleanup days, cosponsoring outhouse installation in high-use areas, and organizing trail-building efforts. They also employ active lobbyists and lawyers to fight legal-access encroachments.

Most access issues involve conflicts with private or public land managers and owners and are often related to perceived climber impact. Although pro-access organizations generally have the environment's best interests in mind, their often uncompromising approach has driven a wedge between some environmental groups and the climbing community. In fact, some conservationists have begun viewing climbing as just another extractive recreation industry, lumping climbers in the same category as, say, snowmobile users. The voice of climbers has sometimes been heard as shouting, *We want to climb where we want, when we want, and how we want.* This is a distressing image, especially for climbers with steadfast conservation principles.

All climbers benefit from negotiations and compromises with environmental groups more than through hard-line opposition. If you're a climber who supports access but also wants environmental values to be fairly represented, join various access organizations and let your voice be heard. Follow the issues and stay informed by getting the facts from both sides. Avoid knee-jerk reactions and take thoughtful stances based on your own principles. When you become aware of issues affecting the backcountry, climbing, or your favorite climbing areas, write your representative and senators; urge your friends and climbing partners to do the same. In addition, support legislative moves to obtain more national recreation land and preserve existing areas.

Afterword

Congratulations. Your journey into traditional lead climbing is well underway with this book's concepts fresh in your mind. Your every effort has one primary purpose: to refine your skills through pure repetition. The nature of trad climbing does not allow you to think your way toward excellence; proficiency grows through logging in hundreds of hours on the rocks. While the concept of "stimulating repetition" might seem an oxymoron outside the sphere of trad climbing, that's just not so on the sharp end as gear-leader. I guarantee no two experiences will ever be the same.

In this book, you've learned about the specific equipment, skills, and techniques that make trad leading a unique experience, rich in adventure and vastly different from other free climbing styles. The overview of specific tools in this book gives you enough facts to make informed choices when you purchase the arsenal of gear you'll need to cope safely with the technical demands on trad terrain. You may be broke after your initial spree, but the experiences ahead come at no significant financial cost.

I hope you have begun your new relationship with trad leading in low-risk settings that allow for a wide margin of error. If you familiarize yourself with your gear's unique capabilities by creating anchor systems under the watchful eye of a seasoned guide on the ground, you'll enjoy a huge pay off once you're on your own and climbing with partners who have entrusted you with their lives. When your gear placement and anchors get a thumbs up from your mentor, the safety net of a top-rope will let you further employ these new skills with movement and additional technical tasks without the worry of making a fatal error. Work out the kinks on top-rope; when you're ready to move on, you'll benefit not only from your technical know-how, but will be more confident.

When you're ready to venture onto easy trad ground sans a top-rope, you'll be primed for learning more technical tasks that are essential to safe and enjoyable leading. Then the stakes are higher: The keys to survival are a smart route and good partner choices, as well as careful attention to detail. If you push your limits safely and sanely, you will cultivate improved ability and technical prowess that will allow you access to the crown jewel of traditional leading: the multipitch adventure. At that point, even more techniques will be introduced, and once again, you will need that all-important careful attention to detail. By that time, your anchoring and protection placement skills will have become intuitive, and you won't struggle as much with the climbing itself. But then the stakes are raised yet another notch forcing you to consider that the higher you climb, the more responsibility you have. Back-up plans are critical, as are basic self-rescue skills. As climbers we don't rely on outside rescue services to save our butts, and we don't sue land managers for mishaps.

Eventually you'll find yourself leading trad routes several pitches from the ground in magnificent settings marveling at having finally achieved the expertise that got you this far. Your elation can fuel plans for bigger, harder, and faster ascents. There's still plenty to learn, from etiquette to improvisation techniques, as well as more advanced skills not covered in this book. Take advantage of every possible chance to continue learning from more skilled climbers, and keep in mind there's rarely only one way to accomplish any technical task. This book provides bare bones knowledge for trad adventures; there's a lot more for you to learn.

Your positive and humble attitude will help you find great partners, learning opportunities, and overall safety and enjoyment. Humility is key—arrogance places a tremendous burden on any climber, especially the new leader. If you're confident, that's great. If you let that confidence slip into arrogance, though, people will expect far more from you than you can deliver as a beginner. Strive for excellence with your ego in check and learn to accept foibles as positive growth opportunities. Every person and every experience teaches you something of value.

Finally, don't give up your other climbing interests in pursuit of the ultimate trad experience. The real beauty of trad climbing is that it incorporates all other styles of climbing. Variety is not only enjoyable but it prevents burnout and is beneficial to your technique. The best trad climbers I know divide their time away from trad stone between bouldering, hard top-roping, sport cragging, aid climbing, and even ice climbing in the winter. Don't miss out on the opportunities to venture away from your home crags and climb on different rock at varied areas; visiting new areas keeps your experience fresh and hones your ability to adapt to different rock, ratings, and conditions. Climb on . . .

Appendix 1

The Clean Climbing Revolution

The Clean Climbing Revolution accomplished two major events in rock-climbing history. It raised consciousness among free climbers about the nonrenewable resource of rock and provided a solution that inadvertently led to some of the sport's most important technological advances. Hammerless protection evolved quickly in the U.S. in 1967 after Royal Robbins returned from a climbing trip to Britain where he'd observed climbers using pebbles as removable lead protection. Back in Yosemite, Robbins and his wife, Liz, completed the famed Nutcracker in what was quite possibly the first, clean first ascent in the country. Shortly thereafter, Robbins wrote a short piece on his experience for *Summit* that inspired his peers to pursue clean climbing.

Climbers began experimenting with the use of common machine nuts for protection, and soon it became possible to order limited removable protection from overseas. In 1971, Doug Robinson completed the first clean Grade IV in Yosemite Valley (East Buttress of Middle Cathedral) with partner Jay Jensen. During this time, Robinson and fellow climbers Tom Frost and Yvon Chouinard began tinkering with design ideas for additional removable-protection options, eventually leading to the production of Chouinard's Hexcentrics and Stoppers. In 1972, these items were offered in the first official Chouinard Equipment Company (since sold and renamed Black Diamond) catalog, along with Robinson's essay "The Whole Natural Art of Climbing Protection," one of the most noted, quoted, reprinted, and influential pieces of climbing literature. "Within months of the article's publication, everyone seemed to be climbing clean," says Robinson. The first paragraph captures the essence of his message:

There is a word for it, and that word is clean. Climbing with only nuts and runners for protection is clean climbing. Clean because the rock is left unaltered by the passing climber. Clean because nothing is hammered into the rock and then hammered back out, leaving the rock scarred and the next climber's experience less natural. Clean because the climber's protection leaves little trace of his ascension. Clean is climbing the rock without changing it, a step closer to organic climbing for the natural man.[14]

Robinson eventually created the tube chock, a large cylindrical device for protecting off-widths. The Lowe Tri-Cam was developed and commercially distributed in the mid-1970s, followed by Yosemite climber Ray Jardine's revolutionary invention in 1978 of the "Friend," the first spring-loaded camming device (SLCD). By the late 1970s, these new options, all relatively lightweight and easy to place, virtually eliminated the average climber's need or desire to use pitons, especially on free routes.

Appendix 2

Lead Ascent Styles

Numerous lead ascent styles exist today, each requiring a certain level of technical assistance. Used in both trad free climbing and sport climbing, these styles include:

- **On-Sight Flash:** This most impressive and bold lead involves a first-time, no-falls ascent by a climber who has neither received any details (beta) regarding the route nor watched another climber ascend it. This ascent style also requires that the leader place all his or her protection on lead (rather than pre-placing it on rappel).

- **Head Point:** A style that originated in Britain and common on bold, runout routes, a head-point ascent is when the leader rehearses the route on top-rope, and leads the route when ready, placing sparse protection from the ground up, hopefully summiting without a fall.

- **Flash:** This ascent denotes leading a route for the first time, placing all protection on lead, and succeeding with no falls or hangs. On a flash ascent, though, the leader may have received previous beta or viewed another leader on the route.

- **Red-point:** In this ascent, the climber works a route by taking frequent tension from the belayer, hanging on the rope, and resting between difficult sections. Once each section is mastered, the climber attempts to lead it from ground to top in one push without falling or hanging. A climber might achieve a red-point after working a route in an afternoon, or years later.

- **Pink Point:** Otherwise similar to the red-point, this ascent style allows the pre-placement of lead protection on rappel.

Appendix 3

Developments Before Sport Climbing

Almost a decade before the advent of sport climbing, worldwide free-climbing styles, particularly in Europe, suggested a change was coming. French climbers were establishing bolted routes via rappel in the Verdon Gorge (in the Provence region of France) in the late 1970s and very early 1980s. Their lack of hesitance to use protection to gain upward purchase on free climbs spawned the term "French-free." Around the same time, climbers Tony Yaniro and Ray Jardine were incorporating rehearsal methods, pre-placed gear, and hang-dogging (resting on gear between difficult moves) into their tactics to establish America's first 5.13s. In Germany, climbers were using similar rehearsal methods for no-fall/hang attempts on the extremely difficult, limestone walls of the Frankenjura (in southeastern Germany). Once a climb had been led in the Frankenjura without falls or hangs, a red dot was painted at the base of each route—hence the term *red-point*.

Appendix 4

The Fixed-Line & Drilled-Bolt Controversy

Between the late 1950s and early 1970s, first-ascent tactics on some of the most renowned Yosemite walls came under fire by a faction of climbers. The controversy focused on two issues: a team's reliance upon fixed lines and excessive use of drilled bolts. Fixed ropes allowed teams to linger on routes for months—even years—letting team members periodically retreat to the Valley floor for supplies, rest, and food. Different partners often rotated in and out of each team, and entire seasons sometimes passed with little or no route progress. What came to be known as siege climbing was then termed by Climber Warren Harding an "expedition-style mentality."

The seemingly high number of bolts placed on some first ascents was also criticized. Bolts provided instant protection and aid points on blank walls, allowing passage up sections that some believed should have been left blank and either unclimbed or climbed by some other means. Most controversial of such ascents was Harding's route up the West Face of the Leaning Tower in 1961, and his establishment of the Dawn Wall (a.k.a. The Wall of Early Morning Light) on El Capitan in 1970. Harding's Leaning Tower ascent involved 111 bolts placed on the 800-foot wall during 18 days over five months; the Dawn Wall had more than 300 holes drilled (some for bolts, others for hooks) during 27 continuous days on 2800 feet of rock. Although Harding and his partner Dean Caldwell didn't use siege tactics on the Dawn Wall, they did place an enormous number of bolts.

Royal Robbins was among those offended by Harding's techniques during this period. The following passage from Pat Ament's *Spirit of the Age*, a 1992 biography of Robbins, best illustrates his view of such tactics: "Given enough bolts and time, any rock of any size and difficulty could be climbed."

Robbins thought that to have the certitude of bolts, and to string fixed ropes from the bottom of the wall to its top, diminished the adventure.

Though Robbins initially denounced Harding's infamous siege and bolting tactics, it later seemed that he had something of a change of heart. On the first ascent of the Salathé Wall on El Capitan in 1961, his team used fixed lines on the lower third of the route (a trend still popular today). Nine years later he set out to remove bolts placed on what he called the "contrived and artificial" Dawn Wall route, on its second ascent. Finding the climb far more technically challenging than he'd anticipated, he and his partner Don Lauria stopped chopping after the first four pitches. Later Robbins admitted he was surprisingly impressed with the route—that it featured some of the hardest nailing he'd ever done. He also acknowledged being wrong in his desire to "erase" the route, calling his initial plan to do so a mistake. Said Robbins after the ascent:

> *Although this climb may not have been done exactly to our taste, and although we might have fretful little criticisms that envy always produces, we can better spend our energy in ways other than ripping and tearing, or denigrating the accomplishments of others . . .*

Glossary

acute mountain sickness (AMS): A non-life-threatening condition occurring as low as 4000 feet (1250 meters) and resulting from the body's adverse physiological reaction to an increase in altitude and barometric pressure, usually relieved by rest, light exercise, and hydration.

alpine climbing: Climbing in a high-altitude mountain environment involving the ascent of snow, ice, and rock. Sometimes referred to as mountaineering.

alpine start: A predawn or early morning commencement of a climbing adventure.

anchor: A configuration of protection points to which climbers connect themselves with the rope for the purpose of belaying, rappelling, or top-roping.

artificial climbing: *See* direct-aid climbing.

ascenders: Mechanical devices used to ascend a fixed rope. *See* Jumars.

autoblock: One of several friction hitches that grip the rope when tightened and weighted. Also known as the French Prusik.

Bachman: A type of friction hitch rigged onto a carabiner. Like other friction hitches, the Bachman possesses gripping qualities that allow it to lock onto a rope when the hitch is tightened and weighted.

back-clip: Erroneous clipping of the lead rope into a quickdraw carabiner so that if a fall were to occur the rope could open the gate of the carabiner and unclip itself.

back off: The act of retreating from a route.

backcountry: Remote site, usually in a wilderness setting, far from civilization.

backward zipper: During a lead fall, failure of several consecutive pieces of protection, closest to belayer beginning with the first piece and shifting to the next highest piece and so on.

bar tack: Rows of zigzags sewn by industrial machines to permanently join webbing together. Most commonly seen on sewn runners (slings).

belay: A backup safety system comprised of a rope, belayer, anchor, and belay device/method that allows a climber's fall to be halted. To belay is to manage such a system.

belay device: Device through which a climber's rope is threaded for the purpose of halting the rope by means of friction during a climber's fall.

belay escape: Initial self-rescue task requiring the tying off of a loaded rope leading to the victim so that the rescuer's hands are free, followed by a complete transfer of the load from rescuer to anchor if necessary. Once the escape is complete, the rescuer is free to conduct ensuing rescue activities.

belay plate: Friction belay/rappel device with a flat metal plate and an oblong hole.

belay stance (belay station): Anchor location.

belay tube: Tube-shaped belay/rappel device that relies on friction for braking.

belayer: The belay management role within a roped climbing partnership.

bergschrund: A large crevasse at the highest point of glacial activity,

usually creating a formidable gap between the final approach and the base area of some alpine routes.

beta: Detailed route information regarding gear specifics, navigation, and/or movement sequences.

Big Bro: A spring-loaded, tube-shaped device used to protect wide cracks.

big wall: A Grade VI route in which the majority of climbing involves direct-aid.

bight: A loop, or fold, of rope formed anywhere, of any size, between the rope's two ends.

bivouac (bivy): A night spent outdoors with minimal or no camping gear, sometimes unplanned.

bolt: A nail-like metal unit placed in a predrilled hole, usually by first-ascent parties, for use as a fixed protection point or anchor component. A permanent hanger, either preaffixed or attached with a threaded nut, provides a clip-in point. Modern bolts are either secured into place by an expanding sleeve, or glue.

bomber: Completely secure and safe without question. From the term "bomb-proof."

bowline on a coil: A knot configuration that allows a nonharnessed climber to tie into the end of a rope.

carabiner: An aluminum alloy snap link with a spring-loaded gate used to connect various equipment components in a roped climbing ascent. Commonly known as a 'biner.

carabiner brake: Several carabiners clipped to a climber's harness assembled to create friction with threaded rope strand(s) for use as a rappel device.

chalk bag: Small cylindrical nylon container worn around a climber's waist to carry gymnast's chalk.

changeover: The process of gear exchange between the follower and the lead climber occurring at belay stations on multipitch routes.

chicken head: A narrow-necked rock protuberance with a broad, rounded head.

chock: *See* Stopper.

chockstone: A rock ranging in size from a pebble to a boulder and wedged in a crack or chimney.

class: A rating system of 1–5 developed by the Sierra Club that reflects terrain difficulty ranging from walking on a trail (1) to technical rock climbing requiring a rope and belay (5).

clean lead ascent: A type of lead ascent in which no pitons are hammered into the rock for protection.

cleaning: The act of removing protection.

clove hitch: An adjustable hitch used for several purposes in climbing, most commonly to secure a rope into an anchor.

cold-shuts: Soft metal hooklike hardware units, sometimes hammered shut, pre-placed on the top of single-pitch routes and used for lowering climbers. Found mostly on sport climbs.

Comité European d'Normalisation (CEN): A European legislative body that oversees standards for climbing equipment used in industrial settings, which is also used by recreational climbers.

cordelette: An 18–25 foot (5–8 meter) loop of accessory cord used for self-rescue applications and to create SERENE anchors.

counterweight rappel: An assisted rappel method used in self-rescue efforts in which the victim, tied to the end of the rope strand opposite the anchor from the rescuer, is lowered by the rescuer who manages the rappel device and simultaneously lowers him or herself.

cow's tail: A runner girth-hitched to a climber's harness and used as an anchor leash at rappel stations.

crack: A rock crevice or fissure.

crack system: A series of continuous sections of cracks leading up a rock face.

crevasse: A deep and usually narrow ice fissure found on glacial terrain, often camouflaged by a layer of snow or ice.

crux: The single most difficult move or series of moves on a route.

daisy chain: An arm's length (approximately) strand of sewn webbing loops designed for use as an adjustable anchor leash in static load situations. Also used as an invaluable tool for aid climbers.

dihedral: Corner.

direct-aid climbing: A method of ascent used commonly on big walls in which climbers directly weight protection to obtain purchase for upward progress. Also known as aid or artificial climbing.

double fisherman's knot: Knot commonly used to join the ends of rope, webbing, or cord. Also known as the grapevine knot.

double-rope leading: Rope technique involving the use of two ropes that can be clipped alternately to lead protection to prevent rope drag. Especially advantageous on meandering routes.

dynamic belay: Force-reducing technique in which the belayer deliberately allows slippage of a small amount of rope through the belay device during a lead fall.

epic: Common term for a climbing incident that evolves into a time-consuming, and sometimes dangerous episode.

escape route: An alternate course of travel allowing climbers to retreat or take a detour from their originally intended route with relative ease.

étrier: A webbing "ladder" with several loops used as rungs to stand in during aid-climbing ascents.

face: A relatively unbroken, featureless rock wall void of cracks. Also, a general term for a large expanse of rock.

fall factor: Fall severity rating determined by the length of the fall and the amount of rope in use at the time of the fall.

figure-eight belay devices: Friction rappel device with two joined metal rings, one larger than the other.

figure-eight follow-through: One of the most common knots used to tie the rope into a harness. Also known as the rewoven figure-eight.

figure-eight on a bight: Knot predominantly used for clipping into an anchor.

fixed gear: Pre-placed, nonremovable gear usually left deliberately for other climbers to use. Includes (but is not limited to) bolts and pitons.

flat overhand: Knot used to join the ends of two ropes of the same diameter in rappel scenarios in which a low-profile knot is advantageous.

follow: The act of climbing after the leader has ascended. May require the cleaning (removal) of protection. Also known as seconding.

follower: The role in a climbing partnership of the climber who follows a route. May require the cleaning (removal) of protection. Also known as the second.

free climbing: Unassisted roped climbing in which climbers rely solely upon their own strength to ascend.

free soloing: Climbing without a rope and protection.

French free: Term used to describe lead tactics on free climbs in which protection is overtly weighted and used as hand- or footholds to assist in making upward progress.

French Prusik: *See* autoblock.

gear sling: A padded loop of webbing designed for carrying climbing hardware, worn over one shoulder and diagonally across the chest.

girth hitch: A simple hitch used to connect two loops of webbing or cord. Also used to secure natural anchor features.

grade: A general route rating that loosely reflects a climb's length and technical difficulty.

grapevine knot: *See* double fisherman's knot.

GriGri: Trade name of a belay device that relies on a spring-loaded cam that grips the rope for automatic braking. Popularized at indoor climbing gyms and outdoor sport climbing settings.

ground-up: An ascent style in which climbers place all gear on lead opposed to establishing pre-placed protection points via rappelling from above. Used primarily to describe first-ascents.

hang-dogging: Resting on gear between difficult moves or using passive gear to assist upward progress on free climbs.

hanging belay: A belay station void of any stances or ledges.

haul loop: A small sewn loop on a harness, pack, or other object used for clipping into a rope with a carabiner.

Hexcentric: Trade name for a hexagonal-shaped passive protection device designed to either wedge or cam into a crack. Known commonly as a Hex and manufactured by Black Diamond.

high-altitude cerebral edema (HACE): A serious, life-threatening form of altitude illness resulting from the body's adverse reaction to an increase in altitude and barometric pressure in which fluid collects around the victim's cerebrum (brain). Occurring at altitudes as low as 8000 feet (2500 meters) but more common at much higher altitudes, HACE treatment requires immediate descent.

high-altitude pulmonary edema (HAPE): A serious, life-threatening form of altitude illness resulting from an increase in barometric pressure in which fluid seeps out of pulmonary capillaries and begins to fill the alveolar spaces in the lungs. Occurring at altitudes of 8000 feet (2500 meters) and above, HAPE treatment requires immediate descent.

hip belay: An old-school belay method used prior to belay devices that relies upon friction created by wrapping the rope around the hips or buttocks for braking.

hueco: A rounded, concave rock feature varying in sizes. Spanish for "hole."

ice climbing: An aspect of alpine climbing (mountaineering) involving the ascent of terrain consisting primarily of ice using crampons and ice axes.

impact force: The actual force on a rope generated by a fall and determined primarily by fall factor and the falling climber's weight but also affected by varying degrees of friction within the system.

impact impulse: During a fall, the length of time over which energy is generated and dissipated throughout the components of a roped climbing system. The longer the fall, the greater the impulse impact.

jamming: The insertion and downward torque of a hand, finger, foot, or toe for the purpose of obtaining purchase in a crack.

Jumars: Trade name for a specific brand of mechanical ascending devices. *See also* ascenders.

Klemheist: Friction hitch with gripping qualities that allows it to lock onto a rope when tightened and weighted. From the German word *Klemme*, meaning "to clamp or jam."

leading/leader: A method of ascent in which a roped climber (the leader) moves up the rock while occasionally placing protection (hardware) or securing fixed gear into which the rope, payed out by a belayer from below, is clipped enroute to an anchor location above, no further than the length of the rope.

load-limiter: Any force-absorbing component of a roped climbing system used to reduce fall forces on equipment. *See also* Yates' Screamer.

locker: A carabiner with a locking gate.

manky: Old, deteriorating, unreliable, unstable, sketchy, and/or unsafe.

mantle: A movement technique for surmounting features lacking positive, incut handholds.

masterpoint: The final, primary link of an anchor where all individual anchor components are joined. The location on a multicomponent anchor where climbers either thread the rope for rappelling or top-roping, or clip into at belays.

mountaineering: *See* alpine climbing.

mule knot: Knot commonly used in self-rescue scenarios to tie off a loaded rope or cord.

multipitch: Description of a climbing route longer than the length of one rope, requiring multiple belays.

Munter belay: A Munter hitch used in combination with a locking carabiner as a substitute belay device.

Munter mule knot: A knot combination consisting of a Munter hitch locked off with a mule knot, commonly used in self-rescue scenarios because it can be easily released under load.

nut: *See* Stopper.

nut tool: Narrow metal pick used to extract Stoppers (nuts). Also known as a "nut key" or "cleaning tool."

off-route: A climbing team's unintentional detour from their originally desired course of travel.

off-width: A crack too large for a fist or cupped-hand jam but too small to enter and climb as a chimney.

on-sighting: Lead ascent in which the leader, having never climbed or viewed the climb before, ascends without the aid of beta.

oppositional placement: Two pieces of protection set to withstand a force from opposing directions, linked together tautly with a clove-hitched runner. Used commonly in vertical cracks when both downward and lateral forces are possible.

overhand on a bight: Multipurpose knot mostly used as a substitution for the figure-eight on a bight although it is slightly inferior in security.

pendulum: A lateral, swinging roped fall. Also, an aid-climbing technique used to swing laterally on an anchored rope to move from one crack system to another.

pitch: The distance between two belays not to exceed (usually) the length of the rope.

piton: A heavy metal peg hammered into cracks and crevices for use as lead protection or an anchor component. Most commonly used today on big walls but also found fixed on some free climbs, many of which at one time were aid routes. Also referred to as a "pin."

primary link: A key link in any climbing system that, without intentionally created redundancy, has no back-up. Two examples include the masterpoint of an anchor, and the carabiner linking a climber's harness to his or her belay/rappel device.

protection: General term referring to a piece of climbing hardware or a runnered natural feature (rock, tree, etc.) used as a component of an anchor, or intermittently for security by lead climbers. Free-climbing protection is either fixed (bolts) or removable (SLCDs, Stoppers, Hexes, etc.) Pitons are removable but are sometimes permanent. Also known as "pro."

Prusik: Friction hitch with gripping qualities that allow it to lock onto a rope when tightened and weighted.

quickdraws: Short versions of runners (slings), sewn or folded into lengths generally ranging from 3 to 12 inches (7.5 to 30 centimeters). Originally a trade name but now used commonly to refer to such runners.

rack: A wide assortment of climbing protection, runners, and carabiners used for creating anchors and setting protection on lead. Organized on the leader's waist attached to harness gear loops or, more often, on a gear sling worn over one shoulder and diagonally across the chest.

rap-bolting: A first-ascent method involving the placement of bolts

as protection points via rappeling from above.

rappel: Self-controlled descent of a rope that allows a climber to lower his or her body by feeding rope through a small friction device connected to his or her harness. Commonly referred to as an "abseil" outside the U.S. Prior to devices, climbers relied upon the classic Dulfersitz rappel method: Friction was achieved by wrapping the rope around one thigh, up across the chest, and down across the back. Painful, insecure, but nevertheless effective.

rappel device: A metal device that creates friction enabling climbers to descend a fixed rope by lowering themselves. Common examples include tube, plate, and figure-eight devices.

rappel ring: An aluminum alloy ring usually found on rappel anchors and used as the masterpoint through which the rope is threaded.

rappel station: An established anchor site used for rappeling.

red-point: Final unassisted lead ascent of a route tried previously by a climber who fell or hung. Often completed after extensive preparation and rehearsal.

ring bend: A knot commonly used to join the ends of webbing or utility cord. Also known as the tape knot or water knot.

rope drag: Rope tension felt by a lead climber usually created by inadequate runnering that prevents the rope from running plumb between leader and belayer.

run it out: The placing of very little lead gear, either by choice, or as dictated by the absence of protection options.

runner: A multipurpose loop of webbing, tied or sewn together, used in numerous applications to link two system components together and/or extend the distance between them. Alternately referred to as a sling. Also, the act of using a runner by a lead climber to reduce rope drag and torque on a protection point: "Be sure to runner (sling) the piece of protection you place under the roof."

runout: Used to describe a leading scenario in which the distance between two pieces of protection is relatively far. Also used to describe a route or section of a route with few protection opportunities.

sandbag: A route that is more difficult than its given rating. Also, the act of suggesting a route is easier than it actually is as in: "She sandbagged me by recommending that route!"

second: The role in a climbing partnership of the climber who ascends after the leader. May require the cleaning (removal) of protection. Also known as the follower.

secondary link: Any redundant link in a climbing system.

seracs: Towers and blocks of ice in an ice fall posing potential hazards for the alpine climber.

SERENE: Common mnemonic used to remember five key elements of a good anchor: S=Safe/Secure; E=Equalized; R=Redundant; E=Easy; NE=No Extension.

sew it up: To place an abundance of lead protection.

shake out: To pause deliberately while climbing to shake arms in a downward fashion, usually one at a time, to achieve increased blood flow to overexerted muscles.

sharp end: Literally, the end of the rope a leader ties in to. Generally, a slang term used to describe the role and responsibilities of a lead climber. For example: "On the second pitch, she had no choice but to take the sharp end when her partner became ill."

shelf: On a pre-equalized cordelette anchor, an alternate clip-in site located directly above the masterpoint knot, incorporating one strand from each protection component.

shock-load: Sudden, direct loading of a piece of protection usually resulting from failure of another piece of equipment.

SLCD: *See* spring-loaded camming device.

sling: *See* runner.

slingshot: *See* top-roping.

smearing: Climbing technique in which the ball and toes of the foot are placed flat against a rock wall as the climber simultaneously stands and weights the foot in an effort to create maximum friction to allow a temporary stance.

splitter: A smooth, parallel-sided crack, usually of significant length.

sport climbing: Widely used to describe free climbing on bolted routes, in which gear placement is secondary to the primary focus of executing difficult moves. Most sport climbs ascend rock faces void of removable protection opportunities and are protected generously by bolts placed by first-ascent parties usually via rappel.

spring-loaded camming device (SLCD): A removable, spring-loaded device used for protection and anchoring. The SLCD, or camming device, has either three or four individual cam components that can be retracted by a trigger to fit into cracks within its size range.

stemming: Climbing technique involving the use of the feet to create opposing force between two distant footholds or walls.

Stopper: A trade name for a metal wedging unit with tapered sides designed to slot into cracks and crevices for use as removable protection. Stoppers are referred to as passive protection because they have no movable parts. Also known as nuts, chocks, and tapers.

tandem rappel: Assisted rappel used in self-rescue efforts in which two climbers are attached with slings of different lengths to one rappel device, but only the lower individual has control of the brake line.

tape knot: *See* ring bend.

taper: *See* Stopper.

tensile strength: The maximum stress a material can withstand without permanently deforming.

testpiece: A notoriously difficult route relative to its rating and other routes with similar ratings.

top-roping: Climbing protected by a rope that leads from the climber up to an anchor. A roped climbing system (known as a yo-yo or slingshot) in which the rope is threaded through a pre-established anchor at the top of a route and the belayer, situated at the base, takes in rope as the climber ascends.

traditional (trad) free climbing: Widely used to describe a free-climbing style involving ground-up lead techniques with an emphasis upon placement of removable protection using existing options such as natural rock features and cracks.

trail line: A second rope trailed by either the leader or more commonly, the follower, used for rappel descents, hauling a pack, and/or as a backup for unplanned retreats.

Tri-Cam: Trade name for an unusually shaped protection device (designed by Lowe) designed to passively cam or wedge into a crack.

topo: Renderings of climbing routes indicating terrain specifics, distance, and sometimes technical information. From the word *topographical.*

Union Internationale des Associations d'Alpinisme (UIAA): An international mountaineering organization that helps govern the standards of climbing equipment.

water knot: *See* ring bend.

Web-o-lette: A 10- to 20-foot strand of Spectra webbing featuring a sewn loop at both ends, created and manufactured by Mountain Tools for use in creating pre-equalized belay anchors.

webbing: Narrow strands of nylon and nylon-blend material used to create items including runners (slings), harnesses, and quickdraws. Sold in most retail climbing shops from bulk spools.

whipper: A lead fall, usually unexpected and long.

Yates' Screamer: A specialized quickdraw made by Yates' Gear with stitching designed to rip under force for the purpose of absorbing force created by a leader fall, and ultimately reducing force on equipment. *See also* load-limiter.

Yosemite Decimal System (YDS): The predominant rock climbing rating system today in North America, originating from the Sierra Club's Class rating system as an extension of Class 5.

yo-yo: *See* top-roping.

Z-rig: A common rescue system used to create a mechanical advantage to raise an incapacitated climber.

Endnotes

1. Achey, Jeff, "Path of the Elders," *Climbing*, June 1999.

2. Robinson, Doug, *A Night on the Ground: A Day in the Open* (La Crescenta, CA: Mountain N' Air Books, 1996).

3. Achey, "Path of the Elders," *Climbing*.

4. Twight, Marc F., and James Martin, *Extreme Alpinism: Climbing Light, Fast, and High*. (Seattle, WA: The Mountaineers, 1999).

5. Soles, Clyde, "Camtasia," *Rock & Ice*, June-July 2001.

6. In 1971, Sierra Club Books published the first guidebook to Yosemite Valley. In this narrative guide, author Steve Roper denounces topos:

   Designed to supplement or even replace the written description, topos are contro-versial in that they tend to make climbing a bit easier on the brain. Route-finding problems are simplified . . . . They encourage climbers onto difficult routes because of their unshakable belief in the topo . . . . Topos assure speed records; they also lessen responsibility. No more querulous statements such as 'I'll just look around this corner,' only 'Here we are and where the hell's the belay bolt.' In other words, part of the adventure of climbing is removed. Topos are not used in this guidebook for the reasons mentioned above . . .

   Subsequent Yosemite guidebooks did eventually include topos, as do most modern guidebooks for other climbing areas today.

7. The late Jack Mileski, a climber who frequented the Shawangunks (a.k.a. The Gunks) in the early 1980s, was known for his incessant shouting of instruc-tions (spewing beta) from the ground to climbers on lead, whether they asked for suggestions or not. Verbosity proliferated at this popular upstate New York climbing area, even after Mileski moved to Colorado. Though Mileski has since died, his legacy of spewing beta reportedly lives on among locals at The Gunks.

8. A UIAA-rated fall involves 176 pounds falling 16 feet on approximately 8 feet of rope.

9. Twight and Martin, *Extreme Alpinism*.

10. Fasulo, David, *Self-Rescue* (Helena, MT: Falcon, 1996).

11. As an alternative, bring a few shoulder-length runners tied with accessory cord. Their length makes them more versatile.

12. For a left-handed brake, follow the same directions, but substitute left for right, and right for left.

13. These unofficial tests were conducted at Black Diamond in Salt Lake City, Utah, on November 9, 2006, by Quality Assurance Manager Kolin Powick. Results were posted in Powick's column, "QC with KP—Off the Record," posted in the "Scene: Beat/Info" section of Black Diamond's Website at http://www.bdel.com/scene/beta/qc_kp_archive.php#110906. Overall test results indicate that using the girth hitch to link two runners reduces the material strength by 30 percent, and in some cases up to 50 percent. Powick observed that, in general, the narrower the material used, the greater the reduction in strength. He also discovered that mixing widths of materials when joining slings via girthing results in a greater reduction in strength. Tests done on any combination involving narrow (6- to 10-millimeter), super-lightweight slings made from Dynex (a Spectra material) resulted in low strength values when girthed. The highest were documented in the girthing of two nylon runners with widths of $^{11}/_{16}$ inch. More research is needed to confirm the results. "These experiments are not all inclusive or totally encompassing by any means," states Powick in his column.

14. Robinson, *A Night on the Ground: A Day in the Open*.

Resources

Achey, Jeff. "Path of the Elders." *Climbing*, June 1999.

Ament, Pat. *History of Free Climbing in America: Wizards of Rock*. Berkeley, CA: Wilderness Press, 2002.

———. *Royal Robbins: Spirit of the Age*. Lincoln, NE: Adventure's Meaning Press, 1992.

American Mountain Guides Association. *Technical Handbook for Professional Mountain Guides*. Golden, CO: AMGA, 1999. (At the time of this book's publication, a 2007 edition was pending release.)

Arce, Gary. *Defying Gravity: High Adventure on Yosemite's Walls*. Berkeley, CA: Wilderness Press, 1996.

Fasulo, David J. *Self-Rescue*. Helena, MT: Falcon, 1996.

Fyffe, Allen, and Iain Peter. *The Handbook of Climbing*. 2nd edition. London: Pelham Books, 1997.

Graydon, Don, and Kurt Hanson, et al., eds. *Freedom of the Hills*. 7th edition. Seattle: WA: The Mountaineers, 2003.

Long, John. *Climbing Anchors*. Evergreen, CO: Chockstone Press, 1993.

———. *Close Calls*. Helena, MT: Falcon, 1999.

———. *How to Rock Climb*. 4th edition. Evergreen, CO: Chockstone Press, 2004.

———, and Bob Gaines. *More Climbing Anchors*. Evergreen, CO: Chockstone Press, 1998.

———, and Craig Luebben. *Advanced Rock Climbing*. Conifer, CO: Chockstone Press, 1997.

Luebben, Craig. *Knots for Climbers*. 2nd edition. Helena, MT: Falcon, 2001.

MacDonald, Dougald, ed. *The Best of Rock & Ice Anthology*. Seattle, WA: The Mountaineers, 1999.

Millman, Dan. *The Warrior Athlete*. Walpole, NH: Stillpoint Publishing, 1979.

Mortimer, Peter. *Return2Sender*. DVD. Boulder, CO: Sender Films, 2005.

Robbins, Royal. *Advanced Rockcraft*. Glendale, CA: La Siesta Press, 1973.

———. *Basic Rockcraft*. Glendale, CA: La Siesta Press, 1994.

Robinson, Doug. *A Night on the Ground: A Day in the Open*. 2nd edition. La Crescenta, CA: Mountain N' Air Books, 2004.

Roper, Steve. *Camp 4: Recollections of a Yosemite Rockclimber*. Seattle, WA: The Mountaineers, 1994.

———, and Allen Steck, eds. *The Best of Ascent*. San Francisco, CA: Sierra Club, 1993.

———, Allen Steck, and David Harris, eds. *Ascent: The Climbing Experience in Word and Image*. Golden, CO: American Alpine Club, 1999.

Rowell, Galen A., ed. *The Vertical World of Yosemite: A Collection of Writings and Photographs on Rock Climbing in Yosemite*. Berkeley, CA: Wilderness Press, 1974.

Soles, Clyde. "Camtasia." *Rock & Ice*, June-July 2001.

———. "The Mother of All Cam Charts." *Rock & Ice*, June-July 2001.

Twight, Marc F., and James Martin. *Extreme Alpinism: Climbing Light, Fast, and High*. Seattle, WA: The Mountaineers, 2003.

Index

About the Author

Heidi Pesterfield lives in the Northern Sierra in Truckee, California, where for 10 years she has been a rock climbing instructor for Alpine Skills International (ASI). Her personal climbing adventures span nearly 24 years, 22 of which involve leading traditional routes. She has climbed throughout the United States, as well as in Canada, Italy, France, and Thailand.

Heidi has taught climbing and outdoor recreation for 17 years, and completed her first American Mountain Guides Association (AMGA) instructor course in 2001. With a bachelor's degree in journalism, Pesterfield has been a freelance writer for 21 years. She has published outdoor adventure articles in numerous magazines including *Climbing, Rock & Ice, City Sports, Summit*, and *Natural Health*. She has also worked closely with the Outdoor Industry Association (OIA) formerly Outdoor Recreation Coalition of America (ORCA), and was a frequent reporter for the *Daily Exposure* at the biannual Outdoor Retailer Markets from 1997 through 1999.

The idea for writing this book came to Heidi several years ago when she noticed a resurgent interest in traditional methods at her home crags of Donner Summit. "Sport climbers and top-ropers were watching trad climbers and saying 'I want to do *that*,'" she remembers. ASI clients were requesting book recommendations on traditional lead craft, but, to her surprise, there wasn't one solely addressing these methods. She found chapters in several books and a video, but no single title devoted to leading trad free climbs. Her own learning years were a school of hard knocks, she recalls with a shudder, "It was trial and error, and I'm truthfully surprised I survived it. If I'd had access to a book like this, I could have avoided a lot of risks."

Heidi enjoys climbing moderate, multipitch free routes in the High Sierra, as well as visiting different areas throughout the world. She likes sport climbing occasionally but admits her passions lie with traditional methods. "You can't beat the exhilaration and adventure woven into the trad experience. And if you stick with it long enough, it'll take you to some of the most beautiful places on the planet."